International Series on Public Policy

Series Editors

B. Guy Peters
Pittsburgh University, Pittsburgh, USA

Philippe Zittoun
Research Professor of Political Science, LET-ENTPE,
University of Lyon, Lyon, France

The International Series on Public Policy - the official series of International Public Policy Association, which organizes the International Conference on Public Policy - identifies major contributions to the field of public policy, dealing with analytical and substantive policy and governance issues across a variety of academic disciplines. A comparative and interdisciplinary venture, it examines questions of policy process and analysis, policymaking and implementation, policy instruments, policy change & reforms, politics and policy, encompassing a range of approaches, theoretical, methodological, and/or empirical. Relevant across the various fields of political science, sociology, anthropology, geography, history, and economics, this cutting edge series welcomes contributions from academics from across disciplines and career stages, and constitutes a unique resource for public policy scholars and those teaching public policy worldwide.

More information about this series at
http://www.springer.com/series/15096

Nicole Herweg

European Union Policy-Making

The Regulatory Shift in Natural Gas Market Policy

palgrave
macmillan

Nicole Herweg
Institute of Political Science
University of Heidelberg
Heidelberg, Germany

International Series on Public Policy
ISBN 978-3-319-49399-2 ISBN 978-3-319-49400-5 (eBook)
DOI 10.1007/978-3-319-49400-5

Library of Congress Control Number: 2016963353

Printed on acid-free paper

This Palgrave Macmillan imprint is published by Springer Nature
The registered company is Springer International Publishing AG
The registered company address is: Gewerbestrasse 11, 6330 Cham, Switzerland

To my family—thank you for being there and for being the way you are.

Acknowledgments

This book would not have evolved into its present form without the support and input from colleagues and reviewers. First of all, my grateful thanks go to Reimut Zohlnhöfer, my doctoral supervisor, whose advice and never-wavering encouragement have substantially contributed to me completing this book.

Furthermore, I was blessed with the opportunity to discuss my research at different stages at workshops and panels dedicated to the multiple streams framework in the last three years. I am very thankful for the many insightful and thought-provoking comments and suggestions I received on these occasions.

From these scientific exchanges resulted research projects and collaborations, which had a strong impact on my understanding of the multiple streams framework and, consequently, on this book. In this regard, I am particularly grateful to Nikolaos Zahariadis, Michael D. Jones, once again, Reimut Zohlnhöfer, Jale Tosun, and Christian Huss.

I also thank my colleagues at the Institute of Political Science at the University of Heidelberg, Germany, for their constant encouragement and support, above all Kathrin Dümig and Fabian Engler. Last but not least, I would like to thank Jemima Warren for her guidance and very pleasant cooperation, James Farrell for language editing, and Svenja Bauer-Blaschkowski and Philipp Mai for assistance with the manuscript. Any shortcomings in this book remain my sole responsibility.

Heidelberg, August 2016 Nicole Herweg

Contents

List of Abbreviations

CCEMG	Consultative Committee of Member States
CEER	Council of European Energy Regulators
CERT	Committee on Energy, Research, and Technology
Commission	European Commission
Council	Council of Ministers
DG	Directorate-Generals
DSO	Distribution system operator
EC	European Community
ECSC	European Coal and Steel Community
EdF	Électricité de France
EEC	European Economic Community
EEU	Effective and efficient unbundling
EP	European Parliament
ERGEG	European Regulators' Group for Electricity and Gas
EU	European Union
GCM	Garbage can model of organizational choice
GdF	Gaz de France
GTE	Gas Transmission Europe
HLG	High-Level Group on Competitiveness, Energy and the Environment
IEM	Internal energy market
ISO	Independent system operator
ITSO	Independent transmission system operator

LNG	Liquefied natural gas
MSF	Multiple streams framework
NRA	National regulatory authority
PCCG	Professional Consultative Committee on Gas
PET	Punctuated equilibrium theory
PSO	Public service obligations
RQ	Research question
SEA	Single European Act
TFEU	Treaty on the Functioning of the European Union (Lisbon Treaty)
TOP	Take or pay
TPA	Third-party access
TSO	Transmission system operator
UK	United Kingdom

List of Figures

List of Tables

CHAPTER 1

Introduction

This book pursues two objectives: First, it addresses the question of how well the multiple streams framework (MSF)[1] is suited for explaining European Union (EU)[2] policy-making in general; and second, it empirically assesses how well it fares in explaining the regulatory shift in the EU natural gas market policy between 1998 and 2009. Until the 1990s, the first question would have been far-fetched, given that it was an established practice to conduct studies of the EU from an international relations perspective (Hix 1994). Mirroring the research interests of this perspective, these studies focused on "understand[ing] how the EU has come about and which factors made it what it is today" (Lelieveldt and Princen 2011, 32). The ongoing deepening of European integration, however, has attracted the attention of public policy scholars, who have since aimed at explaining how the EU actually functions (Lelieveldt and Princen 2011). As the publication of a special issue on theoretical frameworks of the EU's policy process in the *Journal of European Public Policy* in 2013 indicates, the idea to apply theories of public policy and decision-making to political behavior and action in the EU is fully established today.

In this regard, the MSF put forward by Kingdon (1984) and developed further by Zahariadis (2003) ranks as one of the "promising frameworks of the EU policy process" (Zahariadis 2013, 807). In fact, in recent years, analytical interest in the framework has increased with regard to applying it to the EU policy process (Ackrill et al. 2013). The present book contributes to this strand of literature with a systematic translation of the MSF into a

N. Herweg, *European Union Policy-Making*,
DOI 10.1007/978-3-319-49400-5_1

theory of the EU's policy process and its modification in a way which allows for explaining agenda-setting and decision-making.

My main argument is that past MSF applications have not taken sufficiently into account the fact that Kingdon (1984) derived the framework inductively. This inadequacy, in turn, has resulted in an incomplete transfer of the MSF to the EU level. Due to the fact that the MSF was derived from observations of agenda-setting processes in the United States, researchers face several challenges if they apply the framework to the EU: First, they must identify functional equivalents of the MSF's core concepts in the EU; and second, they must assess empirically whether the assumed causal mechanisms also operate at the EU level. Since it is an established practice today to apply the MSF to agenda-setting and decision-making, it is imperative to distinguish two sets of causal mechanisms: one explaining agenda change and another one explaining policy change (Herweg et al. 2015; Howlett et al. 2015). As will be documented in Chap. 2, these challenges have not been dealt with systematically in the Multiple Streams literature so far. Therefore, the present book addresses them one by one and derives a modified MSF. More precisely, it identifies functional equivalents of the MSF's core concepts in the EU's problem stream, political stream, and policy stream. Furthermore, it considers two policy windows (agenda window and decision window) and two different sets of causal mechanisms in order to explain agenda-setting and decision-making. To make the framework's necessary conditions more accessible for the empirical assessment, they are explicitly translated into hypotheses. Summarizing the above, the book's overall research questions are these: Which modifications in the MSF are necessary in order to apply the framework to agenda change and policy change in the EU? How well do the suggested modifications perform in the empirical analysis?

It requires tracing the framework's causal mechanisms leading to agenda change *and* policy change in the EU in order to empirically assess how well the MSF fares in explaining these changes. This calls for analyzing cases in which the phenomenon occurs (here agenda change and policy change), because "[t]racing a nonexistent mechanism in a case where we a priori knew it was not present tells us nothing about how the mechanism works in cases where it is present" (Beach and Pedersen 2016, 4; in a similar vein, see, for instance, Bennett and Elman 2006, 462, Braumoeller and Goertz 2000, 846, Dion 2003, 96 and Mahoney and Goertz 2006, 239).

The cases selected to empirically assess the modified MSF are the three policy processes which led to the EU natural gas directives in 1998, 2003, and 2009 (98/30/EC; 2003/55/EC; 2009/73/EC).[3] These three policy processes have the advantage that they deal with the same policy sector and issue in a (comparatively) stable institutional environment. Regarding the latter, they are all dealt with under the ordinary legislative procedure.[4] This is an important feature, because due to the deepening and widening of European integration over time, there have been various institutional and processual changes regarding EU policy-making. Furthermore, depending on the criteria applied for counting different EU policy processes, Buonanno and Nugent (2013) distinguish between 28 and 100 different policy processes in which the relevant actors or their importance varies. As a consequence, depending on the legislative procedure and the time frame analyzed, the MSF needs to be adapted differently if transferred to EU policy-making. By focusing on the ordinary legislative procedure, this book covers a highly relevant legislative procedure for EU policy-making, given that (by now) it covers 90 percent of all policies adopted in the EU (European Parliament 2014). Furthermore, the focus on the three natural gas directives facilitates tracing the framework's causal mechanisms without getting distracted by idiosyncrasies of different policy sectors and issues.[5]

However, case selection goes beyond exclusively theoretical considerations. EU energy policy is a highly interesting policy sector because it developed from "one of the Community's major failures" (Padgett 1992, 55) until the mid-1990s to a "'hot topic' in the EU's political agenda" (Sandoval and Morata 2012, 4, emphasis in original) today.

This late arrival of European energy policy is noteworthy, given that energy policy and the idea of a common market were pivotal elements in the predecessor treaties of the contemporary EU. More precisely, the Treaty constituting the European Coal and Steel Community (ECSC), signed in 1951, established a de jure common market based on common objectives and institutions for coal and steel (Art. 1 ECSC Treaty). The Euratom Treaty, signed in 1957, aimed at the promotion of Europe's nuclear industries for the benefit of all contracting parties (Art. 1 Euratom Treaty). Finally, the Treaty establishing the European Economic Community (EEC), also signed in 1957, was more generally targeted at harmonizing economic activities by establishing a common market (Art. 2 EEC Treaty).

The disappointing development of the EU's energy policy can, to some extent, be explained by the fact that the energy sources the treaties establishing the ECSC and Euratom had dealt with became less important in the European energy mix, in the case of coal due to technical and economic reasons and in the case of nuclear power due to political reasons.

Furthermore, resulting from the exclusion of energy in the Treaty establishing the EEC, any European energy legislation had to result from legislation in contiguous areas (Prontera 2009, 15; Sandoval and Morata 2012, 2).[6] This also applies to natural gas legislation, particularly since the natural gas era in the then member states began after the signing of those treaties, namely, with the discovery of the Groningen gas field in the Netherlands in 1959 and those in the Southern Basin of the North Sea in the United Kingdom in the mid-1960s (Stern 1992, 2).

Nevertheless, the increasing importance of natural gas in the European energy mix (cf. Fig. 1.1) and the growing import dependency (cf. Fig. 1.2) could have easily justified a further move toward a closer European energy union. The member states treated energy policy as a high-politics issue (Matláry 1997, 25), which had to be shielded from Community action. It

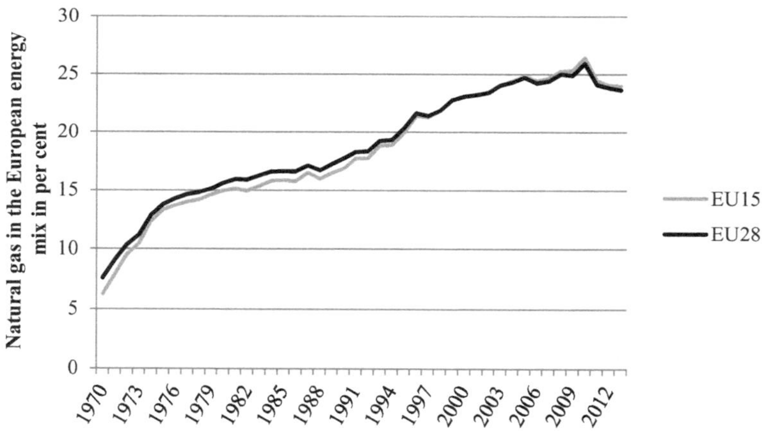

Fig. 1.1 Share of natural gas consumption in the gross inland consumption in the European Union, 1970–2010. *Source*: Own calculation, based on British Petroleum (2014). *Notes*: The graph shows the share of natural gas consumption in the gross inland energy consumption in percentage. There are missing data for EU15 (regarding Luxembourg) and EU28 (regarding Estonia, Croatia, Cyprus, Latvia, Luxembourg, Slovenia, and Malta). On average, these member states' share on the EU15's and EU28's natural gas consumptions was only 0.3 percent (EU15) and 1.6 percent (EU28) between 1990 to 2012. Therefore, the missing data has no impact on the reported consumption trend (percentage calculated from the European energy statistics quantities, http://ec.europa.eu/eurostat/web/energy/data/main-tables, last accessed on February 12, 2014)

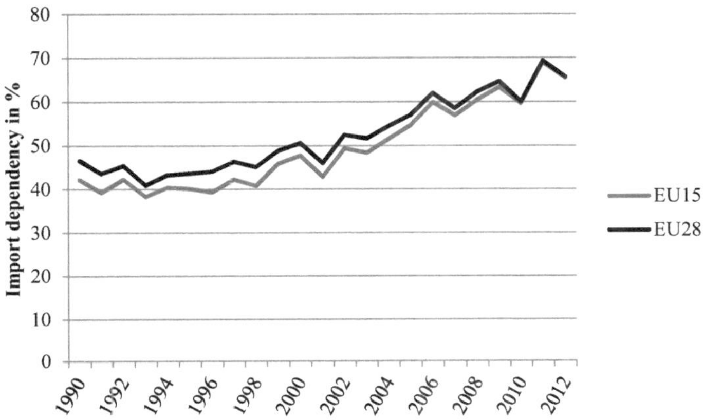

Fig. 1.2 European natural gas import dependency, 1990–2012. *Source*: Own calculation, based on Eurostat energy statistics quantities (http://ec.europa.eu/eurostat/web/energy/data/main-tables, last accessed on February 12, 2014). *Notes*: The natural gas import dependency is calculated as the ratio of net natural gas imports to gross inland consumption of natural gas, whereby the net natural gas imports are natural gas imports minus exports minus stock changes. Due to data restrictions, the numbers reported cover only the time frame from 1990 to 2012.[8] However, since the natural gas era started in the 1960s, the reported shares must have a positive slope for the time before the 1990s

is therefore astonishing that EU natural gas market legislation started to be discussed intensively in 1988, a time when the depletion of natural gas resources was predicted to take place within the next 50 years (British Petroleum 2008).[7] Put differently, natural gas began to lose its high-politics status when natural gas resources were forecast to get scarcer.

The first gas directive (98/30/EC) was passed in 1998 and introduced common rules for the organization of the natural gas sector. This date is referred to as a "decisive breakthrough" (Eberlein 2005, 64) because it marked what Hall (1993, 278) calls a third-order policy change, which means that "the overarching goals that guide policy in a particular field" changed. However, since the passing of the first gas directive, a previously unheard legislative activity evolved dealing with the liberalization of the European natural gas market (see Table 1.1).[9]

Generally speaking, the subject of legislation clusters around three topics: (1) the introduction of common rules (98/30/EC; 2003/55/EC; 2009/73/EC),[10] (2) the introduction of standards concerning the access to the network for cross-border exchanges ((EC) No. 1775/2005; (EC) No. 715/2009), and (3) the institutionalization of European regulators (2003/796/EC; (EC) No. 713/2009; 2011/280/EU). Of these three topics, the introduction of common rules is the centerpiece of the legislation. The last two topics are accompanying measures, which deal with prerequisites for common rules taking full effect.[11] Therefore, the book's focus is on the introduction of the common rules.

1.1 Empirical Research Questions

Apart from its overall research interest—assessing the MSF's capability to be transferred to the EU policy process—the book aims at gaining a better understanding of the above-summarized policy dynamics in EU energy policy-making. Therefore, this chapter also derives a set of empirical research questions.

The first gas directive aimed at far more than just small-scale modifications of the respective national energy sector. To the contrary, it triggered far-reaching adaptation pressures, particularly because the member states played a substantial part in their respective national economies and were used to restricting competition. The common rules introduced in 1998 aimed at removing (or at least at mitigating) these restrictions, which made it inevitable to restructure and reorganize the European natural gas market. Although the affected industry and the member states rejected the introduction of common rules (Padgett 1992, 61), the first gas directive was passed after lengthy negotiations in 1998 (98/30/EC). From a public policy perspective, this change was unexpected. The member states could have easily stopped the directive by blocking it in the Council of Ministers. Therefore, the following research questions arise:

RQ 1: How did the draft directive leading to the first gas directive gain agenda status?

RQ 2: Why did not the member states make use of their right to veto in order to avert this policy change once the gas draft directive entered the decision-making stage?

Regardless of the lengthy negotiations, the passing of the first gas directive was not a one-off exercise; in the subsequent nine years, two more gas directives were passed (2003/55/EC; 2009/73/EC), repealing the previous one. This high regulatory activity regarding the European natural gas

Table 1.1 EU legislation regarding the internal market in natural gas

Date	*Type of legislation*	*Subject of legislation*	*Reference*
July 21, 1998	Directive	Common rules for the internal market in natural gas	98/30/EC
July 15, 2003	Directive	Common rules for the internal market in natural gas	2003/55/EC
November 14, 2003	Decision	Establishing the European regulators' group for electricity and gas	2003/796/EC
November 3, 2005	Regulation	Conditions for access to the network for cross-border exchanges in gas	(EC) No. 1775/2005
July 13, 2009	Directive	Common rules for the internal market in natural gas	2009/73/EC
August 14, 2009	Regulation	Conditions for access to the network for cross-border exchanges in gas	(EC) No. 715/2009
August 14, 2009	Regulation	Establishing the agency for cooperation of energy regulators	(EC) No. 713/2009
May 17, 2011	Decision	On repealing decision 2003/796/EC	2011/280/EU

Source: Own illustration
Note: The date refers to the publication of the final act in the Official Journal of the European Union (or its forerunner)

sector is striking because the idea to liberalize this sector was equated with "the end of civilization" (Stern 1998, 91) in the run-up to the first directive. Therefore, it is astonishing that natural gas regulation returned on the decision agenda in the form of a legislative proposal for a second directive (European Commission 2001) only seven months after the date of transposition of the first directive (98/30/EC, Art. 29–30). Given that a time lag between the implementation of new rules and they taking effect is very likely, just granting seven months for making an impact before discussing revised rules seems unrealistic. Although the time lag between the effective date of the second gas directive and the tabling of the third gas draft directive (European Commission 2007) was longer (just about three years), it still did not grant much time for the provisions of the second gas directive to take full effect. Hence, the book's third research question is this:

RQ 3: How can the return of the gas directive on the EU decision agenda in 2001 and 2007 be explained?

In contrast to the first gas directive, the following ones were of a higher political complexity. Following Kaeding (2006) and Steunenberg and Rhinard (2010), the number of recitals in a directive is a good proxy to estimate the degree of political complexity because member states, the European Parliament, and the European Commission add recitals in order to express reservations or to clarify issues. While the first gas directive contains 32 recitals, there are already 34 recitals in the second one, which culminates in 66 recitals in the third gas directive. Apart from the political complexity, the regulatory provisions increased in terms of scope and detail: Although the number of chapters only increased from seven (first and second gas directive) to ten (third gas directive), the number of articles increased from 31 (first gas directive) to 35 (second gas directive), which finally rose to 56 articles in the third gas directive (see Annexes I and II for an overview). Although one might assume that an increase in political and regulatory complexity involves a higher conflict potential, the negotiation periods were considerably reduced when compared with the first directive process: The decision-making process took two-and-a-quarter years of negotiation regarding the second gas directive and less than two years regarding the third one, while it took six-and-a-half years for the first gas directive. This leads to the fourth research question:

RQ 4: Why did the policy processes accompanying the three gas directives shorten substantially despite a growth in political and regulatory complexity?

1.2 Research Design, Method, and Contribution to the Literature

The book's *overall research interest* is to deliver a theoretical contribution regarding the application of the MSF to the EU's policy process. Reflecting this research interest, it traces the framework's causal mechanisms in the policy processes which led to the three natural gas directives in 1998, 2003, and 2009. Going beyond theoretical considerations and captured in the *empirical research questions* posed above, these policy processes are particularly interesting regarding the timing and duration of agenda and policy change. The MSF is especially suitable for explaining the timing and duration of change because it stresses the importance of timing and sequence of events, and departs from the assumption that policy-making is an exercise in rational problem-solving. Regarding the latter, the framework postulates that it is the combination of compelling problems or political changes, the availability of worked-out alternatives, and the activities of policy-entrepreneurs that lead to (agenda and policy) change. This makes the framework well equipped to explain: first, the timing of the regulatory activity (RQ 1 and 3); second, why member states supported the first gas directive, although they preferred the status quo or at least different contractual provisions (RQ 2). The comparison of the three gas directive processes in turn allows explaining why the policy processes took less time from directive to directive (RQ 4).

In order to do justice to the process-oriented view of the MSF and the book's theoretical and empirical research questions, the book applies the method of process tracing. Unfortunately, process tracing has a "buzzword problem" (Bennett and Checkel 2015, 4): Many researchers refer to this method without being specific about how they define and apply it. At the same time, the more recent literature discusses the existence of various competing definitions and variants of process tracing, best practices, and ways to increase the method's causal inference and validity (for an overview, see Trampusch and Palier 2013). To engage in this discussion goes beyond the book's scope. However, given the method's buzzword problem, it is essential to define clearly how process tracing is defined and applied in this contribution.

Following Bennett and Checkel (2015, 7), process tracing is defined "as the analysis of evidence on processes, sequences, and conjunctures of events within a case for the purposes of either developing or testing hypotheses about causal mechanisms that might causally explain the case". Since the MSF guides this analysis, the process tracing applied is the theory-testing variant (cf. Beach and Pedersen 2013, 11; Checkel 2005, 6; Hall 2006, 25). Put differently, the analysis tests whether the causal mechanisms as hypothesized by the MSF (summarized in Sect. 2.4) are capable of explaining how the issue of introducing and revising common rules for the natural gas market entered the decision agenda and finally led to policy changes in 1998, 2003, and 2009.

In order to properly trace these processes, I conduct a qualitative text analysis based on 586 articles using MAXQDA, a professional software for qualitative and mixed-methods data analysis. The articles considered in the analysis were extracted from the two leading sources of news and analysis on key European topics, *European Voice* and *Agence Europe*, and from the electronic database of LexisNexis for the period 1987 (a year before the internal energy market entered the governmental agenda) to 2009 (the passage of the third gas directive). This was supplemented by available documents from the European institutions and the relevant secondary literature.

With this research design, the book makes a significant theoretical contribution to the current state-of-the-art literature on the MSF. First, it applies the framework fully. According to its citation frequency, the MSF is a widely recognized approach to the study of public policy (Herweg 2013, 322; McLendon and Cohen-Vogel 2008, 31). However, only a few contributions actually applied the framework instead of just citing it (Jones et al. 2016, 9; Herweg 2015, 340). For instance, of all English-language peer-reviewed journal articles referring to the MSF during 2000 and 2013, only 16 percent actually applied the framework. Nevertheless, of these 16 percent, roughly one-third applied all of the framework's elements (Jones et al. 2016, 24).[12] The vast majority of contributions just referred to individual concepts, such as policy windows or policy-entrepreneurs (Herweg 2013, 322; Jones et al. 2016, 18). Hence, this book adds a full MSF application to the literature.

Second, the book explicitly tests the framework's explanatory power. Resulting from incomplete applications and the neglect of the framework's causal mechanisms, most applications only use it for a structured description of processes. Put differently, most contributions deliberately do not exploit the framework's explanatory potential. This corroborates Radaelli's finding that only a few authors have tested Kingdon's (implicitly stated) assumptions (Radaelli 2000, 132). This might be attributable to the fact that the MSF does not offer a set of ready-made hypotheses (Sabatier 2007a, 327). Consequently, in order to test the MSF claims rigorously, they have to be translated into falsifiable hypotheses. Therefore, this contribution derives a systematic set of falsifiable hypotheses and tests how well the MSF fares in explaining the policy processes which led to the passing of the three gas directives.

Since the initial MSF is restricted to the agenda-setting stage, it is necessary to modify the framework in a way which allows for analyzing agenda-setting and decision-making. While it is a common practice to apply the framework to policy stages following the agenda-setting stage (for an overview, see Herweg 2015, 343–46), the respective contributions usually fall short of specifying the causal mechanisms for the policy stage(s) considered in the analysis. This holds particularly true for studies which apply the MSF to

Table 1.2 A quantitative assessment of the multiple streams literature

Peer-reviewed MSF journal articles published between 2000 and 2013	*Contribution*
Reference to MSF	100 % ($n = 1933$)
Filter 1: MSF applications	16 % ($n = 311$)
Filter 2: Full application of the framework	5.5 % ($n = 106$)
Dependent variable analyzed:	100 % ($n = 106$)
Agenda change	50.9 % ($n = 54$)
Policy change	46.2 % ($n = 49$)
Other	2.8 % ($n = 3$)
If the dependent variable is policy change, contributions that introduce theoretical modifications of the initial MSF	16.3 % ($n = 8$)

Source: Own compilation based on the dataset gathered by Jones et al. (2016). MSF stands for multiple streams framework

decision-making. Of the above-mentioned MSF contributions published between 2000 and 2013 that fully apply the framework, 46.2 percent applied the MSF to decision-making (some covering agenda-setting, too). However, only 16.3 percent of these contributions introduced theoretical modifications in order to address their stretched research interest (see Table 1.2).[13] Hence, the book's third value added to the MSF literature is the introduction of a modified MSF which allows for differentiating causal mechanisms for agenda change and policy change.

Fourth, this book adapts the framework's core elements to the EU. Being derived from observations of agenda changes at the federal level of the United States (Kingdon 1984), the MSF is an inductive theory. As such, the framework's generalizable propositions are tailored to explain agenda-setting in this specific institutional setting. Consequently, any transfer of the framework to different institutional settings has to address the question of whether and how the MSF is qualified for this endeavor. Regarding MSF applications to the EU, only few contributions pose that question or explicitly adapt the framework to the EU (cf. Zahariadis 2008; Borrás and Radaelli 2011), although this is a field which has gained momentum since the mid-2000s (Ackrill et al. 2013). To the best knowledge of the author, there is no contribution which engages in both fully transferring and applying the framework to the EU *and* specifying how the causal mechanisms work in this institutional setting.[14] This book aims at filling this research gap.

However, the book's value added is not restricted to contributing to the MSF literature. Table 1.3 informs about the number of publications

Table 1.3 A quantitative assessment of the public policy–oriented research on energy

Political science research on energy		*Political science research on natural gas*		
Web of Knowledge search terms	*Results*	*Web of Knowledge search terms*	*Results I*	*Results II*
Energy	3,282,540	Natural gas	28,504	28,504
Filter 1: Energy policy	29,953	*Filter 1:* Natural gas policy	88	Not applied
Filter 2: Research domain: Social sciences	8630	*Filter 2:* Research domain: Social sciences	45	1755
Filter 3: Political science orientation research areas: government law, public administration, international relations	2959	*Filter 3:* Political science orientation research areas: government law, public administration, international relations	28	506
Filter 4: Search within results for EU/European Union or EC/European Community	183	*Filter 4:* Search within results for EU/European Union or EC/European Community	1	17

Source: Own compilation

Notes: This table summarizes the results of a basic search for contributions referring to "energy" or "natural gas" conducted on January 15, 2016, in the Web of Science databases. The search history for energy is "TOPIC: (energy), Refined by: LANGUAGES: (ENGLISH), Timespan = All years, Search language = Auto" and that for natural gas "TOPIC: (natural near/1 gas), Refined by: LANGUAGES: (ENGLISH), Timespan = All years, Search language = Auto". For natural gas, two searches were conducted: The first replicated the search carried out for energy. Because the first filter already eliminated 99.7 percent of all articles (Result I), a second search was included, which skipped the first filter and left 6.2 percent of the articles for further analysis (Result II)

included in the Web of Science databases that are written in English and deal with (1) energy in general and (2) natural gas in particular. The reported numbers clearly show that energy policy is predominantly analyzed by scholars from other disciplines than political science (for a similar assessment, see Prontera 2009, 1; Strange 1988, 194). Therefore, this book amends the (comparatively little) public policy–oriented research on energy.[15] More precisely, it is a combination of focusing on EU natural gas regulation and on the related policy process, by which it advances public policy research.

Generally speaking, energy policy seems to increasingly attract public policy scholars' attention. For instance, 78 percent of the political science contributions dealing with EU energy policy were published between January 1, 2008, and January 15, 2015. The focus is often on related issues (such as climate policy) or on energy sources other than natural gas. For instance, the liberalization of the electricity and natural gas sectors was addressed simultaneously in the EU. The analysis of the electricity sector has attracted more scientific attention. Whereas the Web of Science databases find 1208 political science contributions dealing with electricity, they find just 506 contributions dealing with natural gas.[16] Of these contributions, 118 consider a European dimension in their analysis of the electricity sector (cf. Eising 2002; Levi-Faur 2011; Padgett 2003), while this is true for only 17 contributions referring to natural gas in their analysis (cf. Bahgat 2006; Schmidt-Felzmann 2011; Talus 2011). In general, contributions that deal with the natural gas sector tend to either include this sector in a broader analysis of EU energy policy or focus on security of supply issues. Thereby, they share common ground with the field of international relations (cf. Aalto and Temel 2014; Proedrou 2011; Waelde 1996; Westphal 2006). Furthermore, it is common to include the natural gas sector in the analysis of different governance modes at work in the EU (cf. Eberlein 2008; Levi-Faur 2011; Maggetti and Gilardi 2011; Schmitt and Schulze 2011). Contributions that exclusively deal with natural gas tend to concentrate on the output or outcome of the European regulatory activity (cf. Brau et al. 2010; Growitsch and Stronzik 2014; Haase 2009).

However, policy process research focusing on EU natural gas regulation is uncommon (for exceptions, see Brutschin 2015; Eberlein 2005; Eikeland 2011). In this context, policy process research is defined as "the study of the interactions over time between public policy[17] and its surrounding actors, events, and contexts, as well as the policy or policies' outcomes" (Weible 2014, 5). Put differently, "the emphasis is much more on the unfolding [of actions, events, and decisions, N.H.] than on the authoritative decision" (Schlager 2007, 293). Consequently, with the above-introduced research design, this book contributes to a better understanding of EU policy processes dealing with natural gas issues.

1.3 The Structure of the Book

Chapter 2 presents the MSF in detail. It starts with a summary of Kingdon's contribution and suggests a way as to how it can be modified in order to explain agenda change and policy change in the EU policy process. Furthermore, this chapter derives a set of hypotheses that guides the analysis of the three gas directive processes. Before this analysis is carried out in Chaps. 4, 5, and 6, some basics about the natural gas market in general, regulatory options, and the content of the three gas directives are presented briefly in Chap. 3. This chapter provides readers unfamiliar with the technical issue of natural gas market regulation with the knowledge to follow the analysis of the policy processes. The analysis of the policy processes tests the theoretical modifications introduced in Chap. 2. Since the book aims at contributing to theory development, each analysis of agenda change and policy change concludes with an overview of how well the MSF in general and its modifications in particular fared in the analysis. Finally, Chap. 7 summarizes these interim conclusions and supplements them with insights gained from the comparison of the three policy processes. In addition, it recapitulates the most important parts of the answers to the research questions posed in this introduction.

Notes

1. Multiple streams has been referred to as a framework (cf. Storch and Winkel 2013; Zahariadis 1999, 2007), approach (cf. Rowlands 2007; Zahariadis 2014), theory (cf. Kingdon 1984, 70, Schlager 2007, 297), and model (cf. Ness 2010; Travis and Zahariadis 2002). Sometimes, these labels are even mingled within one publication (cf. Brunner 2008; Zahariadis 2014), although they are not synonyms (Ostrom 2007, 25–26). A search in Google Scholar, conducted on January 15, 2016, shows that the term "multiple streams framework" (MSF) ($n = 1060$) is most common, followed by the terms "multiple streams model" ($n = 670$), "multiple streams theory" ($n = 412$), and, finally, "multiple streams approach" ($n = 340$). Note that Google Scholar search results include duplicate records. As a consequence, the actual size of search results is lower. By far the most hits delivers the term "multiple streams framework." Therefore, this book follows the path of the majority and uses the descriptor "framework". However, this does not imply that I concede multiple streams as being incapable of explaining an output (e.g., an agenda change). In contrast, as the MSF places values on variables, "posit[s] relationships among the variables, and make [s] predictions about likely outcomes" (Schlager 2007, 297), it matches the definition of theory (in a similar vein, see Cairney and Heikkila 2014).
2. In order to improve the reading flow, this study distinguishes neither between the European Union (EU) and its forerunners, nor

between the earlier equivalents of the European Commission and the Council of Ministers—unless this differentiation is pivotal to the analysis.

3. The decision-making process leading to the first gas directive consists of two policy processes—or decision windows in my terminology: During the first decision window, policy-makers were not able to compromise, which led to the closure of the decision window. The next time the decision window opened, however, policy-makers settled on a compromise. Thus, strictly speaking, there is variance in the dependent variable in this case.
4. This procedure was referred to as the codecision procedure before the entry into force of the Lisbon Treaty.
5. Note that this focus only facilitates the analysis and does not restrict the applicability of the derived modified MSF to the energy sector or the natural gas directives. It is, however, restricted to the ordinary legislative procedure.
6. The first time that energy policy was included in EU primary law was in Article 194 of the Treaty on the Functioning of the European Union (TFEU or Lisbon Treaty), signed in 2007.
7. Note that the depletion scenarios have changed over time due to, for instance, the extraction and use of shale gas. Currently, gas is estimated to peak globally between 2019 and 2035 (for a detailed overview of the different estimate scenarios, see Maggio and Cacciola 2012).
8. Eurostat and the US Energy Information Administration also collect data regarding the energy market. However, their datasets only render possible the calculation of the EU's natural gas import dependency since 1990, while the annual statistical reviews of world energy published by British Petroleum allow for calculating the natural gas import dependency (excluding stock changes) since 1989. As a consequence, regardless of the dataset, it is impossible to present how the European natural gas import dependency developed in earlier periods.
9. Within the EU, the policy output can be distinguished according to its binding force. Whereas recommendations and opinions are noncommittal, the addressees of regulations, directives, and decisions are obliged to follow the issued provisions. The latter differ in terms of the scope of their bindingness: While regulations and decisions are binding in their entirety, directives are only binding with reference

to the target result and leave the member states leeway in implementation form and methods (Art. 288 TFEU). To capture the legislative situation, this contribution focuses on policies with binding force that explicitly address issues concerning the creation and advancement of the internal market in natural gas.

10. In the following, these directives are referred to as the first, second, and third gas directive.
11. Due to being a cross-cutting issue, legislation in related policy areas (such as environment, competition, security) can also affect natural gas regulation. Since the book's focus is on tracing causal mechanisms in the three gas directive processes, and not on providing a legal overview of natural gas legislation, these related policy areas are not taken into consideration (for an overview, see Cameron 2002, 2007; Grunwald 2003). Furthermore, the book also excludes the legislation that was passed before the liberalization of the natural gas sector has been addressed legally. This applies particularly to directives 90/377/EC, 91/296/EEC, and 94/49/EC, given that the Commission had declared them ex post as being part of its liberalization approach of the sector (European Commission 1992).
12. The dataset for this calculation is a result of a meta-review of MSF applications conducted by Jones et al. (2016). The calculation of this percentage was carried out by me. For information regarding data gathering and coding, see Jones et al. (2016).
13. Based on the above-mentioned dataset, this specific coding was carried out by me solely.
14. Zohlnhöfer et al. (2016) deliver a theoretical contribution that deals with how to fully apply the MSF to parliamentary systems and how to outline the framework's causal mechanisms.
15. One contribution that also applies the MSF to EU energy policy-making is that of Eberlein (2012). However, Eberlein (2012, 150) deliberately draws only loosely on the MSF, and does not make use of the framework's explanatory potential.
16. All reported numbers for natural gas publications refer to those which resulted from the second search (Result II). The search results for electricity are reported only in the text, and not included in the table, since the book's focus is on natural gas.
17. Public policy is defined as "the decisions (including both actions and nonactions) of a government or an equivalent authority" (Weible 2014, 4).

References

(EC) No. 1775/2005. *Regulation of the European Parliament and of the Council of 28 September 2005 on Conditions for the Access to the Natural Gas Transmission Networks.*

(EC) No. 713/2009. *Regulation of the European Parliament and of the Council of 13 July 2009 Establishing an Agency for the Cooperation of Energy Regulators.*

(EC) No. 715/2009. *Regulation of the European Parliament and of the Council of 13 July 2009 on Conditions for Access to the Natural Gas Transmission Networks and Repealing Regulation (EC) No 1775/2005.*

2003/55/EC. *Directive of the European Parliament and of the Council of 26 June 2003 Concerning Common Rules for the Internal Market in Natural Gas and Repealing Directive 98/30/EC.*

2003/796/EC. *Decision of 11 November 2003 on Establishing the European Regulators Group for Electricity and Gas.*

2009/73/EC. *Directive of the European Parliament and of the Council of 13 July Concerning Common Rules for the Internal Market in Natural Gas and Repealing Directive 2003/55/EC.*

2011/280/EU. *Decision of 16 May 2011 on Repealing Decision 2003/796/EC on Establishing the European Regulators Group for Electricity and Gas.*

90/377/EC. *Directive of 29 June 1990 Concerning a Community Procedure to Improve the Transparency of Gas and Electricity Prices Charged to Industrial End-users.*

91/296/EEC. *Directive of 31 May 1991 on Transit of Natural Gas Through Grids.*

94/49/EC. *Directive of 11 November 1994 Updating the List of Entities Covered by Council Directive 91/296/EEC on Transit of Natural Gas Through Grids.*

98/30/EC. *Directive of the European Parliament and of the Council of 22 June 1998 Concerning Common Rules for the Internal Market in Natural Gas.*

Aalto, Pami, and Dicle K. Temel. 2014. European Energy Security: Natural Gas and the Integration Process. *Journal of Common Market Studies* 52(4): 758–774.

Ackrill, Robert, Adrian Kay, and Nikolaos Zahariadis. 2013. Ambiguity, Multiple Streams, and EU Policy. *Journal of European Public Policy* 20(6): 871–887.

Bahgat, Gawdat. 2006. Europe's Energy Security: Challenges and Opportunities. *International Affairs* 82(5): 961–975.

Beach, Derek, and Rasmus B. Pedersen. 2013. *Process-Tracing Methods: Foundations and Guidelines*. Ann Arbor: University of Michigan Press.

———. 2016. Selecting Appropriate Cases When Tracing Causal Mechanisms. *Sociological Methods & Research* (online first).

Bennett, Andrew, and Jeffrey T. Checkel. 2015. Process Tracing: From Philosophical Roots to Best Practices. In *Process Tracing: From Metaphor to Analytic Tool*, Strategies for Social Inquiry, ed. Andrew Bennett and Jeffrey T. Checkel, 1–37. Cambridge, UK: Cambridge University Press.

Bennett, Andrew, and Colin Elman. 2006. Qualitative Research: Recent Developments in Case Study Methods. *Annual Review of Political Science* 9(1): 455–476.

Borrás, Susana, and Claudio M. Radaelli. 2011. The Politics of Governance Architectures: Creation, Change and Effects of the EU Lisbon Strategy. *Journal of European Public Policy* 18(4): 463–484.

Brau, Rinaldo, Raffaele Doronzo, Carlo V. Fiorio, and Massimo Florio. 2010. EU Gas Industry Reforms and Consumers' Prices. *Energy Journal* 31(4): 167–182.

Braumoeller, Bear F., and Gary Goertz. 2000. The Methodology of Necessary Conditions. *American Journal of Political Science* 44(4): 844.

British Petroleum. 2008. *Statistical Review of World Energy*. London.

———. 2014. *Statistical Review of World Energy*. London.

Brunner, Steffen. 2008. Understanding Policy Change: Multiple Streams and Emission Trading in Germany. *Global Environmental Change* 18: 501–507.

Brutschin, Elina. 2015. Shaping the EU's Energy Policy Agenda: The Role of Eastern European Countries. In *Energy Policy Making in the EU: Building the Agenda*, ed. Jale Tosun, Sophie Biesenbender, and Kai Schulze, 187–204. London: Springer.

Buonanno, Laurie, and Neill Nugent. 2013. *Policies and Policy Processes of the European Union*, The European Union Series. Palgrave Macmillan: Basingstoke.

Cairney, Paul, and Tanya Heikkila. 2014. A Comparison of Theories of the Policy Process. In , *Sabatier and Weible* 2014, 363–390.

Cameron, Peter D. 2002. *Competition in Energy Markets: Law and Regulation in the European Union*. 1st ed. Oxford: Oxford University Press.

———. 2007. *Competition in Energy Markets: Law and Regulation in the European Union*. 2nd ed. Oxford: Oxford University Press.

Checkel, Jeffrey T. 2005. *It's the Process Stupid! Process Tracing in the Study of European and International Politics: ARENA Working Paper No. 26*. Oslo.

Dion, Douglas. 2003. Evidence and Inference in the Comparative Case Study. In *Necessary Conditions: Theory, Methodology, and Applications*, ed. Gary Goertz and Harvey Starr, 95–112. Oxford: Rowman & Littlefield.

Eberlein, Burkard. 2005. Regulation by Cooperation: The 'Third Way' in Making Rules for the Internal Energy Market. In *Legal Aspects of EU Energy Regulation: Implementing the New Directives on Electricity and Gas Across Europe*, ed. Peter D. Cameron, 59–88. Oxford: Oxford University Press.

———. 2008. The Making of the European Energy Market: The Interplay of Governance and Government. *Journal of Public Policy* 28(1): 73–92.

———. 2012. Inching Towards a Common Energy Policy: Entrepreneurship, Incrementalism, and Windows of Opportunity. In *Constructing a Policy-Making State? Policy Dynamics in the EU*, ed. Jeremy Richardson, 147–169. Oxford: Oxford University Press.

Eikeland, Per O. 2011. The Third Internal Energy Market Package: New Power Relations Among Member States, EU Institutions and Non-State Actors? *Journal of Common Market Studies* 49(2): 243–263.

Eising, Rainer. 2002. Policy Learning in Embedded Negotiations: Explaining EU Electricity Liberalization. *International Organization* 56(1): 85–120.

European Commission. 1992. *Proposal for a Council Directive Concerning Common Rules for the Internal Market in Electricity. Proposal for a Council Directive Concerning Common Rules for the Internal Market in Natural Gas. COM(91) 548 Final.*

———. 2001. *Proposal for a Directive of the European Parliament and of the Council Amending Directives 96/92/EC and 98/30/EC Concerning Common Rules for the Internal Market in Electricity and Natural Gas: COM(2001)125 Final.*

———. 2007. *Proposal for a directive of the European Parliament and of the Council amending Directive 2003/55/EC Concerning Common Rules for the Internal Market in Natural Gas: COM(2007)529 final.*

European Parliament. 2014. *Codecision and Conciliation. A Guide to How the European Parliament Co-Legislates Under the Ordinary Legislative Procedure.*

Growitsch, Christian, and Marcus Stronzik. 2014. Ownership Unbundling of Natural Gas Transmission Networks: Empirical Evidence. *Journal of Regulatory Economics* 46(2): 207–225.

Grunwald, Jürgen. 2003. *Das Energierecht der Europäischen Gemeinschaften: EGKS-EURATOM-EG; Grundlagen—Geschichte—geltende Regelungen.* Berlin: De Gruyter Recht.

Haase, N. 2009. *European Gas Market Liberalisation.* Enschede: Universiteit Twente.

Hall, Peter A. 1993. Policy Paradigms, Social Learning, and the State: The Case of Economic Policymaking in Britain. *Comparative Politics* 25(3): 275–296.

———. 2006. Systematic Process Analysis: When and How to Use It. *European Management Review* 3: 24–31.

Herweg, Nicole. 2013. Der Multiple-Streams-Ansatz—ein Ansatz, dessen Zeit gekommen ist? *Zeitschrift für Vergleichende Politikwissenschaft* 7(4): 321–345.

———. 2015. Der Multiple Streams Ansatz. In *Handbuch Policy-Forschung*, ed. Georg Wenzelburger and Reimut Zohlnhöfer, 325–353. Wiesbaden: VS Verlag für Sozialwissenschaften.

Herweg, Nicole, Christian Huß, and Reimut Zohlnhöfer. 2015. Straightening the Three Streams: Theorizing Extensions of the Multiple Streams Framework. *European Journal of Political Research* 54(3): 435–449.

Hix, Simon. 1994. The Study of the European Community: The Challenge to Comparative Politics. *West European Politics* 17(1): 1–30.

Howlett, Michael, Allan McConnell, and Anthony Perl. 2015. Streams and Stages: Reconciling Kingdon and Policy Process Theory. *European Journal of Political Research* 54(3): 419–434.

Jones, Michael D., Holly L. Petersen, Jonathan J. Pierce, Nicole Herweg, Amiel Bernal, Holly Lamberta, and Nikolaos Zahariadis. 2016. A River Runs Through It: A Multiple Streams Meta-Review. *Policy Studies Journal* 44(1): 13–36.

Kaeding, Michael. 2006. Determinants of transposition delay in the European Union. *Journal of Public Policy* 26(3): 229–253.

Kingdon, John W. 1984. *Agendas, Alternatives, and Public Policies*. Boston: Little, Brown.

Lelieveldt, Herman, and Sebastiaan Princen. 2011. *The Politics of the European Union*. Cambridge: Cambridge University Press.

Levi-Faur, David. 2011. Regulatory Networks and Regulatory Agencification: Towards a Single European Regulatory Space. *Journal of European Public Policy* 18(6): 810–829.

Maggetti, Martino, and Fabrizio Gilardi. 2011. The Policy-Making Structure of European Regulatory Networks and the Domestic Adoption of Standards. *Journal of European Public Policy* 18(6): 830–847.

Maggio, Gaetano, and Gaetano Cacciola. 2012. When will oil, natural gas, and coal peak? *Fuel* 98: 111–123.

Mahoney, James, and Gary Goertz. 2006. A tale of two cultures: Contrasting quantitative and qualitative research. *Political Analysis* 14(3): 227–249.

Matláry, Janne H. 1997. *Energy Policy in the European Union*. London: MacMillan.

McLendon, Michael K., and Lora Cohen-Vogel. 2008. Understanding Education Policy Change in the American States: Lessons from Political Science. In *Handbook of Education Politics and Policy*, ed. Bruce S. Cooper, James G. Cibulka, and Lance D. Fusarelli, 35–50. New York: Routledge.

Ness, Erik C. 2010. The Politics of Determining Merit Aid Eligibility Criteria: An Analysis of the Policy Process. *Journal of Higher Education* 81(1): 33–60.

Ostrom, Elinor. 2007. Institutional Rational Choice: An Assessment of the Institutional Analysis and Development Framework. In *Theories of the Policy Process*, 2nd ed., ed. P.A. Sabatier, 21–64. Boulder: Westview Press.

Padgett, Stephen. 1992. The Single European Energy Market: The Politics of Realization. *Journal of Common Market Studies XXX* 1: 53–75.

———. 2003. Between Synthesis and Emulation: EU Policy Transfer in the Power Sector. *Journal of European Public Policy* 10(2): 227–245.

Proedrou, Filippos. 2011. *EU Energy Security in the Gas Sector: Evolving Dynamics, Policy Dilemmas and Prospects*. Farnham: Ashgate.

Prontera, Andrea. 2009. Energy Policy: Concepts, Actors, Instruments and Recent Developments. *World Political Science Review* 5(1, Art. 7): 1–30.

Radaelli, Claudio M. 2000. Public Policy Comes of Age. *Journal of European Public Policy* 7(1): 130–135.

Rowlands, Ian H. 2007. The Development of Renewable Electricity Policy in the Province of Ontario: The Influence of Ideas and Timing. *Review of Policy Research* 24(3): 185–207.

Sabatier, Paul A. 2007a. Fostering the Development of Policy Theory. In *Sabatier* 2007b, 321–336.

———., eds. 2007b. *Theories of Policy Process*. 2nd ed. Boulder, CO: Westview Press.

Sabatier, Paul A., and Christopher M. Weible, eds. 2014. *Theories of the Policy Process*. 3rd ed. New York: Westview Press.

Sandoval, Israel S., and Francesc Morata. 2012. Introduction: The Re-Evolution of Energy Policy in Europe. In *European Energy Policy: An Environmental Approach*, ed. Francesc Morata and Israel Solorio Sandoval, 1–22. Cheltenham: Edward Elgar.

Schlager, Edella. 2007. A Comparison of Frameworks, Theories, and Models of Policy Processes. In *Sabatier* 2007b, 293–319.

Schmidt-Felzmann, Anke. 2011. EU Member States' Energy Relations With Russia: Conflicting Approaches to Securing Natural Gas Supplies. *Geopolitics* 16(3): 574–599.

Schmitt, Sophie, and Kai Schulze. 2011. Choosing Environmental Policy Instruments: An Assessment of the Environmental Dimension' of EU Energy Policy. Special Mini-Issue 1. *European Integration Online Papers* 15 (9).

Stern, Jonathan P. 1992. *Third Party Access in European Gas Industries: Regulation-Driven or Market-Led?* London: Royal institute of international affairs.

———. 1998. *Competition and Liberalization in European Gas Markets: A Diversity of Models*. London: Royal Institute of International Affairs.

Steunenberg, Bernard, and Mark Rhinard. 2010. The Transposition of European Law in EU Member States: Between Process and Politics. *European Political Science Review* 2(3): 495–520.

Storch, Sabine, and Georg Winkel. 2013. Coupling Climate Change and Forest Policy: A Multiple Streams Analysis of Two German Case Studies. *Forest Policy and Economics*: 14–26.

Strange, Susan. 1988. *States and Markets*. London: Pinter Publishers.

Talus, Kim. 2011. Long-Term Natural Gas Contracts and Antitrust Law in the European Union and the United States. *Journal of World Energy Law & Business* 4(3): 260i–315i.

Trampusch, Christine, and Bruno Palier. 2013. *Process Tracing: A Survey of Practices and Theoretical Contributions*. Amsterdam. Paper Prepared for the Panel: "Process Tracing in Practice", Council for European Studies, Conference 2013.

Travis, Rick, and Nikolaos Zahariadis. 2002. A Multiple Streams Model of U.S. Foreign Aid Policy. *Policy Studies Journal* 30(4): 495–514.

Waelde, Thomas W., eds. 1996. *The Energy Charter Treaty: An East-West Gateway for Investment and Trade. International Energy and Resources Law and Policy Series*. London, Boston: Kluwer Law International.

Weible, Christopher M. 2014. Introducing the Scope and Focus of Policy Process Research and Theory. In *Sabatier and Weible* 2014, 3–21.

Westphal, Kirsten. 2006. Energy Policy Between Multilateral Governance and Geopolitics: Whither Europe? *Internationale Politik und Gesellschaft* 4: 44–62.
Zahariadis, Nikolaos. 1999. Ambiguity, time, and multiple streams. In *Theories of the policy process*, 1st ed., ed. Paul A. Sabatier, 73–93. Boulder, CO: Westview Press.
———. 2003. *Political Decision Making in Modern Democracies*. Washington, DC: Georgetown University Press.
———. 2007. The Multiple Streams Framework: Structure, Limitations, Prospects. *In Sabatier* 2007: 65–92.
———. 2008. Ambiguity and Choice in European Public Policy. *Journal of European Public Policy* 15(4): 514–530.
———. 2013. Building Better Theoretical Frameworks of the European Union's Policy Process. *Journal of European Public Policy* 20(6): 807–816.
———. 2014. Ambiguity and Multiple Streams. In *Sabatier and Weible* 2014, 25–58.
Zohlnhöfer, Reimut, Nicole Herweg, and Christian Huß. 2016. Bringing Formal Political Institutions into the Multiple Streams Framework: An Analytical Proposal for Comparative Policy Analysis. *Journal of Comparative Policy Analysis* 18 (3): 243–256.

CHAPTER 2

Theoretical Approach to the Policy Process: The Multiple Streams Framework

The multiple streams framework (MSF) has been subject to criticism (for an overview, see Herweg 2015a, 334–40). Since its initial publication in 1984, Kingdon's framework has been criticized for being a heuristic device only (cf. Bendor et al. 2001, 186; Mucciaroni 2013, 321; Rüb 2008, 99, 105). Basically, this criticism springs from the fact that (1) Kingdon himself does not offer a set of ready-made hypotheses (Sabatier 2007a, b, 327), and (2) the MSF is applied outside its initial scope (i.e., agenda-setting in the United States) (Herweg 2015a, 340–46; Jones et al. 2016) without having been adjusted accordingly. With regard to transferring the MSF (and other public policy lenses) to the European Union (EU) domain, "there has been scant acknowledgement of (a) the theoretical implications of a 'policy approach' to the EU and (b) the theoretical status of tools and models imported by EU scholars" (Radaelli 2000, 133, emphasis in original). Resulting from the research questions posed in this book, I trace the MSF's causal mechanisms in EU policy processes. As a consequence, the MSF is applied (1) as a framework subject to empirical falsification, (2) to agenda-setting and decision-making, and (3) outside its initial scope. Consequently, the above criticisms must be addressed.

Therefore, this chapter is structured as follows: It first summarizes Kingdon's MSF (Sect. 2.1). Since the initial MSF is only equipped to explain agenda-setting (and the selection of alternatives), Sect. 2.2 introduces a modification of the framework, which allows for analyzing agenda-setting and decision-making. Taking into account that the MSF was derived in order to explain agenda-setting at the federal level of the United States,

N. Herweg, *European Union Policy-Making*,
DOI 10.1007/978-3-319-49400-5_2

Sect. 2.3 extends it to the EU by defining functional equivalents of the framework's core concepts in the EU. Finally, Sect. 2.4 combines these extensions and derives falsifiable hypotheses regarding agenda change and policy change in the EU.

2.1 The Basis: Kingdon's Multiple Streams Framework[1]

As mentioned before in the Introduction, the MSF departs from the assumption that policy-making is an exercise in rational problem-solving. Instead, the framework places ambiguity and contingency at the center of the analysis. Ambiguity indicates that, independent from the available amount of information, there are many ways of thinking about the subject matter of a political decision (Feldman 1989, 5, quoted in Zahariadis 2014, 26). Contingency captures that a concrete political decision is neither necessary, nor impossible—or how Luhmann (1976, 509) put it, "[a] fact is contingent when seen as selection from other possibilities which remain in some sense possibilities despite a selection." As a consequence, there does not exist such a thing as one rational solution to a given problem. Since this implies that a multitude of solutions is possible in principle, the framework's basic aim is not to explain the concrete design of a policy but the timing of an agenda (and policy) change.

The MSF builds on the garbage can model (GCM) of organizational choice developed by Cohen et al. (1972). In particular, Kingdon (1984) adopts three assumptions of the GCM, which he modifies slightly in order to transfer them to the policy process. These assumptions refer to organized anarchies, to a process-oriented conception of decision-making situations, and to the idea that decision outcomes depend on the coupling of processes. The subsequent paragraphs explain the meaning of these assumptions in more detail.

2.1.1 The Concept of Organized Anarchies

Cohen et al. (1972, 1) define organized anarchies as organizations or decision situations that are characterized by problematic preferences, unclear technology, and fluid participation. Translated into economic terminology, problematic preferences do not meet the requirements of a reflexive, complete, and transitive preference order. Typically, the preferences emerge during (inter-)action, which can be traced back to ambiguity. Due to time constraints, politicians all too frequently do not have the opportunity to formulate precise preferences before they have to come to a decision (Zahariadis 2014, 27). Thus, preferences and consequently goals are ambivalent and mutable (Münter 2005, 44)—and, in the worst case, even contradictory.

The second feature of organized anarchies is unclear technology. In organizational theory, technology refers to the applied technique and the organization of work processes (Miebach 2012, 96). Unclear technology is given if members of an organization are only familiar with their individual responsibilities but do not know how they fit in the overall relational structure of the organization. This is complicated by the third feature of organized anarchies: fluid participation in decision-making. In this context, fluidity relates (1) to the changing composition of the decision-making body, which is contingent upon the concrete decision to be taken, and (2) to the varying amount of time and effort members of the decision-making body are willing and able to invest (Cohen et al. 1972, 1).

According to Kingdon, political systems are defined by the same characteristics as organized anarchies, although he puts more emphasis "on the 'organized' than on the 'anarchy'" (Kingdon 1984, 92, emphasis in original), because political processes show structures and patterns. He clarifies this point with the metaphor that the model "is structured in the same sense that a river is fluid, but its banks usually restrict its movement. The process cannot flow just anywhere" (Kingdon 2003, 223). Before elucidating which factors restrict political processes to flow anywhere, it is necessary to introduce the second assumption adopted from the GCM.

2.1.2 *A Process-Oriented Perspective on Policy-Making Situations*

This second assumption is that largely separate processes flow through decision-making situations or more general through the political system (Kingdon 1984, 91). However, Kingdon departs in various aspects from the definitions introduced by Cohen et al. (1972). As mentioned before, Kingdon does not intend to explain decision-making processes in organizations but agenda-setting in political systems. Furthermore, Cohen et al. (1972, 3) base their analysis on four streams: problems, solutions, participants, and choice opportunities. Kingdon distinguishes between processes and participants, because theoretically, each participant could be involved in more than one process. He identifies three processes or streams[2] to be

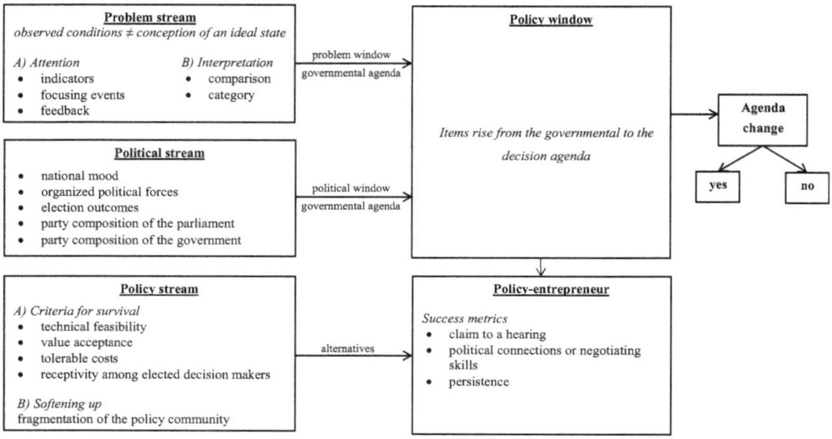

Fig. 2.1 Kingdon's multiple streams framework. *Source*: Own compilation based on Zahariadis (2007)

relevant for explaining agenda-setting at the federal level of the United States: the problem stream, the political stream, and the policy stream (see Fig. 2.1).[3]

The *problem stream* is composed of all conditions that are perceived as problems. More specifically, conditions that are theoretically changeable and desired to be altered (politically) (Kingdon 1984, 119, Kingdon 1994, 218). With his definition of problems as "[a] mismatch between the observed conditions and one's conception of an ideal state", Kingdon (1984, 116) introduces an element of interpretation in problem recognition. Thus, it is useful to distinguish two questions in the problem stream: First, how is attention raised? Second, on which basis is the comparison drawn which leads to the perception that a condition deviates from an ideal state?

Regarding the first question, mechanisms that generate attention are indicators, focusing events, and feedback. For instance, singularly or repeatedly reported indicators addressing energy dependency can raise attention to security of supply issues. Disasters, crises, personal experiences, and symbols count as focusing events.[4] Departing from indicators, focusing events do not have an effect by themselves. They unveil problems if they reinforce preexisting perceptions or if they occur in conjunction with indicators or other focusing events (Kingdon 1984, 119). Finally, channels for feedback on policy outcomes are systematic monitoring and evaluation studies. Besides these more formal channels, feedback can also be received informally or as input from bureaucrats regarding difficulties with policy implementation (Kingdon 1984, 106).

Once attention is raised to an observation, it must be interpreted as problematic to fall in the problem stream. Basically, there are two ways to arrive at this interpretation: First, by comparing one's own performance with that of others' or with one's own past performance on a special subject; and second, by replacing the category on which the comparison has been drawn so far with a new or another category (Kingdon 1984, 117). Indicators raised to measure the functioning of the natural gas market can be evaluated according to its competitiveness or according to matters of security of supply, which might lead to different assessments. If attention is raised to a condition by at least one of the abovementioned mechanisms and this condition does not meet the expectations according to its performance or the applied category, problems are detected.

With regard to problem recognition, the MSF assigns policy-entrepreneurs a pivotal role. Before this role is introduced, a definition of policy-entrepreneurs is needed. Policy-entrepreneurs are defined as "advocates who are willing to invest their resources—time, energy, reputation, money—to promote a position in return for anticipated future gain in the form of material, purposive, or solidary benefits" (Kingdon 1984, 188). This definition implies that it is not the actors' position but their activities that qualifies them for being a policy-entrepreneur. Put differently, each actor can be a policy-entrepreneur in principal (Kingdon 1984, 214). However, deducting from case analyses, Kingdon (1984, 189) concludes that it is more common that only one or a few actors engage in policy-entrepreneurship.

In the problem stream, policy-entrepreneurs have two strategies at their disposal in order to push for a specific problem recognition: First, they attempt to raise attention to specific issues by referring to them in press releases or speeches. Second, they attempt to change the framing of an issue in a way which enforces a specific problem recognition of ambiguous condition (Zahariadis 2007, 77).[5]

The *political stream* refers to the procedural dimension of policy-making, with Kingdon highlighting the importance of the electorate, parties, and interest groups (Kingdon 1984, 152). Thus, it deals with the strife for power (Weber 1985, 852). The national mood, organized political forces, election outcomes, and the party composition, both of the parliament and of the government, illustrate the dynamics in the political stream. The latter is of importance, because the influx of a new government goes hand in hand with new policy perspectives. Organized political forces on the other hand do not promote new ideas but try to influence those ideas that are already under debate. The national mood, defined as "a rather large number of people out in the country (...) thinking along certain common lines" (Kingdon 1984, 153), can promote or hinder problems getting on the agenda. But they do not give impetus to new issues for being considered (Kingdon 1984, 156). Summing up, this stream is characterized by lobbying and group mobilization.

The key elements in the *policy stream* are the policy community and the policy primeval soup. Departing from today's scientific parlance, Kingdon defines a policy community as a loose (instead of a closed, restricted, and stable) relationship of policy specialists who have a shared concern and engage in working out alternatives[6] to policy problems of a specific policy field (Herweg 2013, 8). A prerequisite to become part of a policy community is the interaction with other members of the policy community. Interaction is given if the members of a policy community are familiar with each other's ideas, proposals, and research, which often goes along with personal acquaintance (Kingdon 1984, 123). The policy primeval soup consists of the policy community's ideas, which, in the form of proposals, "are floated, come into contact with one another, are revised and combined with one another, and floated again" (Kingdon 1984, 21).

"Many, many things are possible here [in the policy primeval soup, N. H.]" (Kingdon 1984, 128). Prerequisites for ideas to be considered as eligible alternatives are "technical feasibility, value acceptability within the policy community, tolerable cost, anticipated public acquiescence, and a reasonable chance for receptivity among elected decision makers" (Kingdon 1984, 138). While technical feasibility and tolerable cost address the question of whether implementing an alternative is possible in principle, normative acceptance and receptivity among the decision-makers focus on obstacles that could complicate its passing in the decision-making process.

A pivotal actor in removing obstacles in the way is the policy-entrepreneur. During a process that is called "softening up" (Kingdon 1984, 134), policy-entrepreneurs advocate their ideas in order to gain acceptance and approval from the policy community and the broader expert audience. According to Kingdon (1984, 134), the probability that ideas find their way on the decision agenda is low if they are not accompanied by a softening-up process.

2.1.3 Coupling of the Streams and Agenda Change

The third modified assumption adopted from the GCM is that agenda and policy changes depend on the successful coupling of the problem, political, and policy stream (Cohen et al. 1972, 1; Kingdon 1984, 91). According to the MSF, three necessary conditions must be met to couple the streams: First, the streams must be ripe; second, a policy window is open; and third, policy-entrepreneurs engage in coupling the streams. The streams are ripe if they are receptive to an agenda change. The second prerequisite is that a policy window opens as a result from changes in the problem or political stream. In order to distinguish between the different drivers that open a policy window, Kingdon (1984, 204) distinguishes problem from political windows. Furthermore, policy windows can be distinguished between predictable and unpredictable ones. Examples of predictable windows are negotiations about the budget or elections at the end of a legislative period. A plane crash or new elections as a consequence of a governmental crisis count as unpredictable policy windows. As soon as a policy window has opened, an issue enters the governmental agenda. The governmental agenda is defined as "the list of subjects or problems to which governmental officials, and people outside of government closely associated with those officials, are paying some attention at any given point" (Kingdon 1984, 3).

In this situation, it depends on the third necessary condition whether an issue rises from the governmental onto the decision agenda: the policy-entrepreneurs' coupling activities. The decision agenda is a subset of the governmental agenda and contains those issues that are "moving into position for an authoritative decision, such as legislative enactment or presidential choice" (Kingdon 1984, 211). The way policy-entrepreneurs try to couple the streams depends on the kind of policy window. In the case of problem windows, they attempt to present their favorite policy as a solution to the problem that has opened the policy window and to gain the support of the policy-makers.

For instance, if the recognition of air pollution as an environmental problem has opened a problem window, policy-entrepreneurs present the liberalization of the natural gas markets as a solution to reduce greenhouse gas emissions. They could argue that liberalizing this sector will lead to a decline in natural gas prices, which in turn provides energy consumers with an incentive to substitute other fossil fuels by natural gas. Since natural gas is the cleanest-burning fossil fuel, this would contribute to a better air quality and solve the problem that opened the policy window. If an unexpected interruption in natural gas supply from abroad has reinforced security of supply concerns, this opens a policy window which policy-entrepreneurs use to present the liberalization of the natural gas sector as a solution to this problem. A possible line of argumentation could be that in a proper functioning internal gas market, the network infrastructure is interlinked, which allows for redirecting gas flows in order to compensate for the unexpected interruption. If, more generally, the perception of poor economic growth in the EU opens a policy window, policy-entrepreneurs could frame energy liberalization as a means to boost economic activity. Energy liberalization leads to lower energy prices and translates into competitive advantages, particularly for the energy-intensive industry.

If a political window opens as a consequence of the inauguration of a new government, policy-entrepreneurs try to take advantage of the changed political climate and to sell their favorite policy as a solution to an existing problem (Kingdon 1984, 216–17). If the incoming government has been elected on a manifesto promising to stimulate economic growth, policy-entrepreneurs will come forward with very different proposals on how to achieve this goal, such as a fiscal stimulus package which includes their favorite policies (e.g., tax reduction, increased social spending) or liberalization policies.

Hence, while framing is guided by issue specifics in the context of problem windows, it is guided by policy-makers' receptiveness in the context of political windows. Referring to Kingdon's distinction of problem and political windows, Zahariadis (1996, 405–7) speaks of consequential coupling in the context of problem windows and of doctrinal coupling in the context of political windows.[7] However, policy-entrepreneurs are first and foremost interested in getting their favorite policy on the (governmental and decision) agenda. Therefore, it is highly plausible that a policy-entrepreneur would seize the opportunity and apply both coupling strategies in order to boost his or her chances to change the agenda.

If policy-entrepreneurs succeed in coupling the ripe streams in times of an open policy window, an agenda change takes place. However, policy windows open for a short time span only (Kingdon 1984, 204). They close if a problem has been addressed or solved, if policy-entrepreneurs stop investing their resources, if the conditions that opened the policy window have vanished, if the policy-makers failed to come to a compromise, or if there has not been a worked-out alternative available in the policy stream (Kingdon 1984, 177–78).

2.1.4 *Agenda Change Enabling Factors*

According to Kingdon, specific characteristics of policy-entrepreneurs and policy communities have a beneficial effect on the probability of an agenda change. Whether a policy-entrepreneur succeeds in coupling the streams depends on the person's claim to be heard by the policy-makers and his or her political well-connectedness, negotiating skills, and persistence. The claim to be heard is higher if a policy-entrepreneur (1) is known for being a policy expert, (2) represents an (interest) group, and/or (3) is equipped with decision-making authority (Kingdon 1984, 189–90).[8] But even if a policy-entrepreneur is well-equipped for a successful coupling, he or she can fail due to an overload of the political–administrative system. This happens when too many problems and/or alternatives enter the stage simultaneously.

Additionally, it depends on the level of integration of the policy community as to which ideas remain as a result of the softening-up process. The more integrated a policy community is, the more easily evolve a common language, common outlooks, orientations, and ways of thinking between its members. Since value acceptability within the policy community is one prerequisite for an idea to be considered as an eligible alternative, the broad consensus typical of more integrated policy communities results in the supply of just a few worked-out alternatives. This fosters agenda stability. Less-integrated policy communities lack internal coordination. Consequently, it is easier to float new ideas, which is why in less-integrated policy communities, more and distinct policy alternatives are worked out. From this more abundant supply of worked-out policies follows that agenda instability and disjointed policies are more likely in the presence of less-integrated policy communities (Kingdon 1984, 124–28).

Furthermore, according to Kingdon (1984, 200), "[t]he appearance of a window for one subject often increases the probability that a window will open for another similar subject." He refers to this effect as spillover.[9] A spillover can take place within a given policy area and into adjacent areas. In the former case, a spillover can be traced back to a newly established principle, which policy-makers apply in future arguments in the same policy area. A prerequisite for the spillover into an adjacent policy area is that there is a similarity between the policy areas; for example, that the issue at stake is placed in the same category as the successfully pushed proposal in the precedent policy area (Kingdon 1984, 184). Additionally, it is important that the spillover takes place before policy implementation unveils problems and thereby weakens the arguments to transfer the ideas in question (Kingdon 1984, 202). From the policy-entrepreneur's point of view, it is promising to trigger spillovers for three reasons: First, they assume to be rewarded for the transfer of an already successful policy (for instance, in terms of electoral support); second, there exists a winning coalition that just has to be transferred to a related issue; and finally, the selling of a proposal is facilitated by the possibility to refer to a successful precedent (Kingdon 1984, 204).

2.2 Extension I: Explaining the Policy Decision

Kingdon (1984, 2) explicitly states that the MSF is not about "how issues are authoritatively decided by the president, Congress or other decision makers, but rather how they came to be issues in the first place". Nonetheless, as reported in Table 1.2 (see Sect. 1.2), it is common practice nowadays to expand the framework to explain *agenda-setting and decision-making.*[10] This might largely be attributed to two facts: First, the MSF adopts core assumptions of the GCM, which explicitly aims at explaining decision-making processes. As a consequence of sharing the central core assumptions, it is plausible to assume that the MSF should equally be suited to explain the decision-making stage. Second, Kingdon (2003) himself expands the framework and applies the MSF to agenda-setting *and* decision-making in his analysis of the Reagan budget in 1981 and the Tax Reform Act of 1986 in the second edition of *Agendas, Alternatives, and Public Policies* by (implicitly) referring the policy window to both policy stages.[11]

However, if the MSF is applied to these policy stages, one needs to take into account that they differ in various aspects. From an agenda-setting perspective, more institutional venues are seen to facilitate change by providing actors with venue-shopping opportunities. However, they are seen to prohibit change from a decision-making perspective. The more institutional venues are involved in making decisions, the more likely there are multiple veto actors. Since policy change requires the consent of all veto actors, the presence of multiple veto actors increases the probability of policy stability (Baumgartner et al. 2006). Furthermore, if the MSF is meant to be more than just a heuristic, any expansion of its explanatory potential needs to address the question of causality. The next subsection provides a literature review of previous contributions that extend the MSF to the decision-making stage (2.2.1). Based on the findings of this literature review, the subsequent subsection (2.2.2) introduces a modified MSF suitable for explaining agenda-setting and decision-making.

2.2.1 State of the Art

In contrast to other scientific communities, there is no scientific dialogue within the multiple streams literature yet.[12] As a result, individual contributions remain mostly unconnected to each other (Herweg 2015a, 335; Zohlnhöfer and Rüb 2016b, 12, 15), which makes it difficult to detect which answers to the question of how the MSF can be extended to the decision-making stage have already been found. Additionally, the impressive frequency with which the various editions of Kingdon's monograph are cited makes it impossible to conduct a complete literature review.[13] Therefore, this subsection concentrates on those contributions that are included in the meta-review dataset generated by Jones et al. (2016) and referred to in Sect. 1.2. More specifically, only those applications that (1) apply the MSF fully and (2) to the decision-making stage are considered. It turns out that of the 49 articles fulfilling these two criteria, only eight articles address the need for theoretical modification of the initial MSF when applying it to decision-making. Of these eight articles, two focus on levels of analysis that are too different from decision-making at the federal level of a political system to draw lessons from it relevant for this book (Cook and Rinfret 2013; Lee 2003)[14] and one focuses on policy-entrepreneurship (Bakir 2009). Another article delivers a synthesis of the advocacy coalition framework, the MSF, and the punctuated equilibrium approach (Johnson et al. 2005).[15] Of the remaining four articles, three refer to the theoretical modification delivered by Zahariadis (1995, 1996, 2003) (namely, Blankenau 2001; Storch and Winkel 2013; Travis and Zahariadis 2002), while van Stigt et al. (2013) deliver a modification of their own. Therefore, the next paragraphs concentrate on the theoretical modifications suggested by Zahariadis and van Stigt, Driessen, and Spit.

According to Zahariadis (1992, 359),[16] Kingdon's MSF needs only a small modification in order to be applicable to the decision-making stage: "[P]olicy windows and coupling here refer to decision, not just agenda, choices." Put differently, coupling refers to both, agenda-setting and decision-making. This modification has the advantage that the structural features and logic of the framework remain intact (Zahariadis 1992, 359). Still three streams flow through the political system (problem, political, and policy stream) and policy windows open if changes occur in the problem or political stream. The opportunity for a policy change is given in times of an open policy window provided that a worked-out proposal is available in the policy stream. Whether a policy change actually takes place depends causally on the activities of policy-entrepreneurs. However, this advantage is accompanied by the shortcoming of not allowing to analyze the relevant policy processes appropriately, which provides grist to the mill of those who criticize the MSF of sticking at redescribing policy events (cf. Lodge 2005, 262). [17]

Why does Zahariadis' (1992) suggestion not allow for the analysis of both policy processes accurately? In order to answer this question, it is helpful to recall the difference between the governmental agenda and the decision agenda. The governmental agenda, the "list of subjects that are getting attention", is set in either the problem or political stream, while the decision agenda, the list of subjects "that are up for an active decision" (Kingdon 1984: 4), results from the coupling of all three streams by policy-entrepreneurs (Kingdon 1984: 211). Hence, the coupling process as such explains how the decision agenda is set. In other words, it ends when the formal legislative process begins, during which the policy is formulated and legitimized.[18]

Depending on the political system, policy formulation and legitimation last several months on average. Thus, defining the coupling process in terms of setting the decision agenda and passing a bill involves almost inevitably analytical imprecision. Mainly, there are three reasons for this imprecision: *First*, this theoretical modification implies that (1) the three streams remain constant during the whole investigation period, and (2) the same policy-entrepreneur succeeds in pushing his or her proposal on the decision agenda *and* through the decision process. Knowing that the policy-making process can span several months, these assumptions are not convincing. This holds particularly true for the EU, where policy processes tend to be longer than at the member state level due to the absence of the legislative discontinuity principle (König 2007, 412).[19] According to the legislative discontinuity principle, pending legislation ends with the dissolution of the parliament or the ending of a legislative term. In the EU, elections to the European Parliament (EP) do not prompt a new legislative cycle. Hence, irrespective of the parliamentary session or legislative term, European Commission (hereafter, the Commission) proposals do not vanish from the decision agenda once they are introduced. *Second*, if the coupling process captures agenda-setting and decision-making, it becomes difficult to explain policy stability. More precisely, it is impossible to distinguish whether an issue fails to get on the decision agenda or whether an issue has entered the decision agenda but policy-entrepreneurs fail to find the majority needed for passing the draft proposal during the actual decision-making process. *Third*, if agenda-setting is not kept distinct from decision-making, one cannot assess how much the policy output differs from the initial proposal due to political compromises.

Van Stigt et al. (2013) share with Zahariadis' (1992) approach the idea that decision-making processes are characterized by the MSF's central concepts (problem, political, and policy stream, policy window, policy-entrepreneur). However, they rename policy windows "decision windows", which they define as "a moment or relatively short period of time within a decision round, in which different interests meet and are combined, or in which issues are reframed to arrive at a shared problem definition" (van Stigt et al. 2013, 20). In contrast to Zahariadis, they concentrate exclusively on the decision-making stage. More specifically, van Stigt et al. (2013) aim at explaining decisions which (1) are reached in multiple arenas, (2) span various decision rounds, (3) result from a deliberation process, and (4) are formalized by "a body designated to govern an institutional entity" (van Stigt et al. 2013, 19). Resulting from this broad definition, they cover decision processes that range from those taking place in municipal governments to those of private actors (van Stigt et al. 2013, 19). Due to the inclusion of such diverse decision settings, van Stigt et al. (2013) do not take into account how institutions affect decision-making. This is problematic because state-of-the-art public policy literature finds that a government's scope of action is influenced substantially by institutions (cf. Immergut 1992; Scharpf 1997; Tsebelis 2002).

2.2.2 *A Modified Multiple Streams Framework*

The theoretical modifications suggested by Zahariadis (1992) and van Stigt et al. (2013) share the idea that the structure of the MSF is principally suitable for analyzing decision-making. However, if the MSF is meant to be more than a heuristic device, it needs to be modified in a way that addresses the shortcomings of Zahariadis (1992) and van Stigt et al. (2013). Therefore, I suggest considering two coupling processes (Herweg 2013; Herweg et al. 2015). The first coupling process captures the agenda-setting (hereafter referred to as agenda coupling) and is identical to Kingdon's MSF. The output of this coupling process is a worked-out proposal ready for decision. Since "[b]eing on the decision agenda (...) does not insure enactment or favorable bureaucratic decision, but it is a more active status than being on the governmental agenda" (Kingdon 1984, 175), it is the second coupling process (hereafter referred to as decision coupling) which focuses on the decision-making stage. Decision coupling captures the political struggle about the concrete design of the proposal. It depends on the activities of policy-entrepreneurs as to which of the ideas comprising the policy stream are seen as suitable for gaining the majority needed for a decision. If decision coupling is successful, it ends with the adoption of a bill. Henceforth, the first coupling opportunity is referred to as "agenda window", while the second one is labeled "decision window" (see Fig. 2.2). Since decision coupling captures the (formal) decision-making process, it allows for considering different institutional settings (i.e., stemming for the system of government). The critique can be countered, according to which the MSF is institution-blind (cf. Mucciaroni 1992; Weir 1992, 17–18).[20]

Although the thus-modified MSF keeps the framework's operating structure for both policy processes intact, the concept of policy-entrepreneurs needs to be altered. According to Kingdon (1984, 189), just one or a few persons engage in agenda coupling. However, it is highly plausible that more than just a few persons engage in decision coupling (cf. Roberts and King 1991). Furthermore, while there are actors (and thereby potential policy-entrepreneurs) who participate at both stages of the policy process, there are others who are exclusively engaged in agenda-setting *or* decision-making

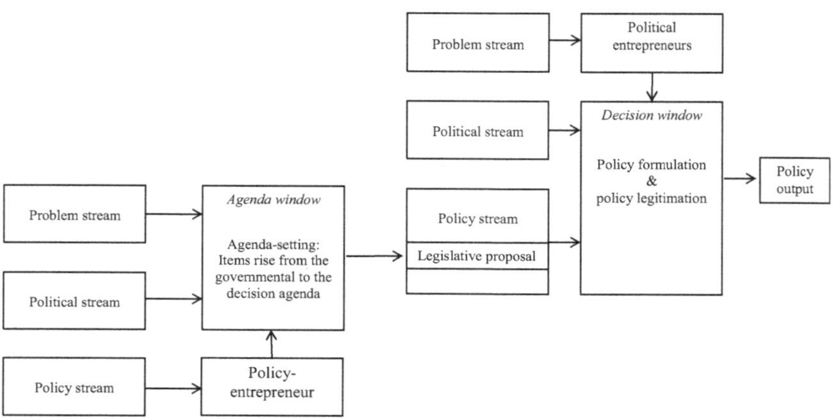

Fig. 2.2 The modified multiple streams framework. *Source*: Herweg et al. (2015: 445). Copyright © 2015 European Consortium for Political Research, published by John Wiley & Sons Ltd. Reprinted by permission of John Wiley & Sons Ltd.

(cf. Saetren 2014, 13). Taking these differences into account, I borrow the concept of collective entrepreneurship from Roberts and King (1991). Central to this concept is the idea that like-minded individuals with different skills, knowledge, and positions work toward policy change both simultaneously and at different stages in the policy process. However, Roberts and King (1991, 152) reserve the term "policy-entrepreneur" for individuals who (1) engage in political entrepreneurship during the creation, design, and implementation phase; and (2) do not hold a formal position in government. In contrast, Kingdon (1984, 129) locates policy-entrepreneurs "in or out of government, in elected or appointed positions, in interest groups or research organizations". While Kingdon's understanding of policy-entrepreneurs works for agenda coupling, it is too broad for decision coupling. This is because a policy-entrepreneur located outside the formal policy-making arena lacks the means to couple the streams, in contrast to an insider policy-entrepreneur who draws on authority qua position.

In order to avoid confusion, I maintain Kingdon's terminology and understanding of the concept of policy-entrepreneurs for the agenda-setting stage. For decision coupling, I replace the term policy-entrepreneurs with "political entrepreneurs" in order to indicate that different persons engage in entrepreneurship. According to Roberts and King (1991, 152), political entrepreneurs are individuals who "hold elected leadership positions in government".[21] The present book stretches this definition in so far as it also considers individuals as political entrepreneurs who (1) hold elected leadership positions and (2) formally belong to the policy-making authorities (i.e., one of the chambers of parliament)—and not just to the government. This slightly changed definition takes into consideration that, for instance, opposition party leaders also try to change draft bills.

Furthermore, the two coupling processes differ in three aspects: (1) the causal mechanisms which open the respective window, (2) the importance of the streams, and (3) the coupling strategies applied. Regarding the causal mechanisms, an *agenda window* is opened by events that trigger changes in the problem and political streams, such as improvements or deteriorations of indicators or the election of a new government. The *decision window* opens in the policy stream. More precisely, it is the worked-out proposal that has risen on the decision agenda as a result of agenda coupling. Put differently, once a draft bill has been introduced in the legislative arena, bargaining about the details of the proposal starts immediately between the actors in the political stream. The reason is that these actors will not pass the chance to influence a policy once an issue is on the agenda, although their personal commitment might vary depending on the importance they attribute to the proposal at stake.

As a consequence, the importance of the streams varies in the two coupling processes.[22] Following Kingdon (1984), all streams are important for *agenda coupling* (see Sect. 2.1.3). Regarding *decision coupling* however, the political stream is of prime importance, while the problem and policy streams are of minor importance. The *political stream* is important because this is where the actors are located whose consent is required in order to adopt a policy. Since decision coupling can only take place if the *policy stream* has been ripened before, it is not very likely that the policy stream changes much during decision coupling. Nonetheless, this stream remains important in so far as political entrepreneurs reach into the policy primeval soup to combine available alternatives in a way with which it is possible to win a majority in parliament.

Concerning the *problem stream*, the reading of a draft bill takes place independently of the given pressure to address the problem the draft bill is meant to solve. On the other hand, the dynamic of the problem stream influences the bargaining process in that a supportive problem stream reinforces the necessity to deal with an issue, while an adverse problem stream dampens it.

With regard to the distinction between *doctrinal* and *consequential coupling*, these coupling strategies become less important during decision coupling. Decision windows are opened by the introduction of a draft bill. This implies that a specific problem–solution connection has prevailed, and extending or changing a frame by enforcing a rival frame or extending the current one (Snow et al. 1986) would impose extra costs to political entrepreneurs. Extra costs arise because political entrepreneurs do not only have to redirect the policy-makers' support toward their pet proposal but also have to convince them from the new framing. This does not exclude the possibility that doctrinal or consequential coupling can take place in decision windows, but it is less likely. Instead, as Herweg et al. (2015, 12) point out, political entrepreneurs use three instruments during decision coupling: package deals, concessions, and manipulation. A political entrepreneur tries to melt different proposals into one *package deal*, provided that his or her pet proposal is part of this package and the inclusion of someone else's pet proposals broadens the support for the package as a whole. Another way to gain the majority needed for passing a bill is to offer *concessions* on the original proposal to other veto actors. Similar to agenda coupling, political entrepreneurs engage in *manipulation* in the sense of providing meaning, clarification, and identity to the issue at stake (Zahariadis 2003, 21).

2.3 Extension II: Explaining the EU Policy Process[23]

Peters (1994, 18, 20) and Richardson (2006, 23) already indicated in the 1990s that the EU policy process shares the characteristics of garbage can decision-making. Nonetheless, it is only since recently that applying the MSF to the EU has gained scholarly attention (Ackrill et al. 2013; Zahariadis 2013). Provided that (1) Kingdon (1984) derived the MSF inductively and (2) (agenda or policy) change is determined by the interaction between context and causal mechanism (Faletti and Lynch 2009), any application of the framework to jurisdictions other than the United States requires the identification of functional equivalents of the MSF's core concepts.

The focus on adapting the framework's core concepts to context specifics rather than its causal mechanisms results from the fact that the latter are contextually insensitive (Faletti and Lynch 2009). Causal mechanisms only inform about the relationship between the framework's elements. Kingdon (1984) differentiates two sets of causal mechanisms: events that open a policy window on the one hand, and coupling activities of policy-entrepreneurs that actually lead to (agenda) change on the other hand. However, as long as the framework's core concepts are not adjusted appropriately, their relation remains ill-defined. For instance, it is easy to identify the government and its partisan composition in nation-states, but it is less obvious if the MSF is transferred to the EU. Mirroring its characterization as a *sui generis* political system, executive power is shared between the Council of Ministers (hereafter, the Council) and the European Council, together with the Commission in the EU (cf. Hix and Høyland 2011). However, simply replacing the government in the political stream with these three executive branches does not clarify which events qualify for a change in government and open an agenda window. Since an open agenda window is a prerequisite for a policy-entrepreneur to succeed in agenda coupling, it is important to know by which events such a window opens.

Although the MSF is increasingly applied as a model for understanding the EU policy process, the existing literature falls short of systematically defining functional equivalents of the framework's core concepts. In this regard, Zahariadis' (2008) contribution is outstanding: He delivers a theory-driven transfer of the framework's elements to the EU, which he supplements with an exemplary discussion of how a policy window opens. However, he does not distinguish between agenda-setting and decision-making. As a consequence, it remains unclear whether the streams' composition varies between these two policy stages (cf. Sects. 2.2.2 and 2.3.2).

As is true for MSF applications in general (Jones et al. 2016), contributions that fully apply the framework to the EU (and as such must define functional equivalents) are rare (Ackrill et al. 2013). Table 2.1 provides an overview of full MSF applications to the EU.[24] These applications share (to a differing degree) the aspect that they do not adapt the framework's core concepts to EU specifics.

Moreover, those applications that transfer the framework's key elements to the EU level arrive at very different definitions. Table 2.2 illustrates how widely these definitions differ at the example of the EU's political stream.

Summing up, in order to apply the MSF to the EU, functional equivalents of the framework's elements must be defined in a theory-informed manner. Furthermore, it is pivotal to be explicit about how the causal mechanisms relate the framework's elements for each policy stage included in the analysis. While the question of causality is addressed in Sect. 2.4, the present chapter engages in the first endeavor: defining functional equivalents. More precisely, it systematically defines them for the elements of the problem stream (Sect. 2.3.1), political stream (Sect. 2.3.2), and policy stream (Sect. 2.3.3). The definitions of policy-entrepreneurs and political entrepreneurs as introduced in the previous chapters also apply to EU policy-making. This is true for agenda and decision windows, too. They only present *opportunities* to make agenda change or policy change happen.

2.3.1 The EU's Problem Stream

The *problem stream* requires only slight adaptations which apply to both policy stages considered in the analysis. This stream needs to be complemented with a European dimension. This means that the problem stream's mechanisms of problem recognition—indicators, focusing events, and feedback concerning previous policy programs—can arise from the member states' and the European level. If it originates from the former, a policy-entrepreneur needs to frame the problem in a way which justifies why it is subject to Community action. A particularity of the EU problem stream is the prominent role the Commission plays in raising attention to specific issues, due to its task of collecting and compiling indicators and feedback, as in the form of benchmarking reports or Green and White Papers.

Table 2.1 Adaptation of the multiple streams framework's core concepts to EU specifics

Contributions	*Streams and stream ripeness*		*Events that open a policy window*		*Policy-entrepreneurs' coupling activities*	
	Adaptation	*Empirical application*	*Adaptation*	*Empirical application*	*Adaptation*	*Empirical application*
Ackrill and Kay (2011)	No	Streams: yes Ripeness: no	Yes (endogenous and exogenous spillovers)		Yes	
Bache (2013)	No	Streams: yes Ripeness: no	No	Yes	No	Yes
Borrás and Radaelli (2011)	Streams: political stream (implicitly) Ripeness: no	Streams: yes	No	Yes	No	Yes
Bürgin (2013)	Streams: political stream Ripeness: no	Streams: yes	No	Yes	Yes	
Copeland and James (2014)	No	Streams: yes Ripeness: no	No	Yes	Yes	
Huisman and de Jong (2014)	No	Streams: yes Ripeness: differentiation between condu-cive and inhibitive factors	No	Yes (focus on the question why the policy window remained open)	No	Yes
Iusmen (2013)	Streams: yes Ripeness: no	Ripeness: implicitly	No	Yes	No	Yes

(continued)

Table 2.1 (continued)

Contributions	*Streams and stream ripeness*		*Events that open a policy window*		*Policy-entrepreneurs' coupling activities*	
	Adaptation	*Empirical application*	*Adaptation*	*Empirical application*	*Adaptation*	*Empirical application*
Kaunert and Giovanna (2010)	No	Streams: implicitly Ripeness: no	No	Yes (problem window)	Yes	
Maltby (2013)	Streams: yes Stream ripeness: no		No	Yes (problem window)	Yes	
Sarmiento-Mirwaldt (2015)	Streams: policy stream	Streams: yes Ripeness: no	No		No	Yes
Zahariadis (2008)	Yes	n.a.	Yes	n.a.	Yes	n.a.

Source: Own compilation

Notes: Adaptation and empirical application of the MSF's core concepts are coded as "yes" if the authors explicitly referred to these core concepts; otherwise, they are coded as "no". If the authors did only refer to a subset of the core concepts, I added which element they considered in their analysis. Since Zahariadis (2008) delivered a theoretical contribution, the columns concerning the empirical application are coded as not applicable (n.a.).

Table 2.2 Adaptation of the political stream to EU specifics

Contributions	*Definition of the political stream*
Borrás and Radaelli (2013: 475)	The political stream is broadly defined as "the time of politics" and includes "elections, public opinion movements and campaigning on issues, based on the electoral cycle". Relevant for the European Union (EU) cycle are "EP [European Parliament] elections, Council summits and the renewal of the European Commission at regular intervals of time".
Bürgin (2013: 2)	"The politics stream refers to interest and power constellations in the Council."
Iusmen (2013: 514)	"[T]he politics stream (...) encompasses both EU internal political conditions and political events occurring in the context of Eastern enlargement."
Maltby (2013: 436)	"The politics stream consists of political developments, in this case a trend of increasing energy imports and prices, along with enlargement of the EU to include NMS [newer member states] which felt their national security was undermined by dependence on gas imports (particularly from Russia)."
Zahariadis (2008: 518)	"Three factors are important in the politics stream: the balance of Council member national and partisan affiliation, the ideological balance of parties in Parliament, and the European mood."
Ackrill and Kay (2011) Bache (2013) Copeland and James (2014) Huisman and de Jong (2014) Kaunert and Giovanna (2010) Sarmiento-Mirwaldt (2015)	These contributions do not include a theoretically derived definition of the political stream.

Source: Own compilation

2.3.2 *The EU's Political Stream*

The *political stream* requires the most far-reaching adaptations because a political system's institutional setting determines the leeway the government, parliament, and interest groups have at different policy stages (cf. Schlager 1999, 247–48). Furthermore, the actors involved in the different policy stages tend to vary (Jann and Wegrich 2007; Saetren 2016). In case some actors participate at both stages of the policy cycle, it is unlikely that their importance remains constant. For instance, whereas an item can rise on the decision agenda against the will of veto actors (such as the majority of the second chamber in parliament), it cannot be passed without their consent (Immergut 1992; Tsebelis 2002). As a first step, the functional equivalents of the government, parliament, interest groups, and the national mood are defined. On this basis, their involvement and importance during agenda-setting and decision-making is discussed. Taking into account that institutions matter, the proposed adjustments are suited to analyze EU policy processes that are subject to the ordinary legislative procedure (ex codecision procedure).

As mentioned above, executive power in the EU is shared between the Commission, the Council, and the European Council. The functional equivalent of the parliament is the EP, and of the national mood, the European mood. Just like in the initial MSF, domestic interest groups (as far as they are concerned with EU policy-making) are relevant. However, they are joined by European representative bodies (such as European umbrella associations of domestic interest groups).

Naming these counterparts is relatively simple (see Table 2.3). Nevertheless, given the vast differences between the political system of the United States and of the EU, it remains to be discussed whether the influence they exert on the EU policy process is sufficiently comparable to the one Kingdon ascribes them in his model. This regards to Kingdon's observations concerning (1) the importance of the partisan composition of the government and parliament, and (2) the influence of interest groups and the national mood.

Regarding the *partisan affiliation* of members of the government and parliament, Kingdon (1984, 160–162) assumes that party membership impacts specific ideas to which officials are receptive (in a similar vein, see Zahariadis 2014, 34). Put differently, parties make a difference (Hibbs 1977). However, it is less clear whether this is the case regarding the EU's executive and legislative powers (Lindberg et al. 2008; for an overview, see Judge and Earnshaw 2008). Given the mixed empirical findings, I refrain from summarizing the state of this research and introduce adjustments, which are tailored to the policy processes analyzed in this book. As a consequence, they might have to be revised for other case studies.

I assume that the *partisan affiliation* does not matter regarding natural gas market regulation, because "[b]oth supporters and opponents of particular regulatory measures usually cast their arguments in the language of 'regulatory science' rather than in the more traditional language of interest or class policies" (Majone 1997, 157, emphasis in original). In contrast,

Table 2.3 The political stream in the EU

The political stream in the initial MSF	*Functional equivalents in the EU*
Government	European Commission Council of Ministers European Council
Parliament	European Parliament
Interest groups	Domestic interest groups and European representative bodies
National mood	European mood

Source: Own compilation

following Zahariadis (2008, 518), the *national affiliation* influences the representatives' receptivity to specific ideas in the EU. This is highly convincing in the case of energy policy, because member states have treated this policy domain "as 'high politics' akin to security policy" (Matláry 1997, 25, emphasis in original; in a similar vein, for instance, Andersen 1993, 137). They tend to put member states' energy interests first (Finon and Surrey 1996, 166). In this respect, the Commission is an exception, because it is usually neither led by national nor partisan considerations but by the promotion of the internal market (Fligstein 2001). As spreading (cost-effective) regulatory activities is a means for the Commission to expand its role (cf. Majone 1998, 202), a similar approach can be expected with a view to natural gas market legislation. Thus, it is the pro-competitive idea of completing the single market that determines the Commission's receptivity to ideas.

Kingdon (1984, 50) defines *interest groups* very broadly and considers "business and industry, professional, labor, public interest groups" as well as "governmental officials as lobbyists" to fall within this category. In the EU, governmental officials are either member states' governmental officials or officials appointed by the member states (such as Commissioners). Since these actors are already included in the political stream via their membership to the Commission, the Council, and the European Council, I do not differentiate whether their actions are those of governmental officials or those of lobbyists.[25] Thereby, I take into account that governmental officials' resources differ tremendously from those of interest groups. In the political stream, their activities are subsumed under the label of government (instead of interest group) actions.

Compared with research on interest groups' influence at the national level, research on EU interest groups has gained less academic attention (Klüver 2013). Furthermore, the studies that empirically examine interest groups' influence in the EU reach contradictory conclusions (Dür 2008). Applying Occam's razor, I adopt Kingdon's (1984, 47) assumption that interest groups enter the scene "as blocking factors" or promoters of their pet solution when an issue has already entered the governmental agenda. Put differently, they aim at influencing which alternatives are seriously considered during agenda and decision coupling but do not engage in pushing an issue on the governmental agenda.[26]

Which type of interest group succeeds in influencing which alternatives are considered during the coupling processes? Once again, research on EU interest groups has produced mixed findings. While one research strand sees business representations as more influential than other interest groups (cf. Cowles 1995; Dür and De Bièvre 2007; Streeck and Schmitter 1991), another strand sees citizen groups in an advantageous position (cf. Dür and Mateo 2014; Mazey and Richardson 1993). Therefore, the following adjustments are derived keeping the policy processes analyzed in this book in mind.

Since previous empirical analyses documented, in contrast to business representations, that environmental and consumer representations had hardly been involved in the policy processes leading to the three gas directives (Eising 2000, 204; Kreutler 2014, 132), I focus on business representations. Dür, Bernhagen, and Marshall (2015, 24–25) find that business representations are more likely to be successful in the case of low-conflict issues and if the EP's role is limited to consultation or approval. The natural gas directives have been conflictual and subject to the ordinary legislative procedure. Departing from Kingdon, I assume that business representations do not play a significant role in the political stream regarding the gas directive processes.

The last element comprising the political stream is the *European mood*. Kingdon (1984, 153) defines the national mood as the perception that "a rather large number of people out in the country are thinking along certain common lines". A prerequisite for the European mood is the existence of an EU public sphere (Princen and Rhinard 2006). As addressed in the Commission's White Paper on a European Communication Policy (European Commission 2006), such a public sphere (as opposed to the sum of the member states' national moods) does not exist yet.[27] Furthermore, it is plausible that highly technical regulatory issues, such as natural gas

Table 2.4 Peculiarities of the political stream regarding the gas directive processes

The political stream in the initial MSF	*Functional equivalents in the EU*	*Peculiarities of the functional equivalents regarding the gas directive processes*
Government	European Commission	Regarding their receptivity for ideas, the Commissioners' partisan and national affiliation can be neglected. Commissioners are, however, particularly receptive to ideas which promote the internal market.
Parliament	Council of Ministers European Council European Parliament	The receptivity to ideas is determined by the actors' national affiliation, while the partisan affiliation can be neglected in the case of natural gas regulation.
Interest groups	Domestic interest groups and European representative bodies	Consumer and environmental representations are neglected. The focus is on business representations, which are expected to play a marginal role only in the political stream. Governmental officials' lobbying activities are regrouped from interest groups to the EU executive.
National mood	European mood	Given the highly technical issue of gas market regulation and the absence of an EU public sphere, the European mood is excluded from the analysis.

Source: Own compilation

regulation, remain unnoticed by the (national as well as) European mood. But even if the existence of a European mood is assumed, it is questionable whether it would exert a similar impact on the policy-makers' receptivity to specific issues. Policy-makers "are less directly accountable to (national or European) publics than are domestic decision-makers in most democracies" (Princen 2007, 31). As a consequence, the European mood is excluded from this analysis. Table 2.4 summarizes the peculiarities of the EU's political stream regarding the gas directive processes.

After having defined the participants located in the EU's political stream, the participants need to be distinguished between those who are important during agenda-setting and those relevant during decision-making (see Table 2.5). Whether they are important or not is determined by the institutional setting. Regarding agenda-setting, the Commission and the European Council are highly important. The former because it enjoys a

Table 2.5 The political stream during agenda-setting and decision-making

Relevant elements of the political stream	*Functional equivalents considered in the analysis of the EU's gas directive processes*	*Importance during*	
		Agenda-setting	*Decision-making*
Government	European Commission	High	Medium
	Council of Ministers	Medium	High
	European Council	High	Scenario I: politics as usual: low Scenario II: used by the Council as a court of final appeal: high
Parliament	European Parliament	Medium	High
Interest groups	Business representations	Low	Low

Source: Own illustration

formal monopoly position to initiate legislation (Pollack 1997, 122), and the latter because primary law tasks it to provide the EU with necessary impetus for its development and to define general political guidelines thereof.[28] The Council and the EP are of medium importance. This is because (1) they exert an indirect right to initiative only and (2) the Commission is not obliged to submit a legislative proposal following those requests.[29]

During decision-making, the Council and the EP are utterly important since their approval is required for the adoption of a legislative proposal. The pivotal position of the Commission vanishes as it lacks formal decision-making power. On the other hand, as long as the Council has not acted, the Commission has the right to "alter its proposals at any time during the procedures leading to the adoption of a Union act" (Art. 293 of the Treaty on the Functioning of the European Union, ex-Art. 250 of the Treaty Establishing the European Community). Apart from altering proposals, the Commission can try to influence the policy decision when submitting an opinion on amendments proposed by the EP at a second reading.[30] Although the Council is not obliged to support the Commission's opinion, Tsebelis et al. (2001, 594–95) stated that once the Commission accepts (respectively rejects) an amendment, the Council follows suit 73 (respectively 67) percent of the time. The European Council's importance varies during decision-making. One would expect that its importance is low, given that it is tasked to define the EU's overall political direction and priorities, which excludes day-to-day politics. However, if ministers in sectoral Council meetings cannot (or are unwilling to) agree on a legislative proposal, "they have developed the habit of passing these dossiers upwards, in effect using the European Council as a court of final appeal" (Hayes-Renshaw and Wallace 2006, 171). In these cases, the European Council is highly important during decision-making. As outlined above, empirical findings regarding (business) interest groups' influence on the three gas directive processes during agenda-setting and decision-making suggest that they play a minor role only in the political stream.

2.3.3 *The EU's Policy Stream*

In contrast to the political stream, the policy stream does not need to be altered differently for agenda-setting and decision-making. Nonetheless, it requires two adaptations in order to adequately cover specifics of the EU policy process: First, functional equivalents of the participants involved in the policy community must be defined at the EU level, and second, the criteria for policy alternatives' survival in the policy primeval soup must be revisited.

According to Kingdon (1984), the so-called hidden participants constitute the policy community (for the following, see Herweg 2016). The hidden participants consist of civil servants, interest groups, academics, researchers, and consultants. Whereas academics, researchers, and consultants can be transferred to the EU without adjustments, civil servants and interest groups need a word of explanation.

Interest groups are highly important in the EU's policy stream, given the Commission's receptivity to input from (national) experts when drafting proposals in general (Mazey and Richardson 1992) and regulatory proposals in particular (Majone 1998). However, it needs to be clarified whether governmental officials should be considered in the category of interest groups (as proposed by Kingdon) or excluded (as suggested in this book for the political stream). Although I exclude governmental officials from the category of interest groups in the political stream, I consider them in the policy stream. There are mainly two reasons for treating governmental officials differently in this stream: First, by regrouping governmental officials from interest groups to the European executive in the political stream, they are still considered in the political stream. By sticking to this definition, it would mean to define the framework's functional equivalents incompletely with regard to the policy stream. Second, the policy stream differs from the political stream in so far as the dominant model of interaction is arguing instead of powering and negotiating (Kingdon 1984, 131–134). Consequently, distinguishing whether a governmental official engages in the discussion as a member of the government or a member of an interest group is not important.

Civil servants in the EU are defined as officials who have "been appointed (...) to an established post on the staff of the institutions of the Union" ((EEC) No. 31, (EAEC) No. 11, Art. 1a). A peculiarity of them is that they are predominantly located within the Commission. This raises the question of whether Kingdon's (1984, 20) assumption that it is possible but unlikely that visible participants (e.g., members of the Commission) join the policy community is accurate with regard to the EU policy process.

Who are the visible participants? Visible participants are, inter alia, the administration, the government, and elections-related participants. Their functional equivalents in the EU are the European Council, the EP, the Council, and the Commission. The Council and the European Council are constituted of member states' governmental officials. Two actors in particular have an outstanding position: The member states' governmental officials and the Commission as they both belong to the visible and hidden group of participants, which means they are engaged in alternative specification, agenda-setting, and decision-making.[31] Consequently, a peculiarity of EU policy communities is that a subset of the visible participants is systematically involved in the policy community.[32]

Furthermore, European policy communities differ from domestic ones insofar as they consist of more stakeholders. For instance, they are composed of stakeholders located at the EU level (Zahariadis 2008, 518) *and* domestic interest representations and firms. This can be illustrated by the example of Eurogas. Eurogas is the European gas industry's interest representation which engages in "an ongoing dialogue with (...) relevant institutions such as the European Commission".[33] Although Verbundnetz Gas AG, a German-based gas firm, is a member of Eurogas,[34] it also has a permanent office in Brussels in order to participate in this policy community (Eurogas 2015a, Landmarks Publications 2008).[35] In addition, Bache (2013) points out that European policy communities have become increasingly transnational, which in the case of the EU natural gas policy community is exemplified, for instance, by the International Association of Oil and

Gas Producers' participation in meetings of the European Regulatory Gas Forum (see subsection 5.1.3).

Thus, the policy stream consists of a policy community in which a multitude of stakeholders work out policy alternatives. According to Kingdon (1984), policy alternatives must fulfill certain criteria (i.e., technical feasibility, tolerable costs, normative acceptance, and receptivity among the policy-makers) in order to survive in the policy primeval soup. Given that the policy community brings together stakeholders from member states (and non-member states), the differences between them (for instance, regarding their policy legacy and socioeconomic conditions) might be too big for a policy community to agree on a short list of prominent policy proposals. Therefore, I do not follow Zahariadis (2008, 518), who argued that Kingdon's criteria for policy alternatives' survival also apply to the EU policy primeval soup. Instead, I follow Peters (1994, 21, 24), who pointed out that the EU is an "agenda-setter's paradise", given that policy-entrepreneurs can select "a high-quality policy alternative from a list of options that have been legitimated in one or more of the member countries". Taking into account that European policy communities have become increasingly transnational, this list of options also includes policies that have been implemented elsewhere and that the EU's policy community is familiar with. Thus, the EU's policy stream counts as ripe if at least one technically feasible policy alternative exists.

2.4 Bringing the Threads Together: Analyzing the EU Policy Process by Applying the Multiple Streams Framework

The previous sections modified the MSF in a way which allows for analyzing agenda-setting and decision-making and adapted the initial MSF's core elements to the EU by defining functional equivalents. According to Capano (2013, 458), "by focusing on sets of causal mechanisms, the study of policy change could be more manageable and better suited to the accumulation of knowledge." Following his suggestion, the next sections explicitly relate the MSF core elements with the causal mechanisms leading to agenda change (subsection 2.4.1) and policy change (subsection 2.4.2) in the EU (see Fig. 2.3).

Furthermore, since contributions that explicitly translate the framework's necessary conditions for change into falsifiable hypotheses are rare (Jones

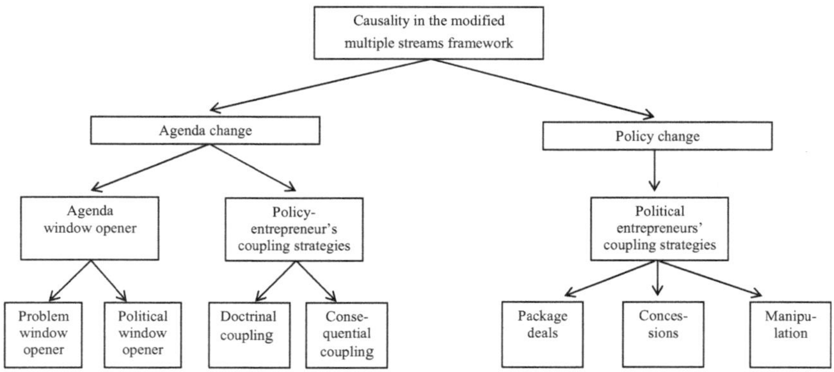

Fig. 2.3 Causality in the modified multiple streams framework. *Source*: Own illustration

et al. 2016; Radaelli 2000), this subsection engages in this endeavor and derives falsifiable hypotheses that will lead the empirical analysis of agenda and policy change.

2.4.1 Agenda Change

Summarizing the previous sections, the MSF contains three implicitly stated necessary conditions for agenda change (for a similar assessment regarding the existence of necessary conditions, see, for instance, Blankenau 2001; Burstein et al. 2005; Stone 2000; Zahariadis 2008). They can be condensed into the following hypotheses.

The likelihood of an agenda change increases if

H1:
the problem stream, political stream, and policy stream are ripe;

H2:
a change in the problem or political stream opens an agenda window; and

H3:
a policy-entrepreneur succeeds in coupling the streams.

Note that all three hypotheses must be met in order for an agenda change to be likely. Since this book aims at contributing to theory development, each hypothesis is tested individually in the empirical analysis. However, before I can test them empirically, they need to be translated from Kingdon's figurative language into falsifiable conditions. Therefore, I now turn to introducing a definition of stream ripeness (Sect. 2.4.1.1) and to deriving more precise hypotheses regarding the occurrence of an agenda window (Sect. 2.4.1.2) as well as a policy-entrepreneur's success in coupling the streams (Sect. 2.4.1.3)

2.4.1.1 The First Necessary Condition: Stream Ripeness

With regard to all streams, ripeness indicates that coupling becomes possible if a policy window opens. As a result of the previous sections, I arrive at the following definitions:

D1:
The problem stream is ripe if (1) attention to an issue relevant for the policy field in question is raised and (2) that issue is interpreted as being problematic.

D2:
The political stream is ripe if the EU government is receptive to a specific issue.

D3:
The policy stream is ripe if the policy community is familiar with at least one alternative to the policy problem in question.

While the framework offers clear guidance on how to empirically assess the ripeness of the problem and policy streams, it does not do so with regard to the political stream, given that the EU's government consists of three executive branches. This gives room for the possibility that just a subset of the three executive branches is receptive to a specific issue. This implies that the ripeness of the EU political stream during agenda-setting differs from Kingdon's conception of political stream ripeness, because the initial MSF is not provided for a government characterized by such a low cohesion. Taking into account that the MSF is derived inductively, it is imperative to adjust this definition on the basis of EU case studies. However, it seems plausible to assume that regarding agenda change, stream ripeness does not necessarily require all three branches of the executive to be receptive to a specific issue. It suffices if the Commission is receptive because of its formal monopoly position to initiate legislation. In order to assess whether this assumption is correct, the receptivity of each branch of the EU government is considered in the empirical analysis.

2.4.1.2 The Second Necessary Condition: An Agenda Window Opens

There are alternative causal paths as to how the agenda window opens. Mirroring this *equifinality* (George and Bennett 2005, 10), next I introduce a set of hypotheses capturing the different causal paths to the opening of an agenda window due to changes in the problem or political stream. With regard to the problem stream, I hypothesize:

H4:

An agenda window opens in the problem stream if

(a) a relevant indicator deteriorates;

(b) an evaluation study points to a discrepancy between a program's goal and the program's effects; or

(c) a focusing event relevant to the policy field in question occurs.

Taking into account that "European clocks matter" (Goetz 2012, 708), changes in the political stream focus on temporal regularities in the EU political system. More precisely, changes that recur regularly and regard the Commission, the Council, the European Council, and the EP are considered.[36]

Since the *Commission* is highly important for agenda-setting, the beginning of its term of office opens a policy window. For the opening of the agenda window, it is irrelevant whether the inauguration of the new Commission results from the regular election cycle or the resignation of the predecessor. From the point of view of proponents of specific policy projects, it is particularly important that the incoming Commission's President and responsible Commissioner in the Directorate-General are receptive to certain policy projects. The former is important because he or she provides political guidance to the entire Commission, while the latter is responsible for formulating draft proposals. In contrast to the member states' level, the Commission publishes its legislative program not only in the beginning of its term in office but also on an annual basis. Thus, I hypothesize:

H5:
An agenda window opens in the political stream if
(a) a new Commission takes office; or
(b) the Commission publishes a working program.

Note that a change in the composition of the *Council* due to national elections does not open an agenda window. This is because, despite the extension of qualified majority voting, the Council still prefers to act unanimously. As a consequence, the replacement of a single national minister neither significantly impacts the probability that an issue enters the agenda nor that a decision is settled.[37] Nevertheless, a change in the *Council Presidency* opens an agenda window. Following Tallberg (2006, 2003), the Council Presidency has the power to structure the agenda. Put differently, the incumbent has the opportunity to "[vary the] emphases put on issues already on the agenda (agenda-structuring)" and "[to deliberately bar] issues from the agenda (agenda exclusion)" (Tallberg 2003, 2). This refers to single meetings of the Council and the setting of policy priorities for its term in office. In 1993, the setting of policy priorities was formalized because the Council's rules of procedure for the first time stipulated that the Council Presidency must present a working program for his or her term in office. In 2002, this task has been supplemented by the provision to draw up multiannual strategic programs by consecutive Presidencies. This leads to:

H6:
An agenda window opens in the political stream if
(a) a new Council Presidency takes office; or
(b) one or consecutive Council Presidencies release their working program(s).

Taking into account that one of the *European Council*'s tasks is to provide the EU with necessary impetus for its development, its acts inform about issues that have risen on the governmental agenda.[38] This results in Hypothesis 7:

H7:
An agenda window opens in the political stream if the European Council publishes acts which provide impetus for the EU's development.

Furthermore, if the European Council requests another branch of the executive to address an issue (such as gathering information or conducting a study on a specific issue), this implies that at least two branches of the EU's executive deal with an issue (and that the third branch, with high degree of certainty, is aware of this). In a similar vein, if the *Council* or the *EP* exerts its indirect right to initiative or tasks the Commission to address an issue, this also signals that governmental officials are paying attention to an issue. Summing up, I deduce the following hypothesis:

H8:
An agenda window opens in the political stream if (at least) one branch of the EU's executive or legislature tasks one (other) branch of the EU's executive to address an issue.

According to Kingdon, parliamentary elections open agenda windows. Note that this does not apply to the EU, because in the *EP*, coalitions are usually formed ad hoc depending on the issue at stake (Decker and Sonnicksen 2011). Consequently, a change in the EP's composition does not make it more likely that the EP makes a more intensive or different use of its indirect right to initiative than it does during the legislative period.

The description of the EU as an "agenda-setting paradise" (Peters 1994, 21) indicates that there are more occasions at which an agenda window opens compared with policy processes at the member states' level (as reflected in Hypotheses 4–8). According to Kingdon (1984), policy windows open for a short time span only. Taking into account that, in the EU, there are more drivers that open agenda windows and that they occur more frequently than at the member states' level, agenda windows do not necessarily close quickly. Instead, I argue that an agenda window stays open as long as an issue remains in the center of governmental attention, for instance, documented by its inclusion in working programs (of the Commission or the Council Presidency) or in the Council meetings' agenda.[39] Hence, I define:

D4:
The agenda window remains open as long as an issue stays on the governmental agenda.

2.4.1.3 *The Third Necessary Condition: A Policy-Entrepreneur Couples the Streams*

Once the streams are ripe and an agenda window is open, the likelihood of an agenda change increases if a policy-entrepreneur succeeds in coupling the streams. Following Kingdon, a policy-entrepreneur engages in doctrinal coupling if an agenda window opens in the political stream and in consequential coupling if an agenda window opens in the problem stream. However, Definition 4 implies that changes in the problem stream and/or political stream keeps the agenda window open. If changes in both streams keep the window open, it does not allow for ascribing a policy-entrepreneur's coupling strategy to a specific change. This is because separating effects that occur in a short time period is next to impossible. Furthermore, it is highly plausible that a policy-entrepreneur would seize the opportunity and apply both coupling strategies in order to boost his or her chances to change the agenda. Therefore, I do not consider the different coupling strategies in my analysis.[40]

Departing from other contributions (cf. Exworthy and Powell 2004; Keeler 1993), I argue that the size of a window does not matter because the potential for a far-reaching (agenda and policy) change does not depend on the size of a window but on the streams' ripeness and on policy-entrepreneurs' (and political entrepreneurs') coupling capabilities.[41]

Whether or not a policy-entrepreneur succeeds in coupling the streams depends on his or her personal skills (i.e., persistence and negotiating skills) and connectedness (in general and with key policy-makers in particular) (cf. Herweg et al. 2015). Since personal skills are difficult to assess empirically, I concentrate on those that are unequivocal to observe. Hence, I hypothesize:

H9:
The policy-entrepreneur is more likely to successfully couple the streams during an open agenda window,
(a) the more persistent he or she is; and
(b) the more access to key policy-makers he or she has.

2.4.2 *Policy Change*

The advantage of the modified MSF is that it allows differentiating between causal mechanisms leading to agenda change from those leading to policy change. In contrast to agenda change, only the activities of political entrepreneurs must be considered as causal mechanisms of policy change, since it is clearly defined how a decision window opens: with the introduction of a draft bill in the legislative arena. Note that a successful agenda coupling reduces contingency in that a draft bill (1) consists of a specific problem-solution linkage and (2) is subject to a specific legislative procedure due to the chosen venue. However, this does not transform decision-making into an exercise in rational problem-solving because structural or institutional reasons often fail to explain why sometimes a draft bill is blocked and sometimes it is passed without disruption. Therefore, policy change causally depends on the activities and skills of political entrepreneurs. Following Herweg et al. (2015), I hypothesize:

H10:
Policy adoption is more likely if a political entrepreneur
(a) manages to combine viable alternatives embraced by different veto actors into one package;
(b) can (and does) offer concessions on the original proposal; and
(c) succeeds in providing meaning, clarification, and identity to the issue at stake.

Package deals and concessions imply that decision-making might be a lengthy process since they render compromising necessary. Insights from agenda coupling allow for deriving a hypothesis when lengthy decision coupling is more likely. Given that the importance of the actors in the political stream varies during agenda coupling and decision coupling, the latter is more likely to be lengthy if agenda coupling has taken place against the will of veto actors. For instance, if the EP opposed a Commission's initiative during agenda coupling, the likelihood of a short decision-making process is low because of its veto potential during decision coupling. Thus, reaching an agreement despite the reluctance of veto actors renders settling time-consuming compromises necessary.

Furthermore, it is possible that decision coupling becomes a lengthy process, because an item is either not included on the policy-makers' agenda, or just with a low priority (cf. Tallberg 2003, 10). The policy-makers' agenda can be conceptualized as (1) the legislative program for a specific period (such as their term in office) and (2) the agenda of actual meetings. The redirection of the policy-makers' attention can result, for instance, from the occurrence of problems, which are perceived to be more urgent, or from activities of political entrepreneurs with agenda-shaping power, who de-emphasize issues on the agenda or even exclude them. Based on these considerations, I derive the following hypothesis:

H11:
Decision coupling is more likely to be lengthy if
(a) agenda coupling has taken place against the will of veto actors; or
(b) policy-makers' attention is redirected to other issues.

Table 2.6 Hypotheses derived from the (modified) multiple streams framework

The MSF's necessary conditions for agenda change

The likelihood of an agenda change increases if

H1 the problem stream, political stream, and policy stream are ripe;

H2 a change in the problem or political stream opens an agenda window; and

H3 a policy-entrepreneur succeeds in coupling the streams.

Specifying H2: Equifinal paths to the opening of an agenda window

H4 An agenda window opens in the problem stream if
- (a) a relevant indicator deteriorates;
- (b) an evaluation study points to a discrepancy between a program's goal and the program's effects; or
- (c) a focusing event relevant for the policy field in question occurs.

H5 An agenda window opens in the political stream if
- (a) a new Commission takes office; or
- (b) the Commission publishes a working program.

H6 An agenda window opens in the political stream if
- (a) a new Council Presidency takes office; or
- (b) one or consecutive Council Presidencies release their working program(s).

H7 An agenda window opens in the political stream if the European Council publishes acts which provide impetus for the EU's development.

H8 An agenda window opens in the political stream if (at least) one branch of the EU's executive or legislature tasks one (other) branch of the EU's executive to address an issue.

Specifying H3: Agenda coupling

H9 The policy-entrepreneur is more likely to successfully couple the streams during an open agenda window,
- (a) the more persistent he or she is; and
- (b) the more access to key policy-makers he or she has.

Explaining decision-making: Decision coupling

H10 Policy adoption is more likely if a political entrepreneur
- (a) manages to combine viable alternatives embraced by different veto actors into one package;
- (b) can (and does) offer concessions on the original proposal; and
- (c) succeeds in providing meaning, clarification, and identity to the issue at stake.

H11 Decision coupling is more likely to be lengthy if
- (a) agenda change has taken place against the will of veto actors; or
- (b) policy-makers' attention is redirected to other issues.

Source: Own compilation

Before the derived hypotheses are empirically tested (for a summary, see Table 2.6), the subsequent chapter informs about European natural gas market's characteristics and its regulation. This allows for focusing the analysis conducted in Chaps. 4–6 on the policy process and for keeping information about technical background knowledge as brief as possible.

Notes

1. This section draws heavily on Herweg (2015a).
2. Following Kingdon (1984), the terms "process" and "stream" are used interchangeably.
3. As the garbage can model (GCM) focuses on decision situation, there are differences between the streams considered both in the GCM and in the multiple streams framework (MSF) (cf. Cohen et al. (1972) versus. Kingdon (1984, 2003, 2010)). Henceforth, Kingdon's understanding of the streams in question is applied.
4. For a critique of this broad definition of focusing events, see Birkland (1997).
5. Rhinard (2010, 40) refers to policy-entrepreneurs engaged in framing as "frame entrepreneurs".
6. Following Kingdon, the terms "alternatives" (cf. Kingdon 1984, 3–4), "solutions" (cf. Kingdon 1984, 21), and "ideas" (cf. Kingdon 1984, 146) are used as synonyms.
7. Boscarino (2009, 429) introduces the terminology of "problem-focused advocacy" for consequential coupling and "problem surfing" for doctrinal coupling.
8. According to Ackrill and Kay (2011, 74), "[i]n the original M[ultiple] S[treams] model—and in much work since—there is both a functional and physical separation of policy entrepreneurs and decision-makers." Since Kingdon lists explicitly the equipment with decision-making authority as one prerequisite that increases a policy-entrepreneur's chance of successfully coupling the streams, I have a different reading of the original MSF and do not see this separation to be plausible.
9. Although Kingdon (1984: 200) explicitly borrows this terminology from the field of international relations, he does not distinguish his usage of the concept from that in international relations. In international relations, three different kinds of spillovers are considered, namely functional, political, and cultivated spillover. For an overview

of the different kinds of spillover, see Lelieveldt and Princen (2011, 35–36).

10. Sabatier (1991, 151) even suggests going a step further by attributing the MSF to be expandable to the entire policy process.
11. By contrast, in the additional case studies of the third edition of his monograph, Kingdon (2010, 231–47) explicitly limits the MSF to agenda-setting and summarizes what happened after the health reform in the Clinton and Obama administrations had entered the decision agenda, in order to give a complete summary of the reform processes.
12. Starting in 2013, various international conferences devoted the MSF panels or workshops (for instance, the American Political Science Association's Annual Meeting 2013 [Panel 25-3], the European Consortium for Political Research's Joint Sessions of Workshops 2013 [Workshop 7], and the International Conference on Public Policy 2015 [Panels TO1P09, TO1P10]). Consequently, a scientific dialogue regarding the MSF seems to be evolving.
13. As of January 15, 2016, Google Scholar lists 14.289 quotations, and the Social Science Citation Index and Science Citation Index list 3.629 quotations.
14. Cook and Rinfret (2013) analyze decision-making in an administration (the US Environmental Protection Agency) and Lee (2003) analyzes decision-making in courts (the US Courts of Appeal).
15. See Cairney and Heikkila (2014, 381–84) and Weible (2014, 397) for an insightful discussion of the value added and theoretical challenges when combining different frameworks.
16. Regarding the question of how to expand the MSF to the decision-making stage, Zahariadis introduces his theoretical modification in Zahariadis (1992), which he refers to in his subsequent contributions. Therefore, this paragraph cites Zahariadis (1992).
17. Most of the following considerations are based on Herweg (2013), Herweg et al. (2015), and Zohlnhöfer and Herweg (2014).
18. An alternative interpretation of Kingdon's MSF could be that the coupling process does not end with the tabling of a draft bill, but it suffices that a worked-out alternative is linked to a perceived problem and that the political stream supports this problem–solution linkage. However, such a reading makes it difficult to nail down when agenda-setting ends and decision-making starts. In his analysis of the Obama administration's health reform, Kingdon (2010)

seems to be closer to the interpretation that coupling ends with the introduction of a draft bill, given that he separates agenda-setting and decision-making as follows: Agenda-setting ends with the Senate and the House of Representatives melding the bills their respective Committees had produced into a single one. Decision-making is about how the two resulting bills could be combined in a way that ensured the support of the Senate and the House of Representatives, given their balance of power. Furthermore, an advantage of defining the end of the agenda-setting process via the introduction of a draft bill is that it is clear enough to be proven wrong, which is "the fundamental precept of science", according to Sabatier (2000, 137).

19. Note that according to Rule 229 of the Rules of Procedure of the European Parliament (EP), the principle of discontinuity is applied as it states: "[a]t the end of the last part-session before elections, all Parliament's unfinished business shall be deemed to have lapsed (...)" (http://www.europarl.europa.eu/sipade/rulesleg8/Rulesleg8.EN.pdf, last accessed: April 6, 2015). In practice, this article is irrelevant because this rule is seen as an abuse of the competences of the EP as laid down in Art. 232 TFEU. Thus, it is not respected by the Council and the Commission (Sierck et al. 2006, 10–11).
20. For a contribution that discusses (1) how far institutions have been considered in the MSF and (2) how institutions can be introduced in the MSF systematically, see Zohlnhöfer et al. (2016).
21. Consequently, political entrepreneurs have, per definition, access to key policy-makers.
22. Ridde (2009, 941) indicates that the importance of the three streams might vary during the policy cycle. Since his focus is on policy implementation, he does not elaborate on the streams' importance during decision-making.
23. Several ideas presented in this chapter built on Herweg (2015).
24. Although Herweg (2015b) is also a full MSF application to the EU, it is not included in this literature review since it summarizes some of this book's findings.
25. Strictly speaking, this is not a peculiarity of MSF applications to the EU but a peculiarity of the political stream in general. In the EU, governmental officials are above all representatives of particular national interests and not of a specific group's vested interests. Furthermore, empirically assessing when a governmental official

acts as a member of government and when as a representative of an interest group is difficult.

26. Note that research on interest groups' influence suggest that business interest groups can be successful in affecting the EU's governmental agenda, too (for an overview, see Dür et al. 2015, 25). Since energy companies opposed the gas directives, it seems plausible to assume that their impact on the prelegislative process had been low.
27. A Citizens' Initiative (as introduced by the TFEU) might be interpreted as an expression of the European mood concerning specific issues. Since the TFEU entered into force after the passing of the third gas directive, this possibility is not included in the theoretical adjustment of the MSF to the EU.
28. The European Council's agenda-setting power is codified in primary law since the Maastricht Treaty (Westlake 1995, 25).
29. The Council's and the EP's indirect right of initiative were included in the Treaty Establishing the European Community of 1992 (see Art. 152 and Art. 138b) for the first time and is retained almost unchanged in the current Lisbon version (see Art. 241 and Art. 225). While this is not questioned in the case of initiatives stemming from the Council, it is disputed in legal literature whether or not the Commission is obliged to submit a legislative proposal following a request of the EP. It is, however, obliged to reason its decision not to submit one (Poptcheva 2013, 3).
30. In April 2015, the Court of Justice of the European Union (henceforth: the Court) ruled that the Commission has the right to withdraw proposals, including those its predecessors have put to the legislators. At the same time, the Court made clear that this ruling does not provide the Commission with veto power. In short, the more a legislative process advances, the more is the Commission constrained in withdrawing proposals (for a detailed summary, see Potcheva 2015).
31. Grøn and Salomonsen (2015, 9) find that hidden participants are also occasionally involved in the political stream, which, according to Kingdon (1984), is the visible participants' realm. More precisely, they find that member states are not always represented by ministers in Council meetings but by civil servants: On average 15 percent of the participants are politically appointed or permanent civil servants. For reasons of simplicity, this finding is not incorporated in the

modified MSF, given that in the vast majority of cases member states are still represented by ministers.

32. The joint membership of participants in various streams raises the question of whether the streams are in fact independent, as assumed by Kingdon (1984). This question is returned to in Chap. 7.
33. The quotation is taken from: "Eurogas: Our mission, vision, objectives", available at: http://www.eurogas.org/about-us/our-mission-vision-objectives/; last accessed: April 6, 2015.
34. Information is taken from: "Eurogas: Our members", available at: http://www.eurogas.org/about-us/our-members/; last accessed: April 6, 2015.
35. Note that this does not imply that domestic stakeholders active at the EU level must be members of European organizations.
36. From this does not follow that the resulting agenda windows are, per definition, predictable agenda windows (Howlett 1998), because whether or not a predictable event (such as a meeting of the Council) opens an agenda window depends on how the involved participants exploit it (for instance, whether the Council makes use of its indirect right to initiative—see Hypothesis 8).
37. This also applies to the European Council, which takes decisions by consensus except where the Treaties provide otherwise.
38. Due to the period of investigation, the President of the European Council as introduced with the Treaty of Lisbon is not considered explicitly. Before 2009, the President of the European Council was an unofficial position covered by the member state in charge of the Council Presidency.
39. Note that policy-making does not automatically transform into an exercise in (rational) problem-solving due to the higher probability of an agenda window to open *and* to remain open.
40. In general, the differentiation between consequential and doctrinal coupling has barely been considered in the MSF literature. Of the empirical MSF applications published between 2000 and 2013, only 9 percent ($n = 28$) refer to these two coupling logics (own calculation based on the dataset gathered by Jones et al. 2016).
41. Furthermore, defining and empirically assessing the size of such a figurative concept in a falsifiable way is difficult to succeed in. Even if the measurement of an agenda window's size were unproblematic, it remains unclear whether it really matters. For instance, Zohlnhöfer and Herweg (2014) show that a seemingly insignificant focusing

event, a scandal regarding wrong placement statistics of the German Federal Labor Office, led to the most encompassing labor market reforms in Germany in living memory, the Hartz reforms.

References

(EEC) No 31, (EAEC) No 11. *Regulation Laying Down the Staff Regulations of Officials and the Conditions of Employment of Other Servants of the European Economic Community and the European Atomic Energy Community (last amended by Council Regulation (EC) No 160/2009 of 23 February 2009).*

Ackrill, Robert, and Adrian Kay. 2011. Multiple Streams in EU Policy-Making: The Case of the 2005 Sugar Reform. *Journal of European Public Policy* 18(1): 72–89.

Ackrill, Robert, Adrian Kay, and Nikolaos Zahariadis. 2013. Ambiguity, Multiple Streams, and EU Policy. *Journal of European Public Policy* 20(6): 871–887.

Andersen, Svein S. 1993. Towards a Common EC Energy Policy. In *Making Policy in Europe: The Europeification of National Policy-Making*, ed. Svein S. Andersen and Kjell A. Eliassen, 133–154. London: Sage Publications.

Araral, Eduardo, Scott Fritzen, Howlett Michael, M. Ramesh, and Xun Wu, eds. 2013. *Routledge Handbook of Public Policy*. London: Routledge.

Bache, Ian. 2013. Measuring Quality of Life for Public Policy: An Idea Whose Time Has Come? Agenda-Setting Dynamics in the European Union. *Journal of European Public Policy* 20(1): 21–38.

Bakir, Caner. 2009. Policy Entrepreneurship and Institutional Change: Multilevel Governance of Central Banking Reform. *Governance* 22(4): 571–598.

Baumgartner, Frank R., Christoffer Green-Pedersen, and Bryan D. Jones. 2006. Comparative Studies of Policy Agendas. *Journal of European Public Policy* 13(7): 959–974.

Bendor, Jonathan, Terry M. Moe, and Kenneth W. Shotts. 2001. Recycling the Garbage Can. An Assessment of the Research Program. *American Political Science Review* 95(1): 169–190.

Birkland, Thomas A. 1997. *After Disaster: Agenda Setting, Public Policy, and Focusing Events. American Governance and Public Policy.* Washington, DC: Georgetown University Press.

Blankenau, Joe. 2001. The Fate of National Health Insurance in Canada and the United States: A Multiple Streams Explanation. *Policy Studies Journal* 29(1): 38–55.

Boscarino, Jessica E. 2009. Surfing for Problems: Advocacy Group Strategy in U.S. Forestry Policy. *Policy Studies Journal* 37(3): 415–434.

Burstein, Paul, Shawn Bauldry, and Paul Froese. 2005. Bill Sponsorship and Congressional Support for Policy Proposals, from Introduction to Enactment or Disappearance. *Political Research Quarterly* 58(2): 295–302.

Cairney, Paul, and Tanya Heikkila. 2014. A Comparison of Theories of the Policy Process. In *Sabatier and Weible* 2014, 363–390.
Capano, Gilberto. 2013. Policy Dynamics and Change. The Never-Ending Puzzle. In E. Araral, S. Fritzen, M. Howlett, M. Ramesh, and X. Wu, Routledge Handbook of Public Policy, 451–461, New York: Routledge.
Cohen, Michael D., James G. March, and Johan P. Olsen. 1972. A Garbage Can Model of Organizational Choice. *Administrative Science Quarterly* 17(1): 1–25.
Cook, Jeffrey J., and Sara R. Rinfret. 2013. The Environmental Protection Agency Regulates Greenhouse Gas Emissions: Is Anyone Paying Attention? *Review of Political Research* 30(3): 263–280.
Cowles, Green M. 1995. Setting the Agenda for a New Europe: The ERT and EC 1992. *Journal of Common Market Studies* 33(4): 501–526.
Decker, Frank, and Jared Sonnicksen. 2011. An Alternative Approach to European Union Democratization: Re-Examining the Direct Election of the Commission President. *Government and Opposition* 46(2): 168–191.
Dür, Andreas. 2008. Interest Groups in the European Union: How Powerful Are They? In *Interest Group Politics in Europe: Lessons from EU Studies and Comparative Politics*, ed. Jan Beyers, Rainer Eising, and William A. Maloney, 110–128. London: Routledge.
Dür, Andreas, Patrick Bernhagen, and David Marshall. 2015. Interest Group Success in the European Union: When (and why) Does Business Lose? *Comparative Political Studies 48(8)*: 1–33.
Dür, Andreas, and Dirk De Bièvre. 2007. Inclusion Without Influence? NGOs in European Trade Policy. *Journal of Public Policy* 27(1): 79–101.
Dür, Andreas, and Gemma Mateo. 2014. Public Opinion and Interest Group Influence: How Citizen Groups Derailed the Anti-Counterfeiting Trade Agreement. *Journal of European Public Policy* 21(8): 1199–1217.
Eising, Rainer. 2000. *Liberalisierung und Europäisierung: Die regulative Reform der Elektrizitätsversorgung in Grossbritannien, der Europäischen Gemeinschaft und der Bundesrepublik Deutschland.* Opladen: Leske + Budrich.
European Commission. 2006. *White Paper on a European Communication Policy: COM(2006)35 Final.*
Exworthy, Mark, and Martin Powell. 2004. Big Windows and Little Windows: Implementation in the 'Congested State'. *Public Administration* 102(12): 2294–2302.
Faletti, Tulia G., and Julia F. Lynch. 2009. Context and Causal Mechanisms in Political Analysis. *Comparative Political Studies* 42(9): 1143–1166.
Feldman, Martha S. 1989. *Order Without Design: Information Production and Policy Making.* Stanford: Stanford University Press.
Finon, Dominique, and John Surrey. 1996. The Future of EU Energy Policy. In *European Energy Policies in a Changing Environment*, ed. Francis McGowan, 165–183. Heidelberg: Physica-Verlag.

Fligstein, Neil. 2001. Institutional Entrepreneurs and Cultural Frames: The Case of the European Union's Single Market Program. *European Societies* 3(3): 261–287.

George, Alexander L., and Andrew Bennett. 2005. *Case Studies and Theory Development in the Social Sciences*. Cambridge, MA: MIT Press.

Goetz, Klaus H. 2012. Political Time in the EU. In *The Oxford Handbook of the European Union*, ed. E. Jones, A. Menon, and S. Weatherill, 703–715. Oxford: Oxford University Press.

Grøn, Caroline H., and Heidi H. Salomonsen. 2015. Who's at the Table? An Analysis of Ministers Participation in EU Council of Ministers Meetings. *Journal of European Public Policy* 22(8): 1071–1088.

Hayes-Renshaw, Fiona, and Helen Wallace. 2006. *The Council of Ministers*. 2nd ed. Houndmills: Palgrave Macmillan.

Herweg, Nicole. 2013. Der Multiple-Streams-Ansatz—ein Ansatz, dessen Zeit gekommen ist? *Zeitschrift für Vergleichende Politikwissenschaft* 7(4): 321–345.

———. 2015a. Der Multiple Streams Ansatz. In *Handbuch Policy-Forschung*, ed. Georg Wenzelburger and Reimut Zohlnhöfer, 325–353. Wiesbaden: VS Verlag für Sozialwissenschaften.

———. 2015b. Explaining European Agenda-Setting Using the Multiple Streams Framework: The Case of European Natural Gas Regulation. *Policy Sciences* 49(1): 13–33.

———. 2016. Clarifying the Concept of Policy Communities in the Multiple Streams Framework. In *Zohlnhöfer and Rüb* 2016a, 125–145.

Herweg, Nicole, Christian Huß, and Reimut Zohlnhöfer. 2015. Straightening the Three Streams: Theorizing Extensions of the Multiple Streams Framework. *European Journal of Political Research* 54(3): 435–449.

Hibbs, Douglas A. 1977. Political Parties and Macroeconomic Policy. *American Political Science Review* 71: 1467–1487.

Hix, Simon, and Bjørn Høyland. 2011. *The Political System of the European Union*. 3rd ed. Basingstoke: Palgrave Macmillan.

Howlett, Michael. 1998. Predictable and Unpredictable Policy Windows: Institutional and Exogenous Correlates of Canadian Federal Agenda-Setting. *Canadian Journal of Political Science* XXXI(3): 495–524.

Immergut, Ellen M. 1992. *Health Politics: Interests and Institutions in Western Europe*. Cambridge: Cambridge University Press.

Jann, Werner, and Kai Wegrich. 2007. Theories of the policy cycle. In *Handbook of Public Policy Analysis: Theory, Politics, and Methods*, ed. Frank Fischer, Gerald Miller, and Mara S. Sidney, 43–62. Boca Raton: CRC/Taylor & Francis.

Johnson, Clare L., Sylvia M. Tunstall, and Edmund C. Penning-Rowsell. 2005. Floods as Catalysts for Policy Change: Historical Lessons from England and Wales. *International Journal of Water Resources Development* 21(4): 561–575.

Jones, Michael D., Holly L. Petersen, Jonathan J. Pierce, Nicole Herweg, Amiel Bernal, Holly Lamberta, and Nikolaos Zahariadis. 2016. A River Runs Through It: A Multiple Streams Meta-Review. *Policy Studies Journal* 44(1): 13–36.

Judge, David, and David Earnshaw. 2008. *The European Parliament*. 2nd ed. - New York: Palgrave Macmillan.

Keeler, John T.S. 1993. Opening the Window for Reform: Mandates, Crises, and Extraordinary Policy-Making. *Comparative Political Studies* 25(4): 433–486.

Kingdon, John W. 1984. *Agendas, Alternatives, and Public Policies*. Boston: Little, Brown.

———. 1994. Agendas, Ideas, and Policy Change. In *New Perspectives on American Politics*, ed. Lawrence C. Dodd and Calvin C. Jillson, 215–230. Washington, DC: CQ Press.

———. 2003. *Agendas, Alternatives, and Public Policies*. 2nd ed. New York: Longman.

———. 2010. *Agendas, Alternatives, and Public Policies*. Updated 2nd ed. Longman/White Plains: Pearson Longman.

Klüver, Heike. 2013. *Lobbying in the European Union: Interest Groups, Lobbying Coalitions, and Policy Change*. Oxford: Oxford University Press.

König, Thomas. 2007. Discontinuity: Another Source of the EU's Democratic Deficit? *European Union Politics* 8(3): 411–432.

Kreutler, Maren. 2014. *The Formation of Coalitions in the European Union: A Comparative Analysis of Initiatives to Influence European Energy Policy*. 1st ed. Baden-Baden: Nomos.

Publications, Landmarks. 2008. *The European Public Affairs Directory 19 (2009): The Comprehensive Guide to Opinion-Formers in the Capital of Europe*. Brussels: Landmarks Publications.

Lee, Emergy G.I. 2003. Policy Windows on the U.S. Courts of Appeals. *Justice System Journal* 24(3): 301–323.

Lelieveldt, Herman, and Sebastiaan Princen. 2011. *The Politics of the European Union*. Cambridge: Cambridge University Press.

Lindberg, Björn, Anne Rasmussen, and Andreas Warntjen. 2008. Party Politics as Usual? The Role of Political Parties in EU Legislative Decision-Making. *Journal of European Public Policy* 15(8): 1107–1126.

Lodge, Martin. 2005. Review: Ambiguity and Choice in Public Policy: Political Decision Making in Modern Democracies by Nikolaos Zahariadis (2003). *Public Administration* 83(1): 260–262.

Luhmann, Niklas. 1976. Generalized Media and the Problem of Contingency. In *Explorations in General Theory in Social Science: Essays in Honor of Talcott Parsons*, ed. Jan J. Loubser, Rainer C. Baum, Andrew Effrat, and Victor M. Lidz, 507–532. New York: Free Press.

Majone, Giandomenico. 1997. From the Positive to the Regulatory State: Causes and Consequences of Changes in the Mode of Governance. *Journal of Public Policy* 17(2): 139–167.

———. 1998. The Rise of the Regulatory State in Europe. In *A Reader on Regulation*, ed. Robert Baldwin, Colin Scott, and Christopher Hood, 192–215. Oxford: Oxford University Press.

Matláry, Janne H. 1997. *Energy Policy in the European Union*. London: MacMillan.

Mazey, Sonia, and Jeremy Richardson. 1993. Environmental Groups and the EC: Challenges and Opportunities. In *A Green Dimension for the European Community: Political Issues and Processes*, ed. David Judge, 109–128. London, England: Frank Cass.

Mazey, Sonia P., and Jeremy J. Richardson. 1992. British Pressure Groups in the European Community: The Challenge of Brussels. *Parliamentary Affairs* 45(1): 92–107.

Miebach, Bernhard. 2012 *Organisationstheorie: Problemstellung—Modelle—Entwicklung*. 2nd ed. Wiesbaden: Springer Fachmedien Wiesbaden.

———. 2013. The Garbage Can Model and the Study of the Policy-Making Process. In *Routledge Handbook of Public Policy*, ed. Eduardo Araral, Scott Fritzen, Michael Howlett, M. Ramesh, and Xun Wu, 320–328. London: Routledge.

Mucciaroni, Gary. 1992. The Garbage Can Model & the Study of Policy Making: A Critique. *Polity* 24(3): 459–482.

Münter, Michael. 2005. *Verfassungsreform im Einheitsstaat: Die Politik der Dezentralisierung in Großbritannien*. Wiesbaden: VS Verlag für Sozialwissenschaften.

Peters, B.G. 1994. Agenda-Setting in the European Community. *Journal of European Public Policy* 1(1): 9–26.

Pollack, Mark A. 1997. Delegation, Agency, and Agenda Setting in the European Community. *International Organization* 51(1): 99–134.

Poptcheva, Eva-Maria. 2013. Parliament's Legislative Initiative. *Library Briefing*, pp. 1–8, October 10.

———. 2015. At a Glance. The European Commission's Right to Withdraw a Legislative Proposal. European Parliament Research Service PE554.204.

Princen, Sebastiaan. 2007. Agenda-Setting in the European Union: A Theoretical Exploration and Agenda for Research. *Journal of European Public Policy* 14(1): 21–38.

Princen, Sebastiaan, and Mark Rhinard. 2006. Crashing and Creeping: Agenda-Setting Dynamics in the European Union. *Journal of European Public Policy* 13 (7): 1119–1132.

Radaelli, Claudio M. 2000. Public Policy Comes of Age. *Journal of European Public Policy* 7(1): 130–135.

Rhinard, Mark. 2010. *Framing Europe: The Policy Shaping Strategies of the European Commission*. Dordrecht: Republic of Letters.

Richardson, Jeremy. 2006. Policy-Making in the EU. Interests, Ideas and Garbage Cans of Primeval Soup. In *European Union: Power and Policy-Making*, 3rd ed., ed. J.J. Richardson, 3–30. Abingdon: Routledge.

Ridde, Valéry. 2009. Policy Implementation in an African State: An Extension of Kingdon's Multiple-Streams Approach. *Public Administration* 87(4): 938–954.

Roberts, Nancy C., and Paula T. King. 1991. Policy Entrepreneurs: Their Activity Structure and Function in the Policy Process. *Journal of Public Administration Research and Theory* 1(2): 147–175.

Rüb, Friedbert W. 2008. Policy-Analyse unter den Bedingungen von Kontingenz: Konzeptionelle Überlegungen zu einer möglichen Neuorientierung. In *Die Zukunft der Policy-Forschung: Theorien, Methoden, Anwendungen*, 1st ed., ed. Frank Janning, 88–111. Wiesbaden: VS Verlag für Sozialwissenschaften.

Sabatier, Paul A. 1991. Toward Better Theories of the Policy Process. *PS: Political Science & Politics* 24: 147–156.

———. 2000. Clear Enough to be Wrong. *Journal of European Public Policy* 7(1): 135–140.

———. 2007a. "Fostering the Development of Policy Theory." In *Sabatier* 2007b, 321–336.

———., eds. 2007b. *Theories of Policy Process*. 2nd ed. Boulder, CO: Westview Press.

Sabatier, Paul A., and Christopher M. Weible, eds. 2014. *Theories of the Policy Process*. 3rd ed. New York: Westview Press.

Saetren, Harald. 2016. Lost in Translation: Re-Conceptualizing the Multiple Streams Back to its Source of Inspiration. In *Zohlnhöfer and Rüb* 2016a, 21–34.

Scharpf, Fritz W. 1997. *Games Real Actors Play: Actor-Centered Institutionalism in Policy Research*. In *Theoretical Lenses on Public Policy*. Boulder, CO: Westview Press.

Schlager, Edella. 1999. A Comparison of Frameworks, Theories, and Models of Policy Processes. In *Theories of the Policy Process*, 1st ed., ed. Paul A. Sabatier, 233–260. Boulder, CO: Westview Press.

Sierck, Gabriela M., Patrizia Robbe, and Carmen Sinnokrot. 2006. *Bessere Rechtsetzung*. Info-Brief/Wissenschaftliche Dienste des Deutschen Bundestages. Berlin: Deutscher Bundestag, Wissenschaftliche Dienste, WD 3.

Snow, David A., E.B. Rochford Jr., Steven K. Worden, and Robert D. Benford. 1986. Frame Alignment Processes, Micromobilization, and Movement Participation. *American Sociological Review* 51(4): 464–481.

Stone, Diane. 2000. Non-governmental Policy Transfer. The Strategies of Independent Policy Institutes. *Governance* 13(1): 45–70.

Storch, Sabine, and Georg Winkel. 2013. Coupling Climate Change and Forest Policy: A Multiple Streams Analysis of Two German Case Studies. *Forest Policy and Economics*: 14–26.

Streeck, Wolfgang, and Philippe C. Schmitter. 1991. From National Corporatism to Transnational Pluralism: Organized Interests in the Single European Market. *Politics & Society* 19(2): 134–164.

Tallberg, Jonas. 2003. The Agenda-Shaping Powers of the EU Council Presidency. *Journal of European Public Policy* 10(1): 1–19.

———. 2006. *Leadership and Negotiation in the European Union*. Cambridge: Cambridge University Press.

Travis, Rick, and Nikolaos Zahariadis. 2002. A Multiple Streams Model of U.S. Foreign Aid Policy. *Policy Studies Journal* 30(4): 495–514.

Tsebelis, George. 2002. *Veto Players: How Political Institutions Work*. Princeton: Princeton University Press

Tsebelis, George, Christian B. Jensen, Anastassios Kalandrakis, and Amie Kreppel. 2001. Legislative Procedures in the European Union: An Empirical Analysis. *British Journal of Political Science* 31(4): 573–599.

van Stigt, Rien, Peter P. Driessen, and Tejo J. Spit. 2013. A Window on Urban Sustainability. Integration of Environmental Interests in Urban Planning Through 'Decision Windows'. *Environmental Impact Assessment Review* 42: 18–24.

Weber, Max. 1985. *Wirtschaft und Gesellschaft: Grundriß der verstehenden Soziologie*. With the assistance of J. Winckelmann. 5., Rev. Aufl.,. Tübingen: Mohr.

Weible, Christopher M. 2014 Advancing Policy Process Research. *In Sabatier and Weible* 2014: 391–407.

Weir, Margaret. 1992. *Politics and Jobs: The Boundaries of Employment Policy in the United States.* Princeton, NJ: Princeton University Press.

Westlake, Martin. 1995. *The Council of the European Union*. London, New York: Cartermill.

Zahariadis, Nikolaos. 1992. To Sell or Not to Sell? Telecommunications Policy in Britain and France. *Journal of Public Policy* 12(4): 355–376.

———. 1995. *Markets, States, and Public Policy: Privatization in Britain and France*. Ann Arbor: University of Michigan Press.

———. 1996. Selling British Rail: An Idea Whose Time has Come? *Comparative Political Studies* 29(4): 400–422.

———. 2003. *Political Decision Making in Modern Democracies.* Washington, DC: Georgetown University Press.

———. 2007. The Multiple Streams Framework: Structure, Limitations, Prospects. *In Sabatier* 2007b: 65–92.

———. 2008. Ambiguity and Choice in European Public Policy. *Journal of European Public Policy* 15(4): 514–530.

———. 2013. Building Better Theoretical Frameworks of the European Union's Policy Process. *Journal of European Public Policy* 20(6): 807–816.

———. 2014. Ambiguity and Multiple Streams. In *Sabatier and Weible* 2014, 25–58.

Zohlnhöfer, Reimut, and Nicole Herweg. 2014. Paradigmatischer Wandel in der deutschen Arbeitsmarktpolitik: Die Hartz-Gesetze. In Rapide Politikwechsel in der Bundesrepublik. Gründe, Akteure, Dynamiken und Probleme, ed. Friedbert W. Rüb. Special issue, *ZfP-Sonderband 6* (6): 91–124.

Zohlnhöfer, Reimut, Nicole Herweg, and Christian Huß. 2016. Bringing Formal Political Institutions into the Multiple Streams Framework: An Analytical Proposal for Comparative Policy Analysis. *Journal of Comparative Policy Analysis* 18 (3): 243–256.

Zohlnhöfer, Reimut, and Friedbert Rüb, eds. 2016a. *Decision-Making Under Ambiguity and Time Constraints: Assessing the Multiple Streams Framework.* Colchester: ECPR Press.

Zohlnhöfer, Reimut, and Friedbert W. Rüb. 2016b. Introduction: Policy-Making Under Ambiguity and Time Constraints. In *Zohlnhöfer and Rüb* 2016a, 1–18.

CHAPTER 3

The European Natural Gas Market and Its Regulation

From the consumer countries' point of view, energy policy aims at fulfilling the three objectives of security of supply, competitiveness, and environmental sustainability in a balanced way (Hoogeveen and Perlot 2005). Since the European Union's (EU) energy dependence rate[1] is growing independent of the energy source, the EU pursues the same energy policy objectives as consumer countries do (cf. European Commission 1988, 2007). For the purpose of analytical clarity, it is useful to distinguish between the general energy policy (e.g., the EU's energy policy), specific policies for the different energy sources (e.g., EU policies dealing with natural gas), and policies addressing traversal or cross-sectoral issues (e.g., research and development policies) (Prontera 2009, 3). As outlined in chap. 1, this book focuses on specific policies for natural gas—more precisely, on the evolution of the European natural gas market regulation. This is a highly technical issue. Therefore, the present chapter aims at providing an understanding of the EU natural gas market (Sect. 3.1), its regulatory requirements (Sect. 3.2), and an overview of its regulation (Sect. 3.3).

3.1 Characteristics of the (European) Natural Gas Market[2]

In general, the natural gas market can be subdivided into an upstream market and a downstream market. The upstream market encompasses "those activities related to natural gas which involve exploration,

N. Herweg, *European Union Policy-Making*,
DOI 10.1007/978-3-319-49400-5_3

development, production, gathering and purification" (Cameron 2005b, lxiv) as well as sales to wholesalers (European Commission 2001, 35). The downstream market refers to the transmission, distribution (Cameron 2005b, lx), and storage of natural gas (European Commission 2001, 35). Due to the strategic importance of the natural gas sector for the economy and the military capability of a state (Cameron 2005a, 7), a high degree of state ownership at all levels of the natural gas industry was (and, to a certain degree, still is) the dominant ownership structure (Stoppard 1996, 8). In the following, the characteristics of this market prior to the liberalization will be outlined. However, since changes in market structure occur rather slowly, many characteristics have only changed slightly or even remained stable. The changes that have occurred are included in this section.

Although there are some similarities between the upstream and the downstream market, the two differ in some important aspects, which is why they will be discussed one by one. Regarding the *upstream market*, natural gas resources are unevenly distributed in Europe, with only a minority of countries having sufficient resources at their disposal to be self-sufficient or to export natural gas. The vast majority of countries depend on imports, mainly from non-EU member states, such as Norway, Russia, and Algeria (Cameron 2005a, 25). As oil and natural gas often co-occur and are extracted by related technologies, the natural gas upstream market is closely linked with the oil market (Stoppard 1996, 5). Generally, the supply contracts between the gas producer and the gas buyer, for instance, the wholesaler, have been long-term contracts inspired by the Dutch Groningen model (Talus 2011, 277). The basic idea of this model is that both the gas producer and the gas buyer profit from long-term contractual agreements. The producer can trust on guaranteed payments for a period long enough to cover (a considerable amount of) the costs incurred from the investment in exploration, production, long-distance transportation, and liquefied natural gas (LNG) liquefaction terminals. The buyer secures its long-term energy supply and is in the position to base investment decisions on predictable transportation needs (Talus 2011, 277). Although competition in the upstream business is possible theoretically, competition is restricted by various anticompetitive clauses that are regularly used in gas supply contracts, such as destination clauses, use restrictions, take-or-pay (TOP) clauses, and oil price indexation (Talus 2011, 277). Destination clauses prohibit the buyer of natural gas to resell it in other areas than initially contracted for. Sometimes, this is combined with the restriction to use natural gas for other purposes than contractually agreed. This keeps the option open for the natural gas seller to become active on its own in hitherto unattended markets. TOP clauses oblige the buyer to pay for a contractually agreed amount of natural gas—usually more than 80 percent of the annual contracted quantity—whether or not this amount is taken to prices that are defined in advance (Hoogeveen and Perlot 2005, 140). Due to the fact that oil and natural gas compete against each other, the natural gas price is usually indexed to the oil price. On the downside, this interfuel pricing policy "[has only been, N.H.] possible because of the absence of gas-to-gas competition" (Stoppard 1996, 16). Notwithstanding the liberalization efforts, even today the "vast majority of international gas trade outside North America is still conducted on the basis of 10–30 years contracts with complex price clauses" (Stern 2014, 43). Taking together the contractual details outlined above, a free play of competitive forces has been limited to such an extent that it would be "misleading to describe it as 'trade' in the generally accepted sense of the term" (Cameron 2005a, 25, emphasis in original).

However, natural gas regulation has paved the way for the emergence of natural gas trading hubs, which means that there is gas-to-gas competition for the small amount of international gas trade not covered by long-term contracts. At the hubs, gas is traded on the basis of transparent prices, which (potential) customers can access via the Internet (Stern 2014, 45). For continental Europe, the Zeebrugge Hub in Belgium is the most important, because it connects the British and Norwegian natural gas markets with those in continental Europe.

The *downstream market* is characterized by a monopolistic market structure (Stoppard 1996, 11). Strictly speaking, this only applies with regard to the required network infrastructure (European Commission 2001, 35) and not to the downstream market per se, as natural gas still competes against alternative energy sources (European Commission 1988, 58). In order to trade natural gas, an appropriate infrastructure is needed. About 75 percent of the European gas imports reach the EU via pipelines (Götz 2007, 7).[3] The construction and maintenance of pipelines is capital intensive. Due to the required high investments, a subadditive cost function is given, which means that once the infrastructure is built, additional customers can be served at low marginal costs. Hence, pipeline networks are natural monopolies (Cameron 2002, 28). Consequently, it is economically reasonable to desist from the construction of another capital-intensive, competing infrastructure as this would not lead to lower prices. Not surprisingly, the prevailing market situation in the European member states prior to the liberalization process has been coined by monopolies in the downstream market (European Commission 1988, 57, 64). On top of that, these monopolies were vertically integrated companies conducting all activities of the downstream market (Cameron 2005a, 28). The monopoly profits that were generated by the ownership of the network infrastructure allowed the vertically integrated companies to cross-subsidize the other company segments, which further limited the competition possible in the downstream market. As the services provided by these vertically integrated companies were seen as essential for the community, governments have used to impose public service obligations (PSO) on them, such as the obligation to supply or to base prices on the incurred costs and to leave them under governmental control. In return, exclusive rights were granted to these companies (Cameron 2005a, 7), most importantly, the rights to import, export, transport, and distribute natural gas (European Commission 1988, 21–22).

In order to amortize the high investments in network infrastructure, gas contracts in the downstream market have shared the main features of those in the upstream market (Talus 2011, 269): The contracts are long term, normally of a duration of 20–30 years (Creti and Villeneuve 2005, 76), which usually contain similar anticompetitive clauses as applied in the upstream market. The long time horizon of the contracts (in addition to the granted exclusive rights) have led to the demarcation of the market, with vertical demarcation meaning "that each operator has its well-defined function and place in the supply chain and generally refrains from entering the markets of its customers and/or suppliers", and horizontal demarcation referring to a situation in which "each importer/wholesaler and/or regional/local distributor has its traditional supply area and (...) generally does not enter the neighbouring supply area" (European Commission 2001, 35). Although the EU natural gas regulation has explicitly attempted to create one internal energy market, there still does not exist one but instead 28 related national energy markets.

3.2 Regulatory Requirements

In summary, the preliberalized natural gas market was dominated by state-owned, vertically integrated companies that were bound in long-term contracts. These contracts included anticompetitive clauses. While the energy companies were granted exclusive rights, they were at the same time obliged to fulfill certain PSO (with regard to the downstream market). As the liberalization of the natural gas market aims particularly at the introduction of competition by removing barriers to trade, it is obvious that a restructuring and reorganization of the European natural gas market has been inevitable. The most important features to introduce competition in this market are (1) introduction of third-party access (TPA) to networks and infrastructure, (2) unbundling of vertically integrated companies, and (3) effective regulatory oversight.

3.2.1 *Introduction of TPA to Networks and Infrastructure*

A means to introduce competition—despite transportation assets being characterized by elements of natural monopolies—is to open networks for third parties. In short, this is "a system where owners of pipelines agree, or are required, to carry gas—which they do not own—through their systems for delivery to third parties" (Stern 1992, 25) against payment of a charge or tariff for the services provided. Consequently, the role of pipeline owners changes "from that of a merchant pipeline company (...) to that of a transportation company providing a range of services" (Stern 1992, 21). Ideally, TPA systems grant equal market opportunities to all parties, and are nondiscriminatory and transparent (Stern 1992, 27). In order to achieve equal market opportunities, the abolition of exclusive rights to construct facilities, to transport and distribute (including related services), as well as to import and export is required. Nondiscrimination refers to equal-access possibilities for (potential) market players to all activities of the natural gas market, which implies a necessity to unbundle the vertically integrated companies (see Sect. 3.2.2). Additionally, nondiscrimination must be exerted with a view to servicing merchant customers and third parties. This can only be achieved if fair charges are invoiced. Closely related to the issue of fair charges is the necessity of granting transparency. The need for transparency is not restricted to prices, but applies to the availability of services. Hence, a transparent methodology for charging for and offering of services is required, which in turn calls for effective regulatory oversight (Stern 1992, 28). TPA does not define a workable commercial agreement; its introduction commands prior clarification of related issues. These issues include defining the following (1) of eligible parties participating in a TPA system, (2) to which facilities TPA has to be granted, (3) of how available capacity and charges for services are calculated, (4) of unbundling requirements, and (5) of regulatory procedures (Stern 1992, 26–27). Furthermore, a decision is needed as to whether TPA is granted on a regulated or negotiated basis. Regulated TPA implies that the tariffs and conditions applied are determined by a regulator (Cameron 2005b, lxiii), while negotiated TPA results from negotiations between the pipeline owner (respectively, pipeline operator) and the access-seeking third party (Cameron 2005b, lxii).

3.2.2 Unbundling Vertically Integrated Companies

Unbundling vertically integrated companies leads to the separation of activities. There are six approaches to unbundling, which differ in terms of rigidity: Account unbundling, functional unbundling, legal unbundling, introduction of independent transmission system operators (ITSOs) or independent system operators (ISOs), and ownership unbundling (cf. Gao 2009, 23). Account unbundling stipulates that a vertically integrated company keeps separate accounts for each activity. This implies that the company has to charge itself the same tariffs for the services received as third parties (International Energy Agency 2000, 81), which eliminates the possibility to cross-subsidize. This form of unbundling counts as the weakest, ensuring that no sensible information flows between the company segments. However, the interruption in the flow of information is essential in preventing vertically integrated companies to gain competitive advantages over third parties (Cameron 2005a, 33). Functional unbundling of vertically integrated companies implies separate management structures for each function, which goes along with unbundled accounts (International Energy Agency 2000, 81) but allows for the same ownership (Cameron 2005a, 33). Legal unbundling can be seen as the advancement of functional unbundling, as it also requires vertically integrated companies to create subsidiaries for the different business divisions (Gao 2009, 23). Ownership unbundling requires that different business divisions do not have the same owner(s), and it counts as the strongest form of unbundling (International Energy Agency 2000, 81). The introduction of an ITSO or an ISO establishes a middle course between legal and ownership unbundling. The latter allows the vertically integrated company to maintain its ownership of network assets, provided that these assets are technically and commercially operated by an ISO, which is an undertaking or entity fully independent from the vertically integrated company (Gao 2009, 23–24). ITSOs are allowed to own and operate the network, provided that the management of the network is carried out by a subsidiary of the parent company.

3.2.3 Effective Regulatory Oversight

As "[t]he most traditional and persistent rationale for governmental regulation of a firm's prices and profits is the existence of a 'natural monopoly'" (Breyer 1998, 59, emphasis in original), the need to establish effective regulatory oversight does not come as a surprise. It aims at ensuring that neither the network owner nor the network operator extracts monopoly rents to the disadvantage of other market players. Generally speaking, the regulatory tasks can be classified according to structure, conduct, and transitional problems. Structure refers to unbundling and the prevention of cross-subsidies, while conduct focuses on the organization of regulation and the control of market behavior, including the granting of security of supply. Transitional problems result from the fact that the extraction of monopoly profits is no longer possible, which is problematic with regard to sunk costs. These arise if competition is introduced before investments in network infrastructure could be recovered. Another example for sunk costs is the introduction of competition during the period of a long-term TOP contract, which was contracted on the assumption that the buyer's market share remains constant and that there will be just one commodity price due to the absence of competitors (Cameron 2005a, 30). Ideally, independent regulatory authorities are entrusted with regulatory oversight. Here, independence refers to the regulator's independence from government authorities and from the regulated companies. This still leaves open a variety of different regulatory designs, ranging from sector-specific single- to multiutility regulators and from the appointment of a regulatory commission to an individual. Furthermore, institutional overlap between the regulatory authority and the competition authority can be handled differently (Cameron 2005a, 31).

3.3 Regulatory Output: The Gas Directives' Provisions

A directive sets out the goals member states have to meet without specifying how to achieve them. However, a directive specifies which general principles member states have to take into account when implementing national law. The more astonishing thing is that none of the gas directives summarizes these general principles in one or a few articles, but have them scattered across various chapters. All three gas directives refer to the following six principles: objectivity, nondiscrimination, transparency, efficiency, competitiveness, and security. The second and third directives add consumer protection, fair prices, cost-reflectiveness, and environmental protection. Although there might be trade-offs between some of these principles, "the Directives' inherent logic suggests they are of equal importance and complementary in nature" (Haase 2009, 191–92, quote on p. 192).

A detailed summary of the three gas directives' content goes beyond the scope of this book.[4] Instead, this section summarizes how the regulation of the above-outlined, most important features for the introduction of competition (TPA, unbundling requirements, and regulatory oversight) changed from directive to directive. This is supplemented by a summary of the provisions regarding legal market opening and PSO, because these topics were highly controversial, particularly during the first and second gas directive process.

The comparison of the gas directives' contents summarized in Table 3.1 shows that (1) they have become more ambitious, and (2) (the large) leeway given to member states regarding the implementation of the directives has diminished from directive to directive (without dissolving completely). The provisions regarding *legal market opening* are a case in point. While the first gas directive stipulates different degrees of market opening to be achieved within different transposition periods for advanced market-openers and latecomers, the second and third gas directives treat all member states equally. Furthermore, the first gas directive aims at a market opening for two groups of customers: gas-fired power generators and final customers consuming more than a fixed amount of natural gas. For instance, advanced market-openers must open their markets equal to at least 43 percent of the total annual gas consumption of their respective gas market by 2008. The remaining member states must achieve a market opening of just 33 percent by 2018. The second and third gas directives stipulate a full market opening for all customers by 2007.

The provisions regarding *TPA* and *unbundling* have become stricter. The first gas directive considers negotiated and regulated TPA, while the second and third only accept regulated TPA (except for access to storage facilities, where member states can opt for negotiated TPA). Regarding unbundling, the first directive stipulates account unbundling for vertically integrated natural gas undertakings, while the second one adds (with few exemptions) functional and legal unbundling of its distribution and transmission activities. Whereas the second directive explicitly states that it does not imply ownership unbundling (2003/55/EC, recital 10), the third directive considers ownership unbundling and the two compromise versions

Table 3.1 The gas directives' main features

Directive	*98/30/EC (first gas directive)*	*2003/55/EC (second gas directive)*	*2009/73/EC (third gas directive)*
Entry into force	August 10, 1998	August 4, 2003	September 3, 2009
Legal market opening	Legal market opening defined for *eligible customers*. These are at least: (1) *Gas-fired power generators* irrespective of their annual consumption level, (2) *Final customers* consuming annually more than (a) 25 million cubic meters (until August 9, 2000) (b) 15 million cubic meters (until August 9, 2003) (c) 5 million cubic meters (until August 9, 2008) The definition of eligible customers must result in a *market opening* equal to at least (a) 20% (until August 9, 2000) (b) 28% (until August 9, 2003) (c) 33% (until August 9, 2018) of the total annual gas consumption of the national gas market If it results in a market opening of more than (a) 30% (until August 9, 2000) (b) 38% (until August 9, 2003) (c) 43% (until August 9, 2008) of the total annual gas	Legal market opening defined for *eligible customers*: (a) As specified by Directive 98/30/EC (until July 1, 2004) (b) All nonhousehold customers (from July 1, 2004) (c) All customers (from July 1, 2007)	

(*continued*)

Table 3.1 (continued)

Directive	*98/30/EC (first gas directive)*	*2003/55/EC (second gas directive)*	*2009/73/EC (third gas directive)*
	consumption of the national gas market, member states are allowed to adjust their definition of eligible customers until the above-listed thresholds		
Third-party access (TPA)	Two *procedures for access* to transmission networks, distribution networks, liquefied natural gas (LNG) facilities, and facilities supplying ancillary services are considered: (1) *Negotiated access* on the basis of voluntary agreements between natural gas undertakings and eligible customers. The natural gas undertakings are obliged to publish their main commercial conditions for the use of the system until August 9, 2001 and annually thereafter (2) *Regulated access* grants natural gas undertakings and eligible customers a right to access to the system on the basis of published tariffs and/or other terms and obligations for system usage In both cases, it does not matter whether the natural gas undertakings	Except for storage facilities: *regulated TPA* based on published tariffs. These tariffs (or the methodologies underlying their calculation) have to be approved ex ante by a regulatory authority In addition to regulated TPA, *storage facilities* can also opt for negotiated TPA *TPA exemption* for major new gas infrastructure granted *Refusal of access* still possible on the same grounds as exemplified in Directive 98/30/EC	

(*continued*)

Table 3.1 (continued)

Directive	*98/30/EC (first gas directive)*	*2003/55/EC (second gas directive)*	*2009/73/EC (third gas directive)*
	and eligible customers are located inside or outside of the territory covered by the interconnected system *Refusal of access* is possible if (a) capacity is lacking; (b) otherwise public service obligations (PSO) could not been carried out; or (c) this would result in economic and financial difficulties with take-or-pay (TOP) contracts		
Unbundling	Whether they are legally obliged or not according to national law, *integrated natural gas undertakings* are required to *separate accounts* for their natural gas transmission, distribution and storage activities, and where appropriate, also for their nongas activities	The directive considers: (a) Account unbundling of integrated natural gas undertakings; this goes along with intense monitoring by national regulatory authorities (NRAs) (b) Functional and legal unbundling of distribution (DSO) and transmission system operator (TSO) *Exemptions:* (1) Integrated natural gas undertakings that serve *less than 100,000 customers* (2) Delay in the implementation of *legal unbundling* of the DSO beyond July 1, 2007	The directive considers: (a) Ownership unbundling (b) Independent system operator (ISO): The ISO is in full control of not only network operations, but also investments (c) Independent transmission system operator (ITSO): Member states can either implement exclusively ownership unbundling or let the TSO opt for an unbundling model by itself

(*continued*)

Table 3.1 (continued)

Directive	*98/30/EC (first gas directive)*	*2003/55/EC (second gas directive)*	*2009/73/EC (third gas directive)*
Public service obligations (PSO)	Member states may impose on a natural gas undertaking PSO relating to *security of supply* and *environmental protection*		
Regulatory authorities	Member states are asked to set up a *competent authority for the settlement of disputes* regarding negotiations and refusal of TPA In the case of cross-border disputes, the dispute settlement authorities concerned shall consult each other The directive does not specify which attributes an authority has to meet to be qualified as competent	Member states are asked to set up *at least one* competent authority for the regulation of the natural gas market Article 25 provides a *list of tasks* falling under the NRA(s)' responsibility	Member states are asked to set up *a single, independent NRA* Articles 39 and 41 provide a *list of tasks* falling under the NRA(s)' responsibility. The directive stipulates *close cooperation* between the NRA and *the Agency for the Cooperation of Energy Regulators*
Date of transposition	August 10, 2000	July 1, 2004	March 3, 2011

Source: Own compilation

of legal and ownership unbundling, the setting up of an ITSO and ISO. Hence, the regulation has become stricter, but still member states have leeway to decide which unbundling model suits them best.

The first directive only touches the issue of setting up one or more *regulatory authorities*. It just refers to an authority for settling disputes regarding negotiations and refusal of TPA, without specifying how this authority should be designed or operate. The second directive asks member states to set up at least one authority for the regulation of the natural gas market and provides a list of tasks this authority should fulfill. In practice, this allowed member states to spread regulatory functions over several authorities "if that [was, N.H.] deemed appropriate by the Member State, permitting, say, local or regional regulatory bodies, but also a combination of NRA [national regulatory authority, N.H.], ministry, and, say, a competition authority" (Cameron 2007, 144). The third directive reduces this variety of regulatory arrangements and stipulates the creation of a single, independent national regional authority (NRA). Furthermore, it specifies the NRA's tasks and stipulates that the NRAs cooperate closely with each other and with the newly established Agency for the Cooperation of Energy Regulators.

Only the provisions regarding *PSO* have barely changed. All directives include the possibility for member states to impose on natural gas undertakings PSO relating to security (which includes security of supply, regularity, quality, and price of supplies) and environmental protection. While the first gas directive generally refers to environmental protection, the second one explicitly lists energy efficiency and climate protection as examples of environmental protection. The third directive adds energy from renewable sources. In addition, all three directives allow member states to introduce the implementation of long-term planning, which is defined as "the planning of supply and transport capacity of natural gas undertakings on a long-term basis with a view to meeting the demand for natural gas of the system, diversification of sources and securing supplies to customers" (98/30/EC, Art. 2, paragraph 23; 2003/55/EC, 2009/73/EC, in both directives included in Art. 2, paragraph 30).

Being familiar with these regulatory details is essential for the analysis of the policy processes which led to the three gas directives, particularly because there were—and there still are—vast differences regarding the degree to which competition in member states' natural gas markets was and still is restricted. The box plots in Figs. 3.1 and 3.2 depict this variety for the EU15 and EU27, respectively, for the negotiation period of the three gas directives (from 1992 to 2009). They show the natural gas market regulation indicator, which is a subindicator of the Organisation for Economic Co-operation and Development's (OECD) sectoral product market regulation indicators in nonmanufacturing product markets. It "quantifies the degree to which regulatory settings (...) are anti-competitive" (Conway and Nicoletti 2006: 6) and ranges from 0 to 6, whereby the higher the indicator is, the more anticompetitive the member state's regulatory setting is. The differences, which the median and interquartile ranges of this index clearly detect, mainly stem from topographical, geological, and cultural differences and impact whether member states are willing to agree on common rules for the natural gas sector. However, resulting from the

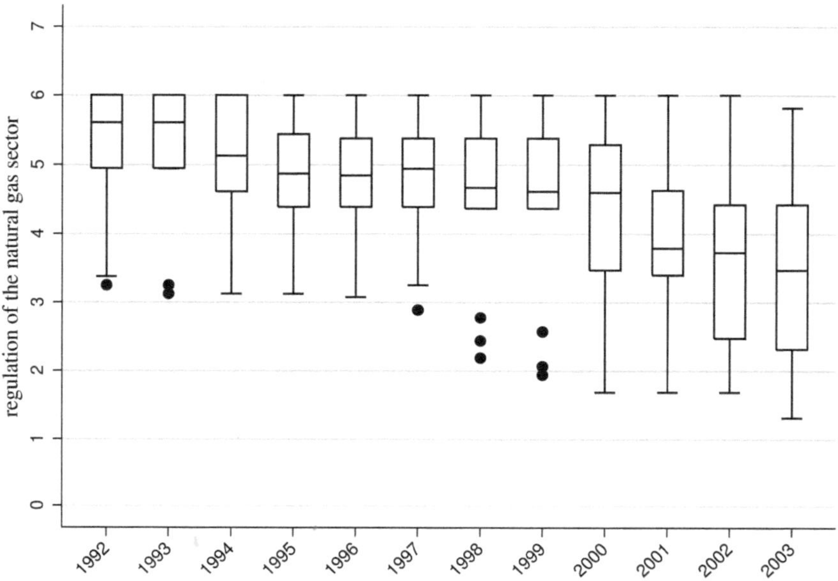

Fig. 3.1 Regulatory diversity in the EU15, 1992–2003. *Source:* Own illustration of the OECD's natural gas market regulation indicator based on Koske et al. (2014). *Notes:* Strictly speaking, from 1992 to 1994, the member states on the negotiation table were those of the EU12. Since the European Council had already concluded in December 1992 to open official enlargement negotiations with Austria, Sweden, and Finland in 1993 (European Council 1992), resulting in their accession to the EU in January 1995, Fig. 3.1 illustrates the development of the natural gas market regulation for the EU15 from 1992 on

multidimensional nature of gas market regulation, member states cannot simply be divided into supporters and opponents. Instead, the composition of these camps varied (and still does) with the aspect of regulation in the past as well as today.

For instance, member states with just a small (or none) natural gas resource base have been highly concerned about securing supply. This applies particularly to member states in Central and Eastern Europe that, due to the legacy of Soviet-era planning, are highly dependent on imports of Russian gas. In order to achieve security of supply, these member states have been willing to defer the introduction (or extension) of competition in the natural gas market. Similarly, member states that have been obliged to pay

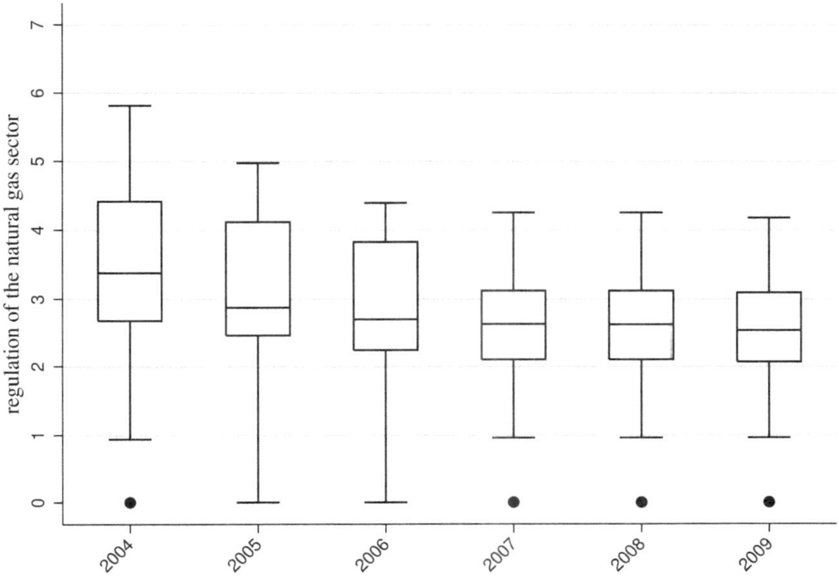

Fig. 3.2 Regulatory diversity in the EU27, 2004–2009. *Source*: Own illustration of the OECD's natural gas market regulation indicator based on Koske et al. (2014). *Notes:* The following data are missing: Italy for the years 2007 to 2009, and France, Romania, Bulgaria, Cyprus, Czech Republic, Malta, Lithuania, and Latvia for the years 2004 to 2009

for a contractually agreed amount of natural gas due to TOP clauses in their ongoing long-term contracts as well as those with emergent natural gas markets have been reluctant to introduce competition. On the other hand, member states that already liberalized substantial parts of their natural gas markets, most prominently the United Kingdom, have pressed for achieving a level playing field in order to avoid disadvantages for their businesses vis-à-vis subsidized national champions located in less liberalized markets. Thus, it is essential for the following analysis of the policy processes to be aware that the policy dynamics might differ with the aspect of regulation currently on the negotiating table.

Notes

1. The energy dependence rate is calculated as the ratio of net energy imports to gross energy consumption.
2. Strictly speaking, one European natural gas market does not exist because the member states' natural gas markets are not sufficiently connected to allow encompassing cross-border trade. For reasons of simplicity, I nonetheless refer to the European natural gas market since the European Union (EU)'s regulatory activity aims at establishing it.
3. The remaining imports (which also require capital-intensive, upfront investments) are delivered in the form of liquefied natural gas (LNG). Since pipeline gas is less expensive than LNG, the former is expected to dominate European gas trade in the long run (Götz 2007, 7). However, at the member states' level, the share of LNG in natural gas consumption varies tremendously. In 2007, for instance, it varied between 0 percent (e.g., Austria, Germany, Sweden) and 68.9 percent (Spain) (own calculation, based on British Petroleum 2008).
4. For an in-depth overview of the directives' contents, see, for instance, Cameron (2005b, 2007), Grunwald (2003), and Johnston and Block (2012).

References

2003/55/EC. *Directive of the European Parliament and of the Council of 26 June 2003 Concerning Common Rules for the Internal Market in Natural Gas and Repealing Directive 98/30/EC.*

2009/73/EC. *Directive of the European Parliament and of the Council of 13 July Concerning Common Rules for the Internal Market in Natural Gas and Repealing Directive 2003/55/EC.*

98/30/EC. *Directive of the European Parliament and of the Council of 22 June 1998 Concerning Common Rules for the Internal Market in Natural Gas.*

Breyer, Stephen. 1998. Typical Justification for Regulation. In *A Reader on Regulation*, ed. Robert Baldwin, Colin Scott, and Christopher Hood, 59–92. Oxford: Oxford University Press.

British Petroleum. 2008. *Statistical Review of World Energy*. London.

Cameron, Peter D. 2002. *Competition in Energy Markets: Law and Regulation in the European Union*. 1st ed. Oxford: Oxford University Press.

———. 2005a. Completing the Internal Market in Energy: An Introduction to the New Legislation. In *Cameron*, 2005b, 7–39.

———., eds. 2005b. *Legal Aspects of EU Energy Regulation: Implementing the New Directives on Electricity and Gas Across Europe.* Oxford: Oxford University Press.

———., eds. 2007. *Competition in Energy Markets: Law and Regulation in the European Union.* 2nd ed. Oxford: Oxford University Press.

Creti, Anna, and Bertrand Villeneuve. 2005. Longterm Contracts and Take-or-Pay Clauses in Natural Gas Markets. *Energy Studies Review* 13(1): 75–94.

Conway, Paul, and Giuseppe Nicoletti. 2006. *Product Market Regulation in the Non-Manufacturing Sectors of OECD Countries: Measurements and Highlights.* OECD Economics Department Working Papers. Paris: OECD Publishing.

European Commission. 1988. *The Internal Energy Market. Commission Working Document: COM(88)238 Final.*

———. 2001. *European Community Competition Policy 2000: XXXth Report on Competition Policy.* Luxembourg: Office for Official Publications of the European Communities.

———. 2007. *An Energy Policy for Europe: COM(2007)1 Final.*

European Council. 1992. *Conclusions of the Presidency: 11–12 December 1992.*

Gao, Anton M.-Z. 2009. The Third European Energy Liberalization Package: Does Functional and Legal Unbundling in the Gas Storage Sector Go Too Far? *Competition and Regulation in Network Industries* 10(1): 17–44.

Götz, Roland. 2007. Russian Gas and European Energy Security. *SWP Research Paper*, 1–21.

Grunwald, Jürgen. 2003. *Das Energierecht der Europäischen Gemeinschaften: EGKS-EURATOM-EG; Grundlagen—Geschichte—geltende Regelungen.* Berlin: De Gruyter Recht.

Haase, N. 2009. *European Gas Market Liberalisation.* Enschede: Universiteit Twente.

Hoogeveen, Femke, and Wilbur Perlot. 2005. *Tomorrow's More: The International System, Geopolitical Changes and Energy CIEP 02/2005.* The Hague: Clingendael International Energy Programme.

International Energy Agency. 2000. *Regulatory Reform: European Gas.* Paris: OECD Publishing.

Johnston, Angus C., and Guy Block. 2012. *EU Energy Law.* Oxford: Oxford University Press.

Koske, Isabell, Isabelle Wanner, Rosmaria Bitetti, and Omar Barbiero. 2014. *The 2013 Update of the OECD Product Market Regulation Indicators: Policy Insights for OECD and non-OECD Countries.* OECD Economics Department Working Papers. Paris: OECD Publishing.

Prontera, Andrea. 2009. Energy Policy: Concepts, Actors, Instruments and Recent Developments. *World Political Science Review* 5(1, Art. 7): 1–30.

Stern, Jonathan P. 1992. *Third Party Access in European Gas Industries: Regulation-Driven or Market-Led?* London: Royal institute of international affairs.

———. 2014. International Gas Pricing in Europe and Asia: A Crisis of Fundamentals. *Energy Policy* 64: 43–48.
Stoppard, Michael. 1996. *A New Order for Gas in Europe?* O.I.E.S. Papers on Natural Gas. Oxford: Oxford Institute for Energy Studies.
Talus, Kim. 2011. Long-term Natural Gas Contracts and Antitrust Law in the European Union and the United States. *Journal of World Energy Law & Business* 4(3): 260–315i.

CHAPTER 4

The First Gas Directive Process

The analysis of the first gas directive process covers the time span between June 1985 (the publication of the Commission's White Paper "Completing the Internal Market" (European Commission 1985)) and June 1998 (the signature of the final act and end of procedure in the European Parliament [EP]). Nonetheless, references to earlier developments are included where necessary in order to capture the dynamics of the streams. The analysis is guided by the hypotheses derived in Chap. 2 (for an overview, see Table 2.6), and it consists of two parts: Sect. 4.1 analyzes the agenda change and Sect. 4.2 the policy change. Due to data restrictions, Hypothesis 6b cannot be assessed empirically. According to this hypothesis, the release of working programs by the Council Presidency opens an agenda window. Since the release of such working programs was only institutionalized in the course of the 1990s, they are not available for the time span investigated (except for the United Kingdom in 1998). The drafting and negotiating of the electricity and gas legislation took place in parallel. The former is only referred to when it is necessary for the explanation of the policy processes concerning the gas directive.

This chapter draws on Herweg (2015), which is a compressed analysis of the first gas directive process.

N. Herweg, *European Union Policy-Making*,
DOI 10.1007/978-3-319-49400-5_4

4.1 Agenda Change

The layout of this chapter is straightforward. Sections 4.1.1 to 4.1.3 summarize the state of the problem stream, political stream, and policy stream, thereby testing whether stream ripeness was a given (Hypothesis 1, specified in Definitions 1–3). The subsequent section discusses by which change the agenda window opened (Hypothesis 2, alternative causal paths specified in Hypotheses 4–8) and how a policy-entrepreneur succeeded in coupling the streams (Hypothesis 3, specified in Hypothesis 9). The final section concludes.

4.1.1 Problem Stream

The definition of problem stream ripeness consists of two aspects: (1) Attention must be raised to an issue relevant for the policy field and (2) that issue must be interpreted as being problematic (Definition 1). Regarding the creation of an internal market in natural gas, the problem stream was not ripe. Until the late 1980s, the most important issue in the problem stream regarding energy had been a perceived scarcity of supply (Eikeland 2004, 3). This perception resulted from the belief that finite resources would soon be depleted, which co-occurred with high demand forecasts (Stern 1992, 2–3). Apart from this depletion scenario, international focusing events—such as the closure of the Suez Canal in 1956 and 1967, the oil crises caused by the Arab oil embargo in 1973, and the Iranian Revolution in 1979—had fostered the impression that energy security was endangered (Daintith and Hancher 1986, 19–31). The fact that the price of crude oil had skyrocketed during the 1970s reinforced that perception. The focus on energy security and the great differences regarding the importance of the distinct energy sources and sectors in their countries (Andersen 1993, 138–39) led member states to treat energy as a strategic commodity, which had to be dealt with nationally (Biesenbender 2015, 22; Pollack 2000, 522).[1] This did not even change when the oil price started to fall in 1986, although this made energy imports (comparatively) cheaper and hence security of supply concerns less pressing (Surrey 1990, 45). Summing up, member states dealt with the question of how to secure energy supply nationally and not as a matter of Community action.

Furthermore, another issue occupied the attention of European Union (EU) officials and media since the mid-1970s, which pushed seemingly less important issues (such as a common energy policy, see below) into the background (cf. Herweg et al. 2015, 3; Jones and Baumgartner 2004, 10): the problem of eurosclerosis. Eurosclerosis refers to a situation of "stagnant growth, rampant inflation, and rising unemployment" (Jabko 2006, 15) and a loss of confidence in European institutions (Moravcsik 1991, 19). Member states, thrown off course by the two oil crises of the 1970s, were confronted with severe economic problems. They attempted but failed to solve them nationally by means of traditional and social–democratic strategies. As a consequence, policy-makers in Western Europe showed "growing interest in and commitment to neoliberal economics" (Cini and L. McGowan 2009, 32). In addition, the member states became receptive for tackling the present economic challenges by means of Community action during the early 1980s (cf. Cini and L. McGowan 2009, 31; Fligstein 2001). This culminated in the publication of the Commission's White Paper "Completing the Internal Market" (European Commission 1988b), which basically was a proposal for a package of neoliberal measures with the objective of creating and completing the internal market by 1992 (referred to as the single market program). The White Paper included a list of obstacles and measures to overcome them. Using the multiple streams terminology, the White Paper introduced a new category: the free movement category, which referred to the removal of physical, technical, and fiscal barriers regarding the free movement of goods, persons, services, and capital (European Commission 1985, 4). Given that the member states' energy markets have been far from complying with that category (Palinkas 1989, 246), it is noteworthy that energy was not included in the single market program (except for in the context of public procurement (European Commission 1985, paragraph 86)). Following Fligstein (2001, 279), this resulted from the Commission's strategy to circumvent potential opposition against the single market program by carefully avoiding to open markets where strong opposition existed.

The Single European Act (SEA), signed in February 1986, incorporated the Commission's proposal regarding the completion of the internal market (excluding energy) and initiated procedural reforms, most importantly, the expanded use of qualified majority voting in the Council regarding internal market matters (Moravcsik 1991, 19–20). In 1988, the widely recognized Cecchini report was published, which the Commission had ordered two years earlier. This report quantified the so-called cost of non-Europe in the areas now covered by the SEA economically. According to this report, the proper implementation of the single market project would lead to "an economic bonus of ECU[2] 200 billion at 1988 prices and the creation of millions of new jobs" (European Commission 1988a, 7). Therefore, the Commission concluded that the completion of the internal market "should be sufficient to transform the Community's economic performance from a less than brilliant one to an outstanding one" (European Commission 1988a, 7). Consequently, with regard to future problem definitions, policy-entrepreneurs from then on could refer to the widely accepted free movement category in order to document the deviation of a condition from its ideal state (cf. Nylander 2000, 310).

To conclude, the definition of problem stream ripeness is not validated: Attention was not raised to the uncompetitive state of the energy markets. Consequently, this was not interpreted as being problematic. However, due to the introduction of the free movement category and a decline in the cost of oil, the problem stream changed insofar as it provided starting points for policy-entrepreneurs to frame the state of the energy market as problematic.

4.1.2 Political Stream

The political stream is defined to be ripe if the EU government is receptive to a specific issue (Definition 2). As discussed in Sect. 2.4.1.1, it is an open question whether all three branches of the EU government or just the Commission needs to be receptive to agenda change. My assumption is that it suffices for the Commission to be receptive. In order to empirically assess whether this assumption is appropriate, each branch of the EU government is considered in the following analysis.

The *Commission* clearly was a proponent of energy liberalization since it had repeatedly aimed at developing a common energy policy (Biesenbender 2015, 23; Hancher 1990, 221; Finon and Surrey 1996, 165; F. McGowan 1989, 548; Maltby 2013, 437–38). Already in 1968, the Commission suggested in its first guidelines for a Community energy policy to take measures "with regard to the free movement of goods, freedom of establishment, application of the rules of competition, and indirect taxation" (European Commission 1968, 10). Regarding natural gas, the Commission specified that this should be achieved (inter alia) by means of recommendations or directives regarding the transport by gas pipelines and the rates charged for this transport (European Commission 1968, 12). This was followed by piles of attempts to push for a common energy policy (cf. European Commission 1972, 1973, 1974a, b, 1976a, b, 1981). After the publication of its White Paper in June 1985, the Commission prioritized the adoption of the Community's energy objectives for 1995 by the

Council in its working program for the years 1986 and 1987 (*Bulletin of the European Communities*, Supplements 1/86 and 1/87).

The above Commission attempts to push for a common energy policy remained unsuccessful (cf. Biesenbender 2015, 27). Notwithstanding their expressions of political will (cf. OJ C 153, July 9, 1975, OJ C 149, June 18, 1980), member states were unable—or unwilling—to arbitrate successfully between their different interests or to agree on how to prioritize different energy measures (Daintith and Hancher 1986, 19–31). As a consequence, neither the European Council nor the Council can be regarded as being receptive to energy liberalization. From June 1985—when the idea of the single market project had taken hold—until June 1988, the *European Council* did not refer to a single market in energy in its conclusions, thereby mirroring the member states' reluctant (or at best hesitant) attitude. However, the same conclusions documented a (growing) support of the single market program as such (European Council 1985, 1986a, b, 1987, 1988b).

Regarding the *Council*, its complete opposition to energy liberalization started crumbling during the late 1980s. As mentioned above, energy was not included in the SEA, the first major amendment of the European Economic Community (EEC) Treaty. Regarding Article 130r of the newly inserted title VII on environment, the Council even published a declaration according to which "the Community's activities in the sphere of the environment may not interfere with national policies regarding the exploitation of energy sources" (OJ L 169/25, June 29, 1987). Put differently, the linkage of energy with the free movement category was still not accepted by the member states in terms of Community action. This changed slightly with the Council agreeing on a resolution concerning energy policy objectives for 1995 in September 1986. One of those objectives clearly reflected the spirit of the SEA as it referred to "greater integration, free from barriers to trade, of the internal energy market with a view to improving security of supply, reducing costs and improving economic competitiveness" (OJ C 241, September 25, 1986). Nonetheless, this resolution lacked a European affirmative call to Community action as it stated that "the framework established by Community objectives is of considerable value as regards the *coordination and harmonization of national energy policies*" (OJ C 241, September 25, 1986, emphasis added; in a similar vein, see Grunwald 2003, 51–52).[3] That the member states addressed energy policy explicitly can be ascribed to the fall of the oil price in 1986 (Andersen 1993, 144) and to the fact that large energy consumers increasingly expressed their disapproval of the great energy price differentials between the member states (Hancher 1990, 221).

It is noteworthy that one member state's attitude toward energy liberalization changed in the early 1980s: that of the United Kingdom. The United Kingdom started to liberalize its energy sector in 1982 (see Sect. 4.1.3) and, since then, acted as an advocate for energy liberalization measures. However, its support was restricted to energy liberalization and excluded the idea of a comprehensive common energy policy (F. McGowan 1996b, 159).

Responding to the above-referred-to Council resolution, the Commission requested the Council's support to carry out a study concerning the current obstacles to a single energy market and means to overcome them in 1987 (Hancher 1990, 222). At this time, the paradigm to answer to any unsatisfactory outcome with "more private ownership, the removal of restrictions on trading, and the promotion of competition" (Helm 2005, 2, in a similar vein Matláry 1997, 19; Scharpf 1996, 17–18) was already established among the involved actors. As a consequence, the Council (as well as the EP and the Economic and Social Committee) backed the Commission's request (European Commission 1988b, 2; Council of the European Communities 1987, 11). According to Pollak et al. (2008, 78), this did not mean that the Council was indeed interested in creating an internal energy market (IEM). To the contrary, the inquiry for further data and information can be seen as a strategy to gain time before being committed to establish an IEM due to the absence of a good justification as to why energy should be omitted from the single market program. Regardless of whether the Council's agreement resulted from a paradigm shift from keynesianism to neoliberalism or from the strategy to delay the creation of an IEM, it entailed that member states could no longer fundamentally question the program itself and that opposition had to be based on technical arguments.

With regard to the definition of stream ripeness, it is fair to say that the Commission was not only receptive to a common energy policy, but also its advocate. The member states, except for the United Kingdom, completely rejected the idea of creating an IEM until the mid-1980s. So far, they had only paid lip service to this idea, but had not moved on from rhetoric to real action. While the European Council simply did not include energy liberalization in its agenda, the Council agreed to the Commission's request to study the obstacles to the creation of an IEM and suggest means to overcome them in 1987. Although it would go too far to say that this means the Council had become receptive to the idea of a single energy market, it "at least tolerated action", to quote Kingdon (2003, 218).

4.1.3 Policy Stream

In the policy stream, members of a policy community engage in working out alternatives to policy problems of a specific policy field. As summarized in Sect. 2.1.2, these members are at least familiar with each other's ideas. Despite its prominence in today's EU founding treaties, energy policy as a matter of Community action had been a neglected subject. As a consequence, the policy community's participants mostly concentrated on generating energy proposals with a national, instead of a supranational, dimension in mind. Of course, some participants had been active with regard to developing European (and international) solutions, such as the E&P Forum,[4] IFIEC,[5] CEFIC,[6] and Unipede.[7] However, their ambitions to come up with worked-out *European* policy proposals were limited. For instance, Unipede focused on technological and scientific cooperation, and barely engaged in political representation (Eising 2000, 203), and IFIEC did not manage to present a united front on the liberalization issue until the early 1990s (Bartle 2005, 97). Furthermore, relevant energy policy specialists did not engage in this exchange due to the prevailing national focus on energy policy. Following a request of the Commission, the Energy Council "held an initial exchange of views on the general problem of the completion of the internal market in the sphere of energy" (Council of the European Communities 1987, 11). This reaction documents a first turn to Community action in the sphere of energy. However, the president's conclusions remained very brief and superficial, which is why it would go too far to classify this initial exchange of views as the Council contributing to the generation of alternatives.

As a consequence, the policy stream was dominated by the policies almost all member states in the natural gas sector had pursued (see Chap. 3). The most important elements of these policies were acceptance of (1) state ownership, (2) vertically integrated monopolies, (3) long-term and partly anticompetitive contracts, as well as the granting of (4) exclusive rights in exchange for the fulfillment of public service obligations (PSO).

This was far from being compatible with the idea of liberalizing the natural gas markets. Although not popular, liberalization pioneers provided proposals in this respect, such as the United States,[8] Canada, and the United Kingdom (Stern 1993, 191). Probably due to its EU membership, particularly the British experiences attracted the policy community's attention (for the following, see Armstrong and Sappington 2006, 328–29). In the United Kingdom, the liberalization of the natural gas market had been one cornerstone of Margaret Thatcher's program of industrial reform. Mirroring the prevailing elements of continental Europe's gas sector, British Gas had been a state-owned and vertically integrated company prior to the reform. Based on its legal monopoly regarding the downstream sector and its legal monopsony in the upstream sector, it had dominated the natural gas market. In 1982, British Gas was privatized in its vertically integrated form, followed by account unbundling in 1991 (and legal unbundling in 1995). With regard to the lack of competitors, a regulation (1) stipulated that British Gas was obliged to grant third parties access to its pipelines in the downstream sector and (2) removed its legal monopsony in the upstream sector in 1982. Furthermore, its customers were divided into two markets, the tariff market and the contract market. The tariff market consisted of customers with a consumption level below 25,000 therms of gas per year (which was reduced to 2500 therms in the early 1990s and removed entirely in 1998) and the contract market of the remaining higher-volume customers. In contrast to the tariff market, prices in the contract market were not regulated, which provided British Gas with the opportunity to practice price discrimination. In order to tackle this problem, provisions stipulated in 1988 that British Gas had to publish ex-ante tariffs regarding the purchase of gas and network access charges, which was supplemented by a provision in the early 1990s that these prices are subject to regulatory oversight. Furthermore, in order to spur competition in the upstream sector, British Gas was prohibited to purchase more than 90 percent of the gas in newly discovered gas fields in 1988. In sum, the core principles of the UK model consisted of (1) unbundling provisions for vertically integrated utilities, (2) regulated third-party access (TPA) to transmission networks on the basis of nondiscrimination and transparency, and (3) regulatory oversight.

Since energy was not explicitly included in the SEA, there had to be a justification for Community action available in the policy primeval soup in order for a EU proposal to evolve. The European Court of Justice had already delivered this justification with its ruling in the case Costa v Enel in 1964, because it implied that electricity had been (and still is) a commodity (which also applies to other energy sources). From this followed, energy must adhere to the free movement category (Smeers 1993, 21; Talus 2013, 288). For the Commission, it had been clear that this could not have been achieved in a one-shot exercise but "step by step through the adoption of specific measures" (European Commission 1978, 15).

It should have become apparent that the policy stream consisted of a loosely fragmented policy community. Was the policy stream ripe? To be ripe, the policy community must be familiar with at least one alternative to the policy problem in question (Definition 3). Thus, given the liberalization experience of other countries and in particular of the United Kingdom, the policy stream was ripe. In addition, the examples of the liberalization pioneers documented that the introduction of competition in the natural gas sector was technically feasible at tolerable costs. Nonetheless, the policy community was split in two: a vast majority with an exclusive focus on national, anticompetitive energy policies and a minority with an interest in liberalization policies (such as the energy-intensive industries, the United Kingdom, and the Commission). While the latter referred to existing liberalization examples as models, the same examples served as deterrents for the former (Stern 1993, 191), particularly for member states' representatives.

4.1.4 *Agenda Window and Coupling*

On January 20, 1988, an agenda window opened in the political stream with the publication of the Commission's working program for 1988 (Hypothesis 5b). In agreement with, inter alia, the Council, the Commission[9] announced in this working program to publish a working document dealing with "the obstacles to a large frontier-free market in the energy sector", which should "serve as a guide for future Commission activities" (*Bulletin of the European Communities*, Supplement 1/88: 50–51). It is beyond debate that energy liberalization thereby entered the governmental agenda. According to Hypothesis 1, it is nonetheless unlikely that this would suffice to also raise energy liberalization on the decision agenda. The reason is that the problem stream had not changed in the meantime, and a prerequisite for successful agenda coupling is that all three streams must be ripe. Therefore, the subsequent section provides a summary of why the agenda window stayed open, which is followed by a section that outlines the policy-entrepreneur's coupling activities.

4.1.4.1 Events That Held the Agenda Window Open

As outlined in Sect. 2.4.1.2, the agenda window stays open as long as an issue remains on the governmental agenda. This had been the case here, because the Commission, implementing its working program for 1988, released a working document entitled and dealing with the IEM (European Commission 1988b, hereinafter referred to as the "IEM document") only three-and-a-half months later, on May 2, 1988. In the multiple streams terminology, this document is an evaluation study in which the Commission had systematically and for the first time applied the provisions formulated in the SEA to the energy sector (Hypothesis 4b). It gave feedback regarding the state of the IEM. More precisely, it took inventory "of the various existing or potential obstacles to a single energy market" and suggested some main subjects to which priority attention should be paid (European Commission 1988b, art. 6). Regarding the natural gas markets, these subjects referred to (1) price transparency and the harmonization of taxation, (2) the avoidance of physical limits on potential trade by concentrating on interconnection capacities, and (3) the facilitation of the free movement of natural gas based on a common carrier system[10] (Annex to European Commission 1988b: 66). While the first two mentioned priorities referred to narrowly defined issues, the implementation of some kind of network access to third parties would entail more far-reaching regulatory changes (see Sect. 3.2), which is the subject and hence focus of the present book.

In its IEM document, the Commission had revealed black in white the deviation of the energy sector from the free movement category and had suggested a further line of action. By raising attention to the fact that the European energy market did not comply with the free movement category, the problem stream had become ripe (Definition 1). Notwithstanding that the member states via the Council had tasked the Commission to carry out this inventory, they lined up with the gas industry in fiercely opposing this document (Nylander 2001, 288; Padgett 1992, 61; Stern 1998, 91), particularly the idea to introduce a common carrier system. It is noteworthy that the Commission had anticipated the member states' and the energy industry's dismissive attitude toward subordinating energy policy to Community action. It had refrained from launching a broad consultation process before it drafted the IEM document in order to avoid documenting the expectable controversy regarding this subject (Schmidt 1998, 195). As the reactions voiced at a public hearing on the IEM document organized by the EP's Committee on Energy, Research, and Technology (CERT) in November 1988 ranged from the reserved to the outright critical, this had been a clever move (European Parliament 1989).[11]

For the next years, energy liberalization in general or the implementation of the Commission's IEM document more specifically remained on the governmental agenda, as signaled by changes in the political stream as well as in the problem stream. Regarding the political stream, from 1988 until the presentation of the gas draft directive on February 21, 1992, the Commission referred to these topics in all of its working programs (Hypothesis 5b).[12] This was no surprise, because the same Commission President, who had been in office when the SEA was passed and had supervised the application of the free movement category to the energy markets, Jacques Delors, was reelected in 1989. Furthermore, the Energy Council referred to the IEM project twice each year (Council of the European Communities 1989a, b; 1990a, b; 1991a, b),[13] while the European Council (1992) referred to it just once explicitly in June 1992 (Hypothesis 7).[14] Given that at this stage of the policy cycle, its task is to provide impetus for the further development of the EU, without a draft directive on the negotiating table, it had been too early for the Energy Council to turn to the European Council as a court of final appeal—unsurprisingly.

In addition to the above-summarized changes in the political stream, several changes in the problem stream also contributed to keep the agenda window open. Most important was the publication of a progress report dealing with the implementation of the IEM document in May 1990 (European Commission 1990b), which raised attention to the uncompetitive state of the energy markets. It is noteworthy that the Commission had tasked itself with the publication of such a progress report in the IEM document (European Commission 1988b, 12). Furthermore, the Commission initiated infringement proceedings against Belgium, Denmark, France, Greece, Ireland, Italy, the Netherlands, Spain, and the United Kingdom in 1991 for granting exclusive rights to import or export gas or electricity, or both (European Commission 1992a, 190). A year later, it decided to send reasoned opinions to these member states (except for Belgium, Greece, and the United Kingdom) after having received their letters of formal notice (European Commission 1993d, 280). Comparable to the progress report, these infringement proceedings also documented the uncompetitive state of the energy markets (Hypothesis 4b).

It is thus evident that the Commission supported energy liberalization without reservations. But how receptive to energy liberalization were the other two branches of the EU government? On the one hand, the Council had been cautious with regard to Community action in the energy sphere in the past. On the other hand, it had given its consent to the Commission's proposal to come up with an analysis of the current state of the energy markets in light of the single market project. Notwithstanding that almost all member states opposed (parts of) the Commission's IEM document, they described it as "a major contribution to the attainment of an internal energy market" at their first energy council meeting after its release (Council of the European Communities 1988, 5). Simultaneously, their reserved position became visible, because at the same meeting they provided an extensive list of challenges, which had to be taken into account when making the IEM real. These challenges included different economic situations and energy policies pursued by the member states as well as special characteristics of the energy market in general, such as its international dimension, import dependency, long-term nature, and investment requirements. Since the Council explicitly asked the Commission for keeping informed regularly of any progress made with regard to the IEM (Council of the European Communities 1988, 5–6), one can conclude that this issue had at least its attention (Hypothesis 8)—though not its unconditional support.

After the Commission had released its working document, the European Council appealed "to the Council to step up its efforts" to create a single market, and named, inter alia, the energy sector as a priority field of action (European Council 1988a, 3) (*Hypothesis 7*). This suggests that the European Council was receptive to energy liberalization. Nonetheless, when speaking for themselves, member states (except for the United Kingdom) voiced their reservations against or even their rejection of the IEM project, casting doubt on the European Council's and the Council's support for energy liberalization.

4.1.4.2 Policy-Entrepreneur's Coupling Activities

With regard to the prospects for an agenda change to actually happen, the fact that the IEM project entered and remained high on the governmental agenda was important. However, it needs a policy-entrepreneur who succeeds in coupling the streams to change the agenda (Hypothesis 3). This policy-entrepreneur was the Commission. This made a coupling of the streams highly probable because the Commission counts as a persistent policy-entrepreneur with direct access to key policy-makers (Hypothesis 9).

Due to institutional ambiguity Ackrill and Kay (2011), energy liberalization touched the boundaries of different Directorates-General (DG), more precisely those of DG Competition (IV), Energy (XVII), General Customs Union and Indirect Taxation (XXI), Single Market and Industry (III), and Environment (XI). It is important to take this institutional ambiguity into account because the respective Commissioners sometimes held different views on how to achieve the goal of completing the IEM. In the subsequent analysis, I refer to the Commission if the cabinet of the Commission President acted cohesively (for instance, when releasing communications or acting on the basis of decisions it had taken as a collegiate body) and to Commissioners individually if they pursued a strategy that differed from that of their colleagues. Moreover, the analysis highlights the activities of the Commissioners of DG Energy and DG Competition because they were the most influential ones in terms of entrepreneurial activities (Andersen 1993, 144).

Concerning these influential Commissioners, there had been a personal turnover with the reelection of Delors as Commission Presidency. In January 1989, António José Cardoso e Cunha replaced Nicolas Mosar as Energy Commissioner, which led to a strengthening of the DG. While Mosar had left "those ambitious to develop energy policy within the Community somewhat impotent", Cardoso e Cunha was seen as an Energy Commissioner with "a desire for action and the will to provide 'a determined lead'" (*EC Energy Monthly* January 1, 1989) right from the start. Under Delors' first term of office, Peter Sutherland had been Competition Commissioner, who was replaced by Sir Leon Brittan during Delors' second term of office. Brittan, "a liberalisation advocate" (Nylander 2001, 306), had served under Margaret Thatcher in different cabinet positions and terms in office. As Sutherland (*Power Europe* March 16, 1989), Brittan took a strong stance for making the IEM real, if necessary, through competition law.

In order to promote political support and to work out a solution acceptable to all stakeholders, the Commission pursued a multitrack strategy. This strategy consisted of (1) manipulating the problem perception by skillfully framing energy liberalization as a means to make substantial efficiency gains as well as to secure supply, (2) initiating a dialogue between everyone involved in gas matters, (3) drafting a gas directive and simultaneously launching infringement proceedings regarding competitive distortions in the gas sector, and (4) threatening to decide on the liberalization issue itself by using its powers under Article 86(3) of the EC Treaty (ex-Art. 90(3) of the EEC Treaty).[15] The next paragraphs summarize these four elements.

Manipulation of the Problem's Perception

Regarding the manipulation of the problem's perception, the Commission faced the challenge that the member states' lack of support for the IEM project stemmed from their perception that energy liberalization would endanger energy security. Therefore, the Commission used two frames[16] in order to achieve a shared problem perception: The deregulation frame and the security of supply frame. The deregulation frame transferred Cecchini's argument of the cost of non-Europe to the natural gas market and highlighted the benefits which would result from the introduction of competition in particular efficiency gains (cf. European Commission 1988b, 5–6; 1990b, 9, 12; 1992b, 3). Apart from the Commission, the large energy-intensive industries, such as the car, chemical, and fertilizer industry, made use of this framing ("European Report" June 12, 1991). The security of supply frame stressed that a competitive natural gas market is a means to secure supply (cf. European Commission 1988b, 6; 1990b, 11–12; 1992b, 4). One of many examples of the security of supply frame usage is the quote of Brittan, "The Commission is rightly concerned about security of supply [in the energy sectors, N.H.] and opening up trade is the best way of giving this concept reality" (quoted in *EC Energy Monthly* April 1, 1991, 1; in a similar vein, for instance, Cardoso e Cunha quoted in *RAPID* October 9, 1992).[17]

Initiation of a Dialogue Between Everyone Involved in Gas Matters

The second element of the Commission's multitrack strategy was the initiation of a dialogue between the Commission, member states, gas industry, and consumers. The Commission adopted the idea for such a dialogue from analyses which it had ordered from Coopers & Lybrand, Belmont, and Prognos AG. The Commission had tasked them to analyze the pros and cons of the introduction of the common carrier principle in the gas and electricity market, after it had become aware of the member states' and gas industry's opposition to this principle. These analyses were completed in January and May 1989 and circulated through the industry, but were not made accessible to the public officially (Stern 1992, 56, 1993, 187).

One suggestion of these analyses was to establish "a separate body responsible to the Commission with sufficient delegated powers to effectively policy common carriage, including policing of dominant positions" (quoted in Black 1993, 134). The Commission took up this suggestion in its Communication accompanying the proposal for a transit directive for natural gas in September 1989, which announced the setting up of two Consultative Committees in order to discuss TPA[18] in depth (European Commission 1989, 3, 14). Furthermore, it was made public that the Commission would base its decision on the desirable degree of TPA going by the insights gained in these Consultative Committees (European Commission

1991b, 56). In the beginning of 1990, the two committees were established, one composed of member states' representatives (referred to as the Consultative Committee of Member States [CCEMG]) and the other one of gas industry and consumer representatives (referred to as the Professional Consultative Committee on Gas [PCCG]). They met monthly for a year and a half (Salter 1994, 92) and were chaired by members of DG Energy (XVII), DG Competition (IV), and DG Single Market and Industry (III) (*International Gas Report* June 13, 1991, European Commission 1992b, 6).

Since in the past energy matters were predominantly dealt with on the national level, the setup of those committees could have contributed to the shift in the policy community's focus from national action to Community action. This shows the example of the preceding establishment of Eurogas, the European association of the natural gas industry representing major transmission and distribution companies (*EC Energy Monthly* July 1, 1991), which participated in the PCCG. With everyone involved in gas matters being brought to one table, all actors had to take a definite position in theory. The report of the CCEMG stated "in terms of balance of opinions, the sceptics of the possible advantages and modalities of implementing TPA outnumbered those who were favorable" (European Commission 1991a, 15), while several representatives refrained from giving their opinion on this matter. The PCCG could not agree on the influence of TPA on security of supply, price developments, and regulatory necessities. In the course of the consultations, the Commission realized that a common carrier system was unrealistic, but TPA for large energy consumers could be within reach (*EC Energy Monthly* April 1, 1991). Both reports refrained from assigning positions to the participants in order to avoid self-commitment (Schmidt 1998, 204). In general,

> the Consultative Committee process appeared both as a major disappointment and a considerable lost opportunity. (...) [F]ar from approaching the process in a constructive manner, virtually all participants—including to some extent those from the Commission[19]—came to the discussions with their negotiating positions mapped out, lacking a willingness to compromise and engage in new thinking. (Stern 1992, 74–75, quotation on p. 74)

Hence, the Consultative Committees did not shift the policy community's emphasis from national solution to EU solutions. Contrary to how the multiple streams framework (MSF) conceptualizes the dynamics in the policy stream, these exchanges of opinions were not content related, but offered just another arena for political struggle. The conflict lines were numerous. Eurogas claimed to speak for the natural gas industry, but its members had conflicting interest (as smaller distributors opposed to monopoly suppliers or British Gas, operating in a liberalized country opposed to the companies enjoying protection from competition) (*EC Energy Monthly* July 1, 1991). In the CCEMG, the United Kingdom had separated itself by speaking in favor of TPA (Stern 1992, 80). The scientific literature, which developed approximately at the same time that the Consultative Committees met, reflected this lack of consensus. This literature attempted to demonstrate that the TPA provisions implemented in the United States, Canada, and the United Kingdom were (at least) unsuccessful and inappropriate for Europe (Stern 1993, 191).

It is striking that the way the Commission summarized the most recent policy community's activities was strongly biased. Despite the given controversies, Cardoso e Cunha stated that, among the member states, "all participants were in favour of increased competition in the electricity and gas sectors" (quoted in *EC Energy Monthly* April 1, 1991), and only disagreed about the impact of TPA on competition. Furthermore, the Commission did not question the introduction of TPA. This documented a quote of Competition Commissioner Brittan, who said that "the most important objective must surely be to open up networks to those who wish to use them, even if they do not own them" (quoted in *EC Energy Monthly* April 1, 1991). The member states only managed to obtain a qualified majority for the Transit Directive (91/296/EEC), passed in May 1991, based on the agreement that this directive did not imply a preliminary decision for a European-wide common carrier system (Schmidt 1998, 199).

To conclude, although the developments in the policy stream summarized above did not result in the involved actors agreeing on one or several worked-out proposals, the Commission benefited from them insofar as they had improved its understanding of the sector and provided a summary of possible arguments in favor of and against liberalization (Lyons 1994, 20).

Drafting a Gas Directive and Simultaneously Launching Infringement Proceedings

During the exchange of views within the Consultative Committees, it became clear to the Commission that the introduction of common rules for the natural gas market, including some kind of TPA, would be a difficult issue (*EC Energy Monthly* April 1, 1991). Nonetheless, the Commission continued to search a common basis for a draft directive that would introduce common rules for the internal market in the course of the Committees' meetings. In fact, the Commission concluded from those meetings that a flexible and gradual liberalization of the natural gas market would be possible. Furthermore, it arrived at the understanding that a corresponding directive should be based on Article 95 (ex-Art. 100a) of the EC Treaty, although it did not rule out the possibility to make use of all its powers under the Treaty (European Commission 1992a, 31).

In the aftermaths of the Committees' meetings, the Commission engaged in working out alternatives itself in the autumn of 1991. Pivotal elements of its alternatives were (1) the removal of monopolies regarding the import, export, production, and transmission of natural gas; (2) account unbundling of vertically integrated companies; and (3) open access to pipelines based on ex-ante published rules and tariffs (*RAPID* September 24, 1991). It is striking that these elements were strongly influenced by the experiences gained from the liberalization in the United Kingdom, although the Commission had announced previously that it would base the regulation of the natural gas sector on the insights gained from the Consultative Committees, in which the United Kingdom had been an outsider (Multinational Service September 8, 1991).

The reason why the Commission's alternatives bore the hallmarks of the British regulation was that the United Kingdom had acted as a successful policy-entrepreneur. It had invested time and effort to convince the Commission of its domestic regulations—even at the cost of isolating itself further from the other member states. Apart from intentions to minimize possible costs resulting from regulatory adjustments, the United Kingdom was motivated by economic disadvantages arising from the possible penetration of its domestic, liberalized natural gas market by European companies that could draw on advantageous (national) monopoly positions (*Europe Energy* June 14, 1991, cf. Héritier et al. 1996, 331). However, it is fair to say that the Commission was not difficult to convince as it was known to be receptive to liberalization policies and a promoter of them itself.

Apart from exchanging views with the stakeholders, the Commission initiated the above-mentioned infringement proceedings against member states that granted exclusive rights to import and export electricity and gas in March 1991 (see Sect. 4.1.4.1). Although the Commission had already announced to apply the competition rules in the energy sector "more strictly than in the past" (European Commission 1990a, 49) in its IEM document and thereafter, the timing for translating these words into deeds was important. This was because it happened (1) before the publication of the Consultative Committees' reports, which more generally had dealt with the question of whether and how TPA could be possible, and (2) a few days after the European Court of Justice had sanctioned the Commission's use of powers under Article 86(3) EC Treaty in the context of liberalizing the market for telecommunications equipment (*Journal of Commerce* March 22, 1991). This Article entrusts the Commission to pass a directive without the participation of the Council and the EP if it aims at dismantling exclusive rights that hamper trade. The similarity between the market for telecommunications equipment and the energy markets was obvious and suggested that the Commission could pursue a similar strategy with regard to energy liberalization.

The Commission's Threat to Decide on the Liberalization Issue Itself

The decisive difference between a proposal based on Article 95 and one based on Article 86(3) EC Treaty is that the former needs the approval of the Council and the EP, while the Commission can pass a directive unilaterally in the latter case. Before the European Court of Justice delivered its judgment regarding the Commission's use of its Article 86(3) powers in the market for telecommunications equipment, the Commission had announced to pursue the same strategy with regard to energy liberalization if the European Court of Justice confirmed its course of action (*Journal of Commerce* March 22, 1991). Consequently, the Commission circulated privately two interconnected proposals regarding common rules for the natural gas market to interested parties: one proposal based on Article 86(3) and one based on Article 95 (Stern 1992, 58). The Commission underlined its determination to achieve an internal natural gas market by all possible means. Furthermore, it changed the involved actors' fallback positions by threatening to decide on the liberalization issues by itself. Following Zahariadis (2003, 89–91, quotation on p. 89), individuals tend to be loss averse, which is why they "tend to choose riskier alternatives when they perceive an alternative will lead to losses". Due to the Commission's threat to decide the issue unilaterally, the member states came to believe that blocking the negotiations would go along with higher losses than trying to change the draft directive in the course of negotiations. Although this reduced their reticence to negotiations, the member states (most prominently the Netherlands, Germany, and France), the EP, and Eurogas openly and harshly criticized the Commission for seriously considering this line of action.

Despite agreeing on the same goal, the completion of the IEM, the Commissioners differed at times on how to achieve it. This became apparent with regard to the question of how to complete the IEM: via competition law and a directive based on Article 86(3) EC Treaty or via political compromises and a directive based on Article 95 EC Treaty. In contrast to DG Competition, DG Energy generally preferred political solutions to implementing the IEM through law (Padgett 1992, 60). Cardoso e Cunha was not restricted to political solutions. To the contrary, he was receptive to making use of competition law. For instance, he substituted the Director of the IEM task force in his DG with a Director from DG Competition after less than a year, because he "favoured a faster, more aggressive approach to the implementation of third party access" (*EC Energy Monthly* April 1, 1991). Unsurprisingly, Brittan and Cardoso e Cunha were described to be close allies and to have worked together in order to make the IEM a reality (*EC Energy Monthly* January 15, 1993). At the same time, Cardoso e Cunha was more cautious regarding the Article 86(3) approach because of the member states' and his colleagues' resistance (Multinational Service October 1991). But he explicitly did not rule out the possibility to implement this approach.

By late 1991, the Commission refrained from using Article 86(3) EC Treaty for the time being. This was mainly for two reasons: First, the Commission had blocked the planned French–Italian takeover of Canadian aircraft maker De Havilland on October 2, 1991 (91/619/EEC), which had caused a storm of protest. At that time, the atmosphere between the member states and the Commission was already heated because of the Commission's considerations to base the gas draft directive on Article 86 (3). Thus, dropping the Article 86(3) approach was a means to avoid alienating the member states from the Commission. Second, a member state's appeal to the European Court of Justice in response to an Article 86(3) usage was highly probable—but whether the ruling would be in favor of the Commission was questioned by some Commissioners (Padgett 2003, 232). Notwithstanding, Brittan, preferring a faster liberalization, still stuck to the Article 86(3) option, while other Commissioners were just willing to go this road in the case that a political compromise would be out of reach (*Multinational Service* November 1991). As a consequence, the Commission decided to take the negotiation route and table a directive based on Article 95 EC Treaty for the time being.

To pass a directive based on Article 95 requires a qualified majority in the Council. Since almost all member states opposed gas liberalization, "the Commission had little choice but to win support for a Council directive on the basis of consensus and unanimity" (Padgett 2003, 232–33, quotation on p. 233), which gave all actors involved the possibility to hamper a British "clear homerun" (Héritier et al. 1996, 332). Despite the necessity to win the Council's support, the Commission only made selective revisions in the draft directive it had prepared in mid-1991. Regarding the overall idea of how to liberalize the natural gas sector, this draft was based on four general principles:

(1) The need for a gradual approach that would allow the affected industry to adjust to the new regulatory environment.
(2) Respect of the subsidiarity principle so that member states could "opt for the system best suited to their natural resources, the state of their industry and their energy policies" (European Commission 1992b, 8).
(3) Avoidance of excessive regulations.
(4) Negotiation of a Council directive in the shadow of the Commission becoming active unilaterally, since it stressed to reserve "the right to make use of all its powers conferred on it by the Treaty as and when appropriate" (European Commission 1992b, 9).

In order to implement these principles, the Commission had opted for a three-stage approach: The first stage referred to the implementation of the price transparency directive and transit directives; the corresponding directives had already been passed (90/377/EC; 91/296/EEC). The second stage aimed at ending exclusive rights by introducing common rules. The third stage, which was a new element in the Commission's proposal, should expand the common rules according to the experience gained during the second stage of the liberalization process (*Bulletin of the European Communities* 10-1991: 33, European Commission 1992b). This approach is an example of a policy-entrepreneur pursuing salami tactics. Salami tactics means that a policy-entrepreneur "cut[s] the process into distinct stages that are presented sequentially to policymakers" (Zahariadis 2014, 39; for a more detailed description, see Zahariadis 2003, 89–95) in order to get his or her desired output adopted.

The introduction of common rules was based on three elements:

(1) The introduction of a licensing system for gas facilities on a transparent and nondiscriminatory basis.
(2) The introduction of management and account unbundling of vertically integrated gas companies.
(3) The introduction of a limited TPA system "whereby the transmission and distribution companies are obliged to offer access to their network to certain eligible entities at reasonable rates, within the limits of available transmission and distribution capacity" (European Commission 1992b, 9). The eligible entities, most importantly large industrial users, should be defined on the basis of consumption thresholds. Furthermore, the draft considered provisions to safeguard take-or-pay (TOP) contracts.

Compared with the Commission's first proposals, this was a scaled-down draft with respect to the high consumption thresholds for compulsory TPA and the consideration of a third stage. On top of that, it left the member states leeway to interpret many provisions in their favor as the same remained vague, for instance, when talking about reasonable charges (*EC Energy Monthly* February 14, 1992; Stern 1992, 67, 82). Although these concessions made the draft directive more acceptable to the member states, they still did not support it. In order to convince the member states, Cardoso e Cunha presented the main elements of the revised draft directive at the Energy Council meeting in October 1991. Furthermore, he toured European Community member states' capitals in order to discuss the proposal with the respective governments before the Commission officially submitting the draft directive on February 21, 1992 (*Bulletin of the European Communities* 10-1991: 33, *EC Energy Monthly* February 14, 1992, *Europe Energy* October 31, 1991). Thereby, a decision window opened.

4.1.4.3 *Interim Conclusion*

How well does the MSF fare in explaining how the draft directive entered the decision agenda? According to Hypotheses 1–3, an agenda change requires that (1) all three streams are ripe, (2) an agenda window opens in the problem or political stream, *and* (3) a policy-entrepreneur couples the three streams. If one of these conditions is not met, the agenda remains stable. Nonetheless, the agenda changed in February 1992, although the prerequisite of stream ripeness was not met.

The agenda window opened by the publication of the Commission's working program in 1988 (Hypothesis 5b). Initially, it had poor prospects of resulting in an agenda change because the problem had not been ripe. With the publication of the Commission's IEM document, the chances for an agenda change had improved because it focused attention to the uncompetitive state of the IEM.[20] Thereby, it made the problem stream ripe.

Following Kingdon (1984, 177), an agenda window closes quickly. The reason why the agenda window stayed open between May 1988 and February 1992 was that the IEM remained high on the governmental agenda (Definition 4). The high agenda status is documented by the inclusion of the IEM project in the working programs or conclusions of all three branches of the EU executive. Additionally, changes in the problem stream (namely the release of a progress report and infringement proceedings) kept the IEM on the governmental agenda.

The Commission, in particular Energy Commissioner Cardoso e Cunha and Competition Commissioner Brittan, acted as a policy-entrepreneur. It exploited the passing of the SEA and enforced the application of the free movement category to the energy sector. This resulted in the perception that the state of the energy markets was problematic. Furthermore, the Commission tested different strategies in order to gain acceptance for its idea to liberalize the natural gas market. It started with communications with affected parties, and when this did not result in support for its position, the Commission tried to change the fallback position of the member states by threatening to use its powers under Article 86(3) and by carrying on infringement proceedings. Under these circumstances, it was the best option for the member states not to block the Commission's initiative from the very start, as this at least granted the member states the opportunity to influence the design of the gas directive.

In addition, the Commission's persistence and access to key policy-makers (see Hypothesis 9) as well as the fact that it was active in all three streams contributed to its coupling success. In the problem stream, the Commission drew attention to the state of the IEM and interpreted it as problematic. In the political stream, it defined the completion of the IEM as one of its major policy projects, included it in its working programs, and thereby pushed it on the governmental agenda. Finally, in the policy stream, the Commission tried to spur the exchange of views between the stakeholders and engaged in working out proposals and in advocating them within the policy community and vis-à-vis the policy-makers.

Table 4.1 How well the multiple streams framework fares in explaining how the first gas directive entered the decision agenda

Directive	*98/30/EC*
The MSF's necessary conditions for agenda change	
The likelihood for an agenda change increases if	
H1 the problem stream, political stream, and policy stream are ripe;	–
H2 a change in the problem or political stream opens an agenda window; ***and***	+
H3 a policy-entrepreneur succeeds in coupling the streams.	+
Specifying H2: Equifinal paths to the opening of an agenda window	
H4 An agenda window opens in the problem stream if	
(a) a relevant indicator deteriorates;	(+)
(b) an evaluation study points to a discrepancy between the program's goal and the program's effects; or	(+)
(c) a focusing event relevant to the policy field in question occurs.	
H5 An agenda window opens in the political stream if	
(a) a new Commission takes office; or	
(b) the Commission publishes a working program.	+
	(+)
H6 An agenda window opens in the political stream if	
(a) a new Council Presidency takes office; or	
(b) one or consecutive Council Presidencies release their working program(s).	
H7 An agenda window opens in the political stream if the European Council publishes acts which provide impetus for the EU's development.	(+)
H8 An agenda window opens in the political stream if (at least) one branch of the EU's executive or legislature tasks one (other) branch of the EU's executive to address an issue.	(+)
Specifying H3: Agenda coupling	
H9 The policy-entrepreneur is more likely to successfully couple the streams during an open agenda window	
(a) the more persistent he or she is; and	+
(b) the more access to key policy-makers she or he has.	+

Source: Own compilation
Note: "–" indicates that a hypothesis is falsified, "+" indicates that a hypothesis holds, and "(+)" indicates that the hypothesis' independent variable had kept the agenda window open

Although derived in order to explain decision coupling, Hypothesis 10c performs surprisingly well regarding the explanation of agenda coupling. Translated to agenda coupling, this hypothesis postulates that coupling is more likely if a policy-entrepreneur succeeds in providing meaning, clarification, and identity to the issue at stake. Strategies to achieve this are framing the problem–solution linkage as a gain in comparison with alternative linkages and pursuing salami tactics. The credible threat of the Commission to resort to Article 86(3) in order to introduce common rules to the natural gas market made the member states perceive the negotiation of these rules as a gain. Furthermore, that the Commission presented the common rules as the second of three stages in the completion of the IEM is an example of salami tactics. This applies particularly to the move to introduce a third stage at which the common rules should be expanded, according to the experiences gained at the second stage.

Regarding the question of when the political stream counts as ripe (Definition 2), the analysis of this agenda-setting process suggests that it suffices if the Commission is receptive to a specific issue. I understand receptivity in the sense of taking a favorable view of a specific issue instead of just being willing to discuss an issue (as had been the case with the Council and the European Council). Table 4.1 summarizes how well the MSF fares in explaining the agenda-setting process of the first gas directive.

4.2 Policy Change

Two decision windows were needed in order to adopt the gas draft directive. I analyze these windows in Sects. 4.2.1 and 4.2.2. The focus is on the bargaining dynamics since this allows for testing the hypothesis dealing with the likelihood of policy adoption (Hypothesis 10). More precisely, these sections summarize the activities of those involved in decision-making and their attempts to gain support for their preferred solutions. In order to assess whether decision coupling is more likely to be lengthy if policy-makers' attention is redirected to issues they perceive to be more urgent (Hypothesis 11), each section includes an analysis of whether the respective Council President included the IEM in the meetings he or she presided over. This is supplemented by a summary of the activities of the EP and of the Commission. The former is important, because the EP's consent was required in order to pass the gas draft directive. The analysis of the Commission's activities is essential for two reasons: (1) because it had threatened frequently to decide on the issue unilaterally if it deemed this necessary, and (2) because as long as the Council has not acted, the Commission has the right to alter its proposals. Furthermore, changes resulting from the EU's political time cycle (such as the election of a new EP or Commission) are considered since they entail a disruption of ongoing negotiations. Section 4.2.3 concludes.

4.2.1 *The First Decision Window and Coupling: A Case of Deadlock*

The first decision window spans the time from February 1992 until the spring of 1994. As agreed in the Treaty of Maastricht, signed in February 1992, from November 1993 on, the gas draft directive (as well as many other pending legislations) would no longer be subject to the consultation but to the cooperation procedure (European Commission 1993b, 79). Thereby, a new venue, the EP, gained in importance, because without its consent, the gas draft directive could not be passed. With regard to the EU's political time cycle, a new Commission's term in office started in January 1993. Delors was reelected as President. Since the IEM had been highly prioritized in his former two tenures, it did not come as a surprise that the Commission's working program for the years 1993 and 1994 referred to the gas draft directive as a principal legislative proposal (*Bulletin of the European Communities*, Supplement 1/93: 20). With regard to the Energy and Competition Commissioner, there had been a change in personnel: Energy Commissioner Cardoso e Cunha and Competition Commissioner Brittan no longer served as Commissioners. Abel Matutes took over DG Energy from Cardoso e Cunha and Karel van Miert DG Competition from Brittan.

The Energy Council's negotiations of the draft directive were presided over by Portugal (January to June 1992), the United Kingdom (July to December 1992), Denmark (January to June 1993), Belgium (July to December 1993), and Greece (January to June 1994). Given the resistance against the draft directive, the timing for its submittal could not have been better, because both the Portuguese and the British Presidency were judged to be favorable. The former coincided with the fact that the draft came from a Portuguese Commissioner (*EC Energy Monthly* February 14, 1992). And the latter, with the fact that the United Kingdom was a known proponent of the Commission's proposal. Hence, these Presidencies promised to push the gas draft directive high on the decision agenda.

In May 1992, the Council, presided over by the Portuguese Luis Fernando de Mira Amaral, discussed the issue for the first time. It became clear that the member states could only agree on three general principles: security of supply, environmental protection, and the principle of subsidiarity (Council of the European Communities 1992a, 4). With regard to the TPA provisions, the cornerstone of the draft directive, most member states voiced reservations concerning

> the challenge to the guarantees relating to the system of property ownership; protection of the interests of small consumers; non-discriminatory treatment in respect of tariffs; the introduction of a suitable infrastructure, and if necessary, of the related funding; definition of transparency of costs; application of the rules of competition in order to avoid price distortion; advisability of having an evaluation report from the Commission on the introduction and operation of the transit of electricity and natural gas as recommended by the Council directives of 1990 and 1991; an adequate transition period; an evaluation of progress at the end of the 2nd stage before beginning an examination of the 3rd stage. (Council of the European Communities 1992a, 5)

Put differently, the majority of the member states strongly opposed the proposal—the Netherlands, Germany, and France to the point of blockage and demanding a redraft. Due to this resistance, the Portuguese Presidency did not even manage to find support for the Council conclusions and passed a set of general Presidency conclusions instead (*European Energy Report* June 12, 1992).

The Community's Economic and Social Committee and the EP's CERT debated the proposal in parallel. Their reactions were equally daunting as both committees signaled strong reservations ("European Report" May 23, 1992). While the Economic and Social Committee approved the idea to liberalize the energy sector, it questioned the introduction of TPA. CERT was skeptical about energy liberalization in general and particularly concerned with the protection of consumer interests and environmental protection (European Parliament 1989, 57–58; Matláry 1997, 124). From a public hearing it had organized one day before the Energy Council had met in May 1992, the rapporteur and chairman of CERT, Claude Desama, had concluded that "the Commission's proposals could not be accepted as such, nor rejected, but that it was necessary to propose amendments, involving possibly a transitional period" (European Commission 1993c, 15). Notwithstanding the apparent resistance against the gas draft directive, the European Council mentioned energy as a priority field of action in the context of the single market program at its first meeting, after the Commission had submitted its legislative proposal, in June 1992 (European Council 1992, 11).

The next Council meeting took place in late November 1992 and was presided over by Timothy Eggar. Although the United Kingdom counted as the strongest supporter of the gas draft directive in the Council, the progress of the discussions was limited (*International Gas Report* December 11, 1992; *Platts Oilgram News* December 7, 1992; *Power Europe* December 4, 1992). While at the preceding Council meeting, the member states could only agree on three points (security of supply, environmental protection, and principle of subsidiarity), they managed to settle on the following six principles, which should be respected when making the IEM a reality (Council of the European Communities 1992b, 8–9):

(1) *Security of supply*, in terms of national safeguard measures regarding (a) the choice of primary fuels for electricity generation, (b) the granting of long-term investments, and (c) the maintenance of the transmission systems' and distribution systems' safety and integrity.
(2) *Environmental protection*, which should not be negatively affected by the IEM.
(3) *Protection of small consumers*, particularly preventing cross-subsidies for large consumers and allowing for the possibility to maintain PSO as well as to regulate tariffs where appropriate.
(4) Gradual introduction of *transparency and nondiscrimination*.
(5) *Implementation* of the gas draft directive should be possible in a way which would allow member states to choose the structure and instruments best suited to their own circumstances.
(6) Inclusion of *transition periods* for the introduction of TPA.

However, the member states still opposed the draft directive's TPA provisions. The discussion ended with the Council asking the Commission to modify its legislative proposal by taking into account the position of the EP and the Council discussions (Council of the European Communities 1992b, 9). Despite the member states' remaining reservations, the discussions had nonetheless moved on. This was mainly because the member states had explained explicitly the nature and scope of their reservations. Only on this basis, political entrepreneurs would be able to offer concessions or package deals, which made policy adoption more likely (Hypothesis 10a–b). In line with this reasoning, Cardoso e Cunha concluded that the discussion had shifted from technical points questioning the feasibility of energy liberalization as such to political and philosophical points, entering "pure political discussions" (Cardoso e Cunha quoted in *EC Energy Monthly* December 4, 1992).

At the end of 1992, the Commission's term of office ended and, with it, Cardoso e Cunha's presence in the College of Commissioners. The newly appointed Energy Commissioner, the Spaniard Abel Matutes, was more willing to compromise than his predecessor. One reason for the increased willingness to compromise was that the entry into force of the Maastricht Treaty came closer, and with it, the EP gained in importance due to its right to veto the gas draft directive. Additionally, a new category of EU legislation became mandatory: the principle of subsidiarity. Since the Commission had drafted the gas proposal before this principle was inserted in the revised Maastricht Treaty in December 1991, the Commission itself now considered its legislative proposal as being too detailed and interventionist and not in line with the principle of subsidiarity. Therefore, the Commission intended to revise it and aimed at a minimum essential harmonization (*EC Energy Monthly* April 8, 1993), or as Matutes put it, "I am prepared to talk to all interested parties to find the formula which would combine both realistic considerations with meeting the Commission's objectives" (*EC Energy Monthly* August 4, 1993). Furthermore, Matutes stressed that the Council, the EP, and the Commission should cooperate closely. On the one hand, this made settling an agreement more likely. On the other hand, this would only be possible at the cost of watering-down some of the draft directive's main elements. Since Matutes suggested to base further discussions of the gas draft directive on the report authored by Desama (henceforth: Desama report), this was a likely scenario (*Power Europe* April 9, 1993).

Bilaterally, the Commission and CERT, and the Council and CERT were involved in discussing the draft of the Desama report (*EC Energy Monthly* August 4, 1993). Although highlighting differences (for instance, regarding the necessity to harmonize tax and environmental measures as a precondition for further liberalization steps, as foreseen by Desama), Matutes documented his willingness to compromise by giving up the insistence at compulsory TPA. Instead, he considered a voluntary, negotiated TPA (*EC Energy Monthly* March 11, 1993, *Platts Oilgram News* May 5, 1993). According to Hypothesis 10a, this made policy adoption more likely because Matutes combined viable alternatives, here different organizations of TPA, into one package.

Contrary to earlier announcements, the Energy Council met in late June 1993 under the Danish Presidency. The reason for the delayed Council meeting was the Danish referendum on the Maastricht Treaty in May and a political alliance between Denmark and Norway regarding the opposition against a directive that dealt with the authorizations for the prospection, exploration, and production of hydrocarbons (*Platts Oilgram News* March 4, 1993).[21] Put differently, because the Danish Presidency's attention was redirected to issues it perceived more urgent, the Council meeting was delayed, which according to Hypothesis 11b accounts for a lengthy coupling process. However, it can be doubted that negotiations would have taken less time without this delay because the Commission and the Council had already stated earlier that the gas proposal should be redrafted on the basis of the still pending suggestions from the EP. This reading is confirmed by the fact that, at this Council meeting, negotiation barely moved forward: The Council conclusions basically repeated that the Commission should modify its proposals in accordance with the EP's and the Council's suggestions (Council of the European Communities 1993, 8; *RAPID* June 25, 1993). At the same meeting, the Commission took the chance to present its second progress report on the IEM. With regard to the gas proposal, this progress report summarized the state of negotiations. While it explicitly referred to four of the six principles the Council had agreed upon in November 1992 (principle of subsidiarity, environmental protection, protection of smaller consumers, and security of supply), it remained silent with regard to granting transitional periods and implementation leeway (European Commission 1993c, 14–15).

Under the incoming Belgian Presidency, the political discussion on the liberalization of the energy markets was speeding up because Belgium intended to take the chance to enforce a total reorientation concerning TPA based on the report of its compatriot, CERT rapporteur Desama (*Europe Energy* June 24, 1993). Mirroring the findings of a public hearing organized by the EP in October 1992 (European Commission 1993c, 15), the EP came forward with numerous suggestions for amendments. Desama managed to reduce them from 580 to 240 (referring to the electricity and gas draft directives) before parliamentary debate took place as late as mid-November 1993 (for a summary, see European Commission 1993a, 4–5). Despite the large number of amendments, the EP still failed to present a united front and approved the report by a vote of 145 for, 18 against, and 57 abstentions. Although more than 100 amendments were acceptable to the Commission (for instance, those stressing the concept of subsidiarity), the majority were not (such as the suggestion to allow distribution companies to keep their supply monopoly) (*EC Energy Monthly* April 8, 1993, November 19, 1993; *Power Europe* December 3, 1993).

The delayed voting on the Desama report gave the Commission only a few weeks to revise its legislative proposal for the next Energy Council meeting, which was announced for December 10, 1993. Three days before the meeting of the Energy Council, the Commission agreed on the amended proposal. The main changes the Commission made to the gas draft directive concerned the following issues (European Commission 1993a, 7–11):

(1) Inclusion of a chapter concerning production, transport, and distribution.
(2) Greater reference to PSO as suggested by the EP.
(3) Allowance of negotiated TPA to networks.
(4) Requirement of account unbundling instead of management unbundling.
(5) Simplification of the rules concerning the operation of transmission and distribution companies.
(6) Compliance with the six principles put forward by the Energy Council in December 1992.

Thereby, this draft included package deals (Hypothesis 10a) documented by the inclusion of negotiated TPA and concessions (Hypothesis 10b), that is, documented by abstaining from management unbundling. Accordingly, the revised draft directive differed substantially from the Commission's draft of January 1992—but also from the EP's opinion. As a consequence, the Council just took note of Energy Commissioner Matutes' presentation and left further discussions for the next Council meeting in May 1994 (*European Report* December 10, 1993, December 15, 1993, Salter 1994, 96).

During the above-mentioned Energy Council meetings, the Commission revived its threat to decide on gas liberalization without the involvement of the EP and the Council. In 1992, the credibility of this threat was backed by the Commission's decision to send reasoned opinions to Denmark, France, Ireland, Italy, the Netherlands, and Spain after having examined their replies to the letters of formal notice concerning exclusive rights to import and export gas and electricity (European Commission 1993d, 40). As had been the case during agenda coupling, this threat aimed at making the member states perceive the blockage of negotiations as a loss. It would put them into danger to lose any say on the issue. This should make them more willing to compromise (Hypothesis 10c). Unmistakably, the new Energy Commissioner Matutes stressed that from a failure to agree on the proposal would follow

> that instead of developing a policy by the normal procedure [a directive process, N.H.], elements of energy policy will then be developed via judgments or competition cases in a rather disorderly way (...) because the complaints are there and Articles 85 [today's Article 105, N.H.] and 86 [today's Article 106, N.H.],[22] as well as Article 90 [today's article 86, N. H.] apply to the energy sector. Nowhere in the Treaty or anywhere else is there an indication that the energy sector is exempt. (van Miert quoted in *EC Energy Monthly* August 4, 1993)

Following Zahariadis (2014, 39), the Commission acted cleverly because political entrepreneurs "will have greater success if they present them [policymakers, N.H.] with options that recoup perceived losses". In this case, the option would be to enter negotiations with a will to settle a compromise.

Nonetheless, the progress of the draft negotiations remained slow, which was why Competition Commissioner van Miert announced to carry on the pending infringement proceedings regarding exclusive import and export rights in the energy sector in May 1993. From van Miert's point of view, this "frontal clash" was a second-best solution only (quoted in *EC Energy Monthly* August 4, 1993). Drawing on his experiences as Transport Commissioner in the previous Commission, he pointed to the successful stepwise liberalization of the aviation sector, which he believed should be possible in the energy sector, too. This explains why he delayed legal actions as a response to (1) the Energy Council meeting in June 1993 (in which he sensed a change in attitude of some member states) and (2) indications of two of the member states concerned (namely France and the Netherlands) that they would review their legislation. Matutes conditioned the preliminary stop of legal actions on reaching an agreement on common rules for the internal market in electricity and natural gas in the Council (*EC Energy Monthly* August 4, 1993; *Power Europe* August 4, 1993). Since the Council meeting in December 1993 failed to achieve progress on that issue, the Commission decided in January 1994 to enter the final stage of the infringement proceedings against France, Ireland, Italy, the Netherlands, and Spain. The Commission excluded Denmark from these infringement proceedings because it had repealed the exclusive right to import natural gas granted to Dansk Naturgas A/S (European Commission 1995, 133). Finally, in mid-June, the Commission took the dispute to the European Court of Justice—much to the disgust of the national governments and utilities involved, as well as of the EP. Two months earlier, in April 1994, the

European Court of Justice had ruled that electricity is to be treated as a good (C393/92 Almelo v Ijsselmij). This made van Miert's threat to develop energy policy via judgments and competition cases more credible (*EC Energy Monthly* September 26, 1994, *Europe Energy* July 1, 1994, *Power Europe* March 11, 1994) and worsened the perceived fallback option of the member states regarding the ongoing negotiations about common rules.

Because of the slow pace of the negotiations so far, the Commission and the Council decided to leave aside the proposal concerning the natural gas market and concentrate on the electricity draft instead. To choose the electricity over the gas directive accounted for the fact that the latter was even more controversial. The gas directive was to be scheduled again after substantial progress had been made on electricity liberalization ("European Report" November 26, 1994; *Financial Times* May 25, 1995). Thus, the decision window closed in the spring of 1994 because the policy-makers had decided to prioritize the electricity draft.

4.2.2 The Second Decision Window and Coupling: A Spillover from the Electricity Directive

Until the decision window for the gas draft directive opened again in the autumn of 1996, there had been some changes in the political stream due to the EU's political time cycle:

(1) In June 1994, elections to the EP had taken place. In the newly elected parliament, Claude Desama remained CERT rapporteur. But the elections had triggered a change in personnel in the Commission because Energy Commissioner Matutes had been elected to the EP and had therefore been replaced by Marcelino Oreja.
(2) In January 1995, the ninth Commission had been elected with Jacques Santer as its Presidency.[23] As its predecessors, Santer included the IEM project in its working programs (*Bulletin of the European Union*, Supplements 1/95: 34, 58, 1/96: 12, and 1/97: 9), except for in 1998, probably because a compromise on the gas draft directive was already within reach in mid-1997. In the working program for 1995, Santer had revived the threat that the Commission could "take the matters into its own hands" if the Commission would find "that the Council has made no progress" (*Bulletin of the

European Union, Supplement 1/95: 58) regarding the gas and electricity drafts.

(3) In the Santer Commission, van Miert remained Competition Commissioner, but the Energy Commissioner changed with Christos Papoutsis replacing Oreja. Hence, within two years, the Energy Commissioner had changed four times. This implied a temporary weakening of this portfolio because all Commissioners required a period of training. Furthermore, none of Cardoso e Cunha's successors followed a hard line as he had done, but were more willing to compromise (*Platts Oilgram News* November 2, 1994).

(4) Due to EU enlargement in 1995, when Austria, Finland, and Sweden joined the EU, the composition of the European Council and Council had changed slightly. With regard to the negotiation of the gas draft directive, Finland and Sweden strengthened the position of those pushing for exemptions in the opening up of the gas markets because their gas markets as such or some of its regions were still limited to the extent of being classified as emerging (*EC Energy Monthly* December 13, 1996, *Energy Economist* June 1, 1997).

During the second decision window, the Energy Council meetings were presided over by Ireland (July to December 1996), the Netherlands (January to June 1997), Luxembourg (July to December 1997), and the United Kingdom (January to June 1998). This decision window already opened in the autumn of 1996, which was a result of Energy Commissioner Papoutsis' entrepreneurial activities. As soon as it became clear that a common position concerning the electricity draft was within reach for the subsequent Energy Council meeting on June 25, 1996, he started pushing the gas draft directive back on the decision agenda by immediately suggesting its revision. The revisions should take into account "the opinions of all interested parties—governments, producers, consumers and employees— in order to form the best possible view of the situation and achieve a valid and credible compromise" (Papoutsis quoted in *European Report* July 17, 1996). As a consequence, the Council's energy working group and the Committee of Member States' Permanent Representatives to the EU started reviewing the legislative proposal in its latest version and the electricity draft directive as recently agreed upon in the Energy Council. Key elements of this electricity draft directive were:[24]

(1) The definition of a gradual market opening for high and medium consumers, which went along with access to the networks based on a single buyer system,[25] negotiated TPA, or regulated TPA.
(2) The provision to unbundle the accounts of vertically integrated companies, and in case a member state opted for the single buyer model, management unbundling was also compulsory.
(3) Allowance to impose PSO relating to security of supply and environmental protection.
(4) Allowance for two options regarding the construction of new facilities: application of an authorization procedure or a tendering procedure, whereby both had to be objective, transparent, and nondiscriminatory.

The directive was planned to be effective for nine years. During this time, the Commission was instructed to assess the success of the directive. This assessment should provide the basis for further discussions regarding the future adjustment of the market opening (96/92/EC; Padgett 2003, 234).

The Irish Energy Council President, Emmet Stagg, circulated a compromise text for a revised gas directive in October 1996, which adopted most of the electricity draft directive and largely superseded the last gas draft directive (Cameron 2002, 166). Finally, he set this compromise text on the agenda of the Energy Council meeting two months later. The Energy Council welcomed it as "an important step in the right direction" and "a good basis for progress in further discussions" (Council of the European Union 1996, 5). In Kingdon's (1984) wording, this was an example for a successful spillover because the winning coalition and successful arguments were transferred from the electricity debate to the gas debate. Particularly, the writing of the compromise text was facilitated by the experiences those involved had gained during the electricity debate, which was also reflected by a dynamic and positive atmosphere of negotiation (*European Report* January 11, 1997). However, where arguments could not be transferred due to the inherently given differences between electricity and natural gas, the need of further negotiations became obvious (Council of the European Union 1996, 6). This primarily concerned the following issues (for the following, see *Agence Europe* November 29, 1996, December 3, 1996, December 4, 1996; Council of the European Union 1996, 5–6; *Energy Economist* June 1, 1997; *Financial Times* December 4, 1996, December 5, 1997):

First, while there was consensus that electricity has a universal nature, the majority of member states doubted that this also applies to natural gas. Nonetheless, they agreed that PSO regarding prices, quality, environmental issues, and security of supply should be possible in general. This was an important aspect for France, while the United Kingdom, Germany, and the Netherlands highlighted the need to keep in mind the anticompetitive effects extended PSO would have.

Second, regarding access to the networks, the participants agreed to focus on negotiated and regulated TPA and to leave aside the single buyer model. But, as the access question touched on one of the most controversial issues, TOP contracts, negotiating of TPA provisions promised to be controversial. A danger for large gas distributors was that opening their networks would probably go along with a decreased market share. As a consequence, they would have to buy gas due to their TOP contracts without having sufficient customers.

Third, regarding the question of how to deal with TOP contracts, the current compromise text provided that the Commission, on application by the relevant member state, could grant derogations from the TPA provisions for contracts entered into force before July 25, 1996 (Cameron 2002, 167). Basically, three different positions had to converge concerning this issue: (1) the producers' position (the United Kingdom and the Netherlands, supported by Germany); (2) the consumers' position, most prominently regarding those countries that were dependent on gas imports (France, Belgium, and Spain); (3) the position of member states without a gas market or with an emergent gas market only (Portugal, Sweden, and Greece). As the latter assumed that they could only expand their networks on the basis of TOP contracts, they were asking for derogations to be interpreted broadly.

Forth, due to the huge differences regarding the development of the markets and the customer base, the definition of market opening was discussed controversially, too. The current gas draft directive provided for a yet unspecified initial market-opening percentage and for the Commission to adjust this percentage annually for the subsequent year (Cameron 2002, 166). The United Kingdom and Germany favored a rapid, substantial opening, while France championed a gradual approach. In this context, the definition of eligible customers, including possible exemptions, would be crucial.

Finally, the unbundling of accounts of vertically integrated gas companies (according to its activities in production, transport, storage, and distribution) was accepted to be necessary. Still, it needed to be settled as to how to achieve transparency without providing competitors with confidential and commercially sensitive information. At the same time, red tape should be kept to a minimum.

As had been the case during the negotiations of the electricity directive, the United Kingdom and France had opposing opinions on the degree of liberalization, with the United Kingdom pressing for competition and France trying to keep it down. As the only member state, France was concerned with domestic resistance since it was confronted with strikes by gas and electricity workers and approaching elections for the National Assembly between May 25 and June 1, 1997. Hence, France's negotiating range was restricted, and its willingness to liberalize was of a modest nature. The remaining member states took positions between the United Kingdom and France.

The Netherlands took up the Presidency in January 1997 and stressed that, during its term of office, "[p]riority will be given to the gas directive and development of renewable energy sources" (Peter Scholten, Dutch Deputy Director-General of Energy, quoted in *Oil & Gas Journal* December 9, 1996). During the Dutch Presidency, two compromise texts were circulated. The first was in April before the Energy Council meeting in late May, and the second was in its aftermath, in June 1997, documenting the results or the extent of disagreement (Cameron 2002, 167). At the Council meeting in May, the Presidency focused on the issues of market opening, TOP, and emergent markets and regions.

Although the discussions moved forward, these issues were not conclusively settled. Regarding market opening, the April compromise text defined a first stage for the market opening. At this stage, power generators and customers using more than 25 million cubic meters annually were defined as eligible customers. After five years, this threshold should be reduced to 10 million cubic meters, and after ten years, to 1 million cubic meters. This definition of eligible customers should lead to a market opening of at least 30 percent initially, 40 percent after five years, and 50 percent after ten years (Cameron 2002, 167). In the course of the Council meeting, the member states agreed on (1) setting a lower limit for the market opening and the possibility to limit market opening if a certain level would be exceeded, (2) defining power generators and large industries with a certain annual consumption level as eligible customers, (3) opening the market progressively by means of reducing the volume thresholds for eligible customers and/or increasing the minimum percentage of market opening, and (4) incorporating a safeguard clause. However, they could neither agree on how to quantify the degree of market opening nor on how to define eligible customers. The revised compromise text of June 1997 documented this disagreement because it referred to the degree of market opening without quantifying it. Instead, the Dutch Presidency inserted letters of the alphabet as placeholders for concrete numbers. Furthermore, this compromise text lacked a definition of the concept of eligible customers (Cameron 2002, 167). This indicated that there was room for concessions or package deals (or even both) with regard to market opening (Hypothesis 10a–b).

The Council also discussed the provisions regarding TOP contracts. The Irish gas draft directive had stipulated that the Commission could grant derogations regarding TPA for TOP contracts entered into force before July 25, 1996, on application by the relevant member state. The Council had discussed this issue controversially, which was why the Dutch Presidency suggested in April 1997 that such derogations could be granted regardless of when the TOP contracts entered into force (Cameron 2002, 167). At its May meeting, the Council expressed its support for a system characterized by transparency and well-formulated criteria without going into details (Council of the European Union 1997a, 1–2). But still, the details of how to grant derogations were not settled because the member states opposed the suggestion that it fell under the Commission's responsibility to grant derogations. Thus, the Presidency's June draft incorporated a compromise by offering concessions to both sides (Hypothesis 10b): It stipulated that derogations could be granted by the member states without reference to the Commission if the contract entered into force before July 25, 1996. Only contracts which entered into force after this date would need the Commission to grant a derogation (Cameron 2002, 167). Furthermore, with regard to emergent markets, the Council agreed on granting temporary exemptions, which should be listed in an Annex to the Directive. The member states were invited to inform the Council Presidency which regions they would want to be included in this Annex (Council of the European Union 1997a, 2).

Although determined to achieve substantial progress, serious negotiations were hampered by the French elections (*Energy Economist* June 1, 1997). After the Council meeting, the Dutch Presidency deferred the decision on whether to organize an additional Council meeting in June. His decision depended on the progress of the Permanent Representatives Committee and whether France's new administration would be prepared to enter the negotiations. As France did not indicate its willingness, the next Council was scheduled on October 27, 1997, under the Luxembourg Presidency (*Energy Economist* June 1, 1997, *RAPID* May 29, 1997). This confirms Hypothesis 11b, because decision coupling was interrupted by the redirection of France's attention to national elections, an issue it perceived to be more urgent at that moment.

Luxembourg started its presidency with a revised gas draft directive. Among other things, this draft specified thresholds for eligible customers and minimum figures for market opening, which were less ambitious than those the Irish Presidency had suggested in October 1996. This is a clear example of offering concessions on a previous proposal (Hypothesis 10b). More precisely, eligible customers were defined as those with a consumption threshold of (a) 25 million cubic meters initially, (b) 15 million cubic meters after five years, and (c) 5 million cubic meters after 10 years, which should lead to a market opening of (a) 28, (b) 40, and (c) 45 percent, respectively. In addition, power generators also counted as eligible customers (Cameron 2002, 167). At the Energy Council meeting in October, the majority of the member states agreed on the consumption thresholds. Only France opposed to including gas-fired power generators as eligible customers. As it did not have such generators, France would have to include more industrial consumers in order to comply with the proposed percentage of market opening (*Financial Times* October 27, 1997). With this position, France had isolated itself from the other member states in the Council ("European Report" October 28, 1997).

With regard to imposing PSO on natural gas undertakings, the member states managed to agree at the same Council meeting that this was allowed for the general economic interests (being operationalized as security, regularity, quality and price, as well as environmental protection). Furthermore, they reaffirmed that member states could opt for negotiated and/or regulated TPA to the system and specified that the latter should be based on published tariffs and/or other terms and obligations for system usage (Council of the European Union 1997b, 2). The subject of TOP contracts was addressed as well. According to the current compromise text, transmission companies were granted a derogation of giving third parties access to their networks if that would result in serious economic or financial difficulties. Before a member state could approve a request for derogation, it had to notify the Commission, which would have the possibility to reject it (Cameron 2002, 167). Although the Energy Council managed to achieve agreement on that issue, it was interpreted differently. While France assumed the

Commission would have to turn to the European Court of Justice if it did not agree, the Commission and the Council Presidency believed the Commission to have the last word. According to them, it would be the national authority that had to turn to the European Court of Justice (*European Report* October 28, 1997).

The next Energy Council meeting was scheduled for December 1997. In its runup, it became clear that member states with more than the qualified majority of votes needed for adopting the draft directive supported the current Presidency compromise (*EU Neues Bulletin* December 8, 1997). As a consequence, the Luxembourgian Presidency openly considered relinquishing a unanimous vote and opting for a qualified majority vote in order to reach a common position (*Financial Times* December 8, 1997). Particularly for France, which still asked for concessions, this would mean a loss in the sense of losing the possibility to influence the design of the draft directive. According to Hypothesis 10c, this should make France more willing to compromise.

Indeed, as the French government was keen on avoiding a decision under a pro-competitive British presidency, the prospects to reach an agreement were good (*European Energy Report* October 27, 1997). Against some member states' and industry's expectation that a left swing in France would harden the fronts, its new government followed the line of its predecessor (*Energy Economist* July 1, 1997). Owing to the participants' willingness to compromise in the sense of offering and accepting concessions (Hypothesis 10b), all unresolved questions could be settled at this Council meeting (Council of the European Union 1997c, 1–5). France accepted the Commission's role in granting derogations from TPA when harming TOP contracts, while the other member states moved toward France as regards the degree of market opening (*European Report* December 10, 1997).

Compared with how long and winding the road to an agreement had been so far, the subsequent decisions were fairly easy. The common position was endorsed by the next Energy Council meeting on February 12, 1998, and by the EP, without any amendments, on April 30, 1998. Although some conceivable amendments were discussed, CERT rapporteur Desama stressed that major points of the EP were already incorporated in the gas draft directive since it was built on the electricity directive. Furthermore, the Council Presidencies, particularly the Luxembourgian one, had consulted parliamentarians regarding the main aspects of the future gas directive (*EU Neues Bulletin* December 10, 1997). In order to avoid breaking the compromise, Desama suggested refraining from amending the proposal and managed to push this through (*Agence Europe* April 30, 1998). This is another example for a political entrepreneur who presented a problem–solution linkage (namely amending the gas draft directive) as a loss and thereby made risk-averse policy-makers willing to settle a compromise (Hypothesis 10c). The Commission recommended the Council to adopt the text, which happened on May 11, 1998.

Summing up, the most important results of the new directive were the following: The minimum degree of market opening was set at 20 percent of annual consumption in the year 2000, which would increase to 28 percent in 2005 and to 33 percent in 2010. This went along with the extension of the definition of eligible customers, starting with customers consuming annually more than 25 million cubic meters of gas, which would decrease to 15 million cubic meters after five years and to 5 million cubic meters after ten years. Gas-fired power generators counted as eligible customers independently of their consumption. Network access had to be granted via regulated TPA or negotiated TPA, both to be characterized by transparency and nondiscrimination. Network access could be refused because of PSO, due to a lack of capacity, or in the context of TOP contracts. In the latter case, member states had to notify the Commission about such a refusal, which would have the final say on that issue. Some derogations were granted for member states, in particular to those that (a) lacked interconnection to gas networks of another member state, (b) had just one main outside supplier, or (c) were defined as an emergent market (namely Greece and Portugal) (98/30/EC; Agence Europe May 11, 1998).

4.2.3 Interim Conclusion

Almost six years and three months after the Commission had introduced the gas draft directive, the Council, the EP, and the Commission finally passed the first gas directive (98/30/EC). Is the MSF able to explain this policy change and the length of decision-making? With regard to the likelihood for a policy to be adopted, I hypothesized that this is more likely if a political entrepreneur manages to achieve package deals (Hypothesis 10a), offers concessions (Hypothesis 10b), and provides meaning, clarification, and identity to the issue at stake (Hypothesis 10c).

To start with, who acted as a political entrepreneur? In Sect. 2.2.2, I defined political entrepreneurs as individuals who hold an elected leadership position and formally belong to the policy-making authorities. This implies that any member states' representative in the Council, any member of the

EP, and any Commissioner could theoretically act as a political entrepreneur—provided he or she invests resources to promote his or her favorite policy (in a similar vein, see Ackrill et al. 2013, 882). During decision coupling, the most visible political entrepreneurs in the Council had been most of its Presidencies (see below). Regarding the Commission, the Energy and Competition Commissioners in charge were engaged in political entrepreneurship, as had been the case during agenda coupling. In the EP, particularly CERT rapporteur Desama stood out as a political entrepreneur. Of all political entrepreneurs, he was the only one who did not change his position during the entire policy process. Hence, he was involved in agenda coupling and decision coupling.

Basically, decision coupling can be divided into three stages. The *first stage* covers the period from February to December 1992. During this time, negotiations moved slowly forward from blockage to political discussions. The most visible political entrepreneurs were Competition Commissioner van Miert, the Portuguese Council President de Mira Amaral, and the British Council Presidency Eggar. It was De Mira Amaral's and Eggar's merit to unveil the nature and scope of the member states' reservations. This was an important achievement because most member states had opposed the gas draft directive in a nonconstructive manner during agenda coupling. But in order to be able to offer concessions or package deals (Hypothesis 10a–b), political entrepreneurs-to-be needed to know which room for maneuver existed. Hence, the Council Presidencies paved the way for a successful decision coupling at a later stage of the policy process. That this room for maneuver had to be revealed in the first place suggests that Hypothesis 11a holds: If the veto actors had supported the agenda change despite existing differences regarding the policy preferred, it would (at least) have been easier from the outset to figure out where and (eventually) how compromises could be settled. In this case, political entrepreneurs had to convince the gas draft directive's opponents that it was technically feasible and falling within EU competence in the first place. This necessarily led to a prolonged decision-making process.

While the above-mentioned Council Presidencies were especially involved in discussions about technical feasibility, the Commission drove the point home that the IEM in general and the gas draft directive in particular fell within EU competence. By the Commission, I refer to the Commission as such, but above all to Competition Commissioner van Miert. The Commission documented that the gas draft directive was subject to Community action by referring to it in its working programs. However, van Miert was the principal proponent of resorting to infringement proceedings in order to make the IEM real. This line of action should increase the member states' willingness to compromise by making them perceive the blockage of the draft negotiations as a loss when compared with the possibility to lose their say on that issue completely (Hypothesis 10c). In terms of successful polical entrepreneurship, this strategy produced mixed results: On the one hand, it proved the Commission's willingness for action and thereby forced the member states to deal with issues touching the IEM. On the other hand, the member states did not respond to the Commission's strategy by adjusting the policies upon which the legal actions were based.

The *second stage* spans the period from January 1993 to June 1994 and the most important political entrepreneurs were the Commission (by including the IEM in its working programs) and Competition Commissioner van Miert as well as Energy Commissioner Matutes (by threatening to act unilaterally in order to achieve the IEM). This stage was initiated by the entry into force of the Maastricht Treaty, which introduced the principle of subsidiarity and upgraded the EP to a colegislator on an equal footing with the Council. These changes made the Commission more willing to compromise because the Commission's legislative proposal of 1992 had been written before the insertion of the principle of subsidiarity in the Maastricht Treaty. As a consequence, the Commission's favorite policy no longer counted as a viable alternative because it did not consider this principle adequately. Additionally, it would no longer suffice to settle a compromise in the Council, but the gas draft directive would also have to take on board possible amendments by the EP. This is mirrored in the Commission's draft of December 1993, which included some package deals (e.g., consideration of regulated *and* negotiated TPA and emphasis of the principle of subsidiarity, Hypothesis 10a) and concessions (e.g., dropping of management unbundling, Hypothesis 10b). In contrast to the Commission, the member states' willingness to compromise did not increase substantially. This might relate to the fact that they had the backing of CERT, which was equally skeptical about energy liberalization in general. Furthermore, the Council had already stated in late November 1992 that it planned to base further negotiations on a revised Commission draft, which should take into account amendments suggested by the EP. But it took until mid-November 1993 for the EP to put its amendments to a plenary vote. Hence, for all practical purposes, there was one year of gridlock, which accounts for a prolonged decision coupling process. During this time, the Commission revived its threat to resort to its powers under the Treaty and thereby exclude the member states from policy formation. It even linked pushing the infringement proceedings forward to the failure to reach a common position regarding the gas draft directive (Hypothesis 10c). Nonetheless, the Council did not manage to make any progress until the second half of 1993, which was why the Commission entered the next stage of the ongoing infringement proceedings. Put differently, as had been the case in the first stage of decision coupling, this strategy did not have the intended effect, although pursued skillfully by van Miert and Matutes. Even worse, the differences between the actors involved proved to be (at least seemingly) unbridgeable. Hence, the actors decided to concentrate on the less controversial electricity draft. To conclude, Hypothesis 10c does not hold with regard to the Commission's threat scenario. Nevertheless, the turn to the electricity draft corroborates Hypothesis 11b, according to which the redirection of the policy-makers' attention accounts for a more lengthy decision coupling process.

The *third stage* covers the time from the autumn of 1996 to May 1998. Energy Commissioner Papoutsis managed to direct the policy-makers' attention back to the gas draft directive when the Energy Council's common position concerning the electricity draft directive appeared to be feasible in the summer of 1996. This resulted in a redrafting of the gas proposal by using the current electricity draft as a template. The subsequent negotiations of the revised draft directive took place in a climate which differed completely from that of the previous two stages. Instead of blockage, package deals (Hypothesis 10a) and concessions (Hypothesis 10b) shaped the Council's negotiations during that time. The reason for this change of climate was that the agreement on the electricity directive (which was formally approved by the Council in late December 1996) had broken down the legitimacy barrier entirely. Neither feasibility nor EU competency regarding the gas draft directive was questioned any more. Applying Kingdon's (1984) terminology, this was a spillover. All Council Presidencies, the Irish, Dutch, and Luxembourgian, acted as political entrepreneurs, which was documented by their efforts in producing compromise texts in order to reach an agreement. The Luxembourgian Presidency and CERT rapporteur Desama, who also acted as a political entrepreneur, even applied the strategy to frame prolonging the negotiations as a loss (Hypothesis 10c). Addressing in particular France, the Luxembourgian Presidency threatened to opt for a qualified majority vote in order to settle an agreement. The perceived necessity to adopt a threatening position resulted from France' attempts to limit competition in the gas sector to the minimum degree possible and to the fact that France had been the only member state that protracted negotiations because of national elections (thereby confirming Hypothesis 11b). Desama managed to discourage the EP from amending

Table 4.2 How well the multiple streams framework fares in explaining how the first gas directive was passed

Directive		*98/30/EC*
Explaining decision-making: decision coupling		
H10	Policy adoption is more likely if a political entrepreneur	
	(a) manages to combine viable alternatives embraced by different veto actors into one package;	+
	(b) can (and does) offer concessions on the original proposal; and	+
	(c) succeeds in providing meaning, clarification, and identity to the issue at stake.	(−)
H11	Decision coupling is more likely to be lengthy if	
	(a) agenda change has taken place against the will of veto actors; and	+
	(b) policy-makers' attention is redirected to other issues.	+

Source: Own compilation
Note: "+" indicates that a hypothesis holds and "(−)" indicates that a hypothesis does not hold for the entire policy process analyzed

the gas draft directive because of the danger to break the Council's compromise. In contrast to the former decision coupling processes, the strategy to frame prolonged (or blocked) negotiations as a loss worked this time as it led France to settle a compromise and the EP to refrain from suggesting amendments. Table 4.2 summarizes these findings.

Notes

1. For an analysis of the (absent) European response to the energy crisis of the 1970s, see Jegen and Mérand (2013, 6–7) and F. McGowan (2011, 496–97).
2. ECU is the abbreviation for European Currency Unit. It was used as the unit of account of the European Community before the introduction of Euro coins and banknotes in 2002.
3. For a detailed discussion of this Council resolution, see Palinkas (1989).
4. The E&P forum was a Brussels-based association of the upstream industry world's oil and gas exploration and production companies. It was founded in 1974 and became the International Association of Oil & Gas Producers in 1999 (http://www.iogp.org/About-IOGP#3880677-notable-events, last accessed on March 11, 2015).

5. IFIEC is the International Federation of Industrial Energy Consumers, founded in 1983 and Brussels-based (Bartle 2005, 97).
6. CEFIC is the Brussels-based "forum and voice of the chemical industry in Europe", founded in 1972 (http://www.cefic.org/About-us/Cefic/, last accessed on March 11, 2015).
7. Unipede, the Union internationale des producteurs et distributeurs d'électricité, was already founded in 1925 in Paris (Eising 2000, 203).
8. For a summary of the development of natural gas regulation in the United States, see Correljé et al. (2013, 4) and Gao (2010, 23–96).
9. Due to institutional ambiguity, it would be misleading to assume that the Commission acted as a coherent actor (cf. Ackrill and Kay 2011). Although differences between different Directorates-General exist, I refer to the Commission if they are irrelevant for the broader argument.
10. A common carriage system obliges pipeline companies to carry as much gas as the pipeline's capacity allows for third parties. If the demand is higher than the capacity of the pipeline, capacity pro rata must be offered to all parties (Stern 1992, 23).
11. After the public hearing then-Rapporteur, Rolf Linkohr, and then-Chairman of CERT, Michel Poniatowski, concluded that the creation of the IEM would be difficult to achieve because of the given national diversity with regard to (inter alia) energy supply capabilities, energy consumption structures, national energy objectives, and economic characteristics. Furthermore, they did not see the issues of environmental protection and consumer interests addressed adequately in the IEM document. Interestingly, Linkohr referred to a judgment by the European Court of Justice dealing with third-party access (TPA) in the telecommunication sector and guessed that from this would follow that TPA in the energy sector could become mandatory if the issue would end up in court (European Parliament 1989, 56–58).
12. See *Bulletin of the European Communities*, Supplements 2/89: 22, 1/90: 20, 1/91: 7, and 1/92: 41.
13. As mentioned above, the working programs of the Council Presidency are not available. However, the fact that no incumbent made use of its agenda-structuring power to bar the IEM from the agenda indicates that this issue had the Council's attention.

14. The European Council referred to energy in other contexts, more specifically in the context of public procurement (European Council 1989, 1990b) and energy infrastructure (European Council 1989, 1990a). Although a proper energy infrastructure is a prerequisite for a frontier-free IEM, I did not count it as a reference to energy liberalization. The reason is that it does not touch the introduction of common rules, which is the centerpiece of energy liberalization.
15. Please note that the EC Treaty was signed at the end of this agenda coupling and entered into force during decision coupling. Before the EC Treaty became valid, Article 90(3) of the EEC Treaty had established the legal frame for the Commission's threat to decide on the liberalization issue itself. Since Article 86(3) of the EC Treaty correlates with Article 90(3) EEC Treaty, I only refer to Article 86(3) EC Treaty to improve the reading flow.
16. The Commission also used an environmental frame, according to which gas-to-gas competition would lead to fuel switching from oil and solid fuels to natural gas, thereby reducing CO_2 emissions (Cardoso e Cunha quoted in *RAPID* September 24, 1991 and October 9, 1992; European Commission 1992b, 4). However, compared with the deregulation frame and the security of supply frame, the Commission rarely made use of this framing.
17. Another example for the linkage of energy security to energy trade is the Energy Charter Treaty. This treaty was initiated by the European Union (EU) in 1991 and signed by 51 states. It aims (inter alia) at creating open and nondiscriminatory energy markets. Initially, it was designed as a means to stimulate growth in Eastern European and former Soviet Union countries, on the one hand, and to increase the EU's energy security, on the other hand. For more information on the Energy Charter Treaty, see Wälde (1996).
18. Note that at the beginning of the discussion of how to open networks for third parties, there were "substantial problems and confusion – even among English language speakers – as to the meaning of common carriage and third party access" (Stern 1993, 184). This might explain why the terms were (apparently) used interchangeably in the late 1980s. Being fully aware that common carriage and TPA describe different ways of opening access to pipelines, I nonetheless adopt the terminologies used in the primary and secondary literature because they document the state of the debate of that time.

19. Since the Commission's position had already been in July 1989, "If they [the United Kingdom, N.H.] can do it [common carriage, N. H.], you [European gas producers and distributors, N.H.] can do it" (quoted in *Energy Economist* July 1, 1989), it becomes apparent that their willingness to compromise was limited, too.
20. Note that Herweg (2015, 94) interpreted the release of the IEM document as the moment when the agenda window opened. This interpretation was based on two considerations: (1) Space restrictions did not allow for discussing the entire agenda-setting process in detail and (2) the Commission's working program was only published three months before the release of the IEM document. This implies that policy-entrepreneurs barely had time to take advantage of the change in the political stream. Furthermore, the Commission itself was the policy-entrepreneur. Therefore, the change in the problem stream, the release of the IEM document, was more important in terms of agenda dynamics.
21. This directive was finally passed in May 1994 (94/22/EEC).
22. Today's Article 105 of the Treaty on the Functioning of the European Union (TFEU) summarizes the Commission's powers to interpret the competition rules of the Treaty, and Article 106 limits the extent to which member states may intervene in the market through public undertakings.
23. Note that the tenure of the third Delors Commission spanned only two years in order to align the mandates of the Commission with those of the European Parliament (EP).
24. For a comprehensive summary of the electricity directive, see Cameron (2002, 143–65).
25. A single buyer "is any legal person who, within the system where it is established, is responsible for the unified management of the transmission system and/or for centralized electricity purchase and sale" (Cameron 2007: lxiii).

References

90/377/EC. *Directive of 29 June 1990 Concerning a Community Procedure to Improve the Transparency of Gas and Electricity Prices Charged to Industrial End-users.*

91/296/EEC. *Directive of 31 May 1991 on Transit of Natural Gas Through Grids.*

91/619/EEC. *Decision of 2 October 1991 Declaring the Incompatability with the Common Market of a Concentration: Case No IV/M.053 - Aerospatiale-Alenia/de Havilland.*

94/22/EEC. *Directive of the European Parliament and of the Council of 30 May 1994 on the Conditions for Granting and Using Authorizations for the Prospection, Exploration and Production of Hydrocarbons.*

96/92/EC. *Directive of the European Parliament and of the Council of 19 December 1996 Concerning Common Rules for the Internal Market in Electricity.*

98/30/EC. *Directive of the European Parliament and of the Council of 22 June 1998 Concerning Common Rules for the Internal Market in Natural Gas.*

Ackrill, Robert, and Adrian Kay. 2011. Multiple Streams in EU Policy-Making: The Case of the 2005 Sugar Reform. *Journal of European Public Policy* 18(1): 72–89.

Ackrill, Robert, Adrian Kay, and Nikolaos Zahariadis. 2013. Ambiguity, Multiple Streams, and EU Policy. *Journal of European Public Policy* 20(6): 871–887.

Andersen, Svein S. 1993. Towards a Common EC Energy Policy. In *Making Policy in Europe: The Europeification of National Policy-Making*, ed. Svein S. Andersen and Kjell A. Eliassen, 133–154. London: Sage Publications.

Armstrong, Mark, and David E. M. Sappington. 2006. Regulation, competition, and liberalization. *Journal of Economic Literature* XLIV: 325–366.

Bartle, Ian. 2005. *Globalisation and EU Policy-Making: The Neo-Liberal Transformation of Telecommunications and Electricity*. Manchester: Manchester University Press.

Biesenbender, Sophie. 2015. The EU's Energy Policy Agenda: Directions and Developments. *In Tosun, Biesenbender, and Schulze* 2015: 21–40.

Black, Alexander J. 1993. Direct Sales of Gas in the European Community. *Tulsa Journal of Comparative and International Law* 1(1): article 10.

Cameron, Peter D. 2002. *Competition in Energy Markets: Law and Regulation in the European Union*. 1st ed. Oxford: Oxford University Press.

———. 2007. *Competition in Energy Markets: Law and Regulation in the European Union*. 2nd ed. Oxford: Oxford University Press.

Cini, Michelle, and McGowan Lee. 2009. *Competition Policy in the European Union*. 2nd ed. Basingstoke: Palgrave Macmillan.

Correljé, Aad, Martijn Groenleer, and Jasper Veldman. 2013. Understanding Institutional Change: The Development of Institutions for the Regulation of Natural Gas Transportation Systems in the US and the EU. *EUI Working Papers RSCAS 2013/07*, 1–18.

Council of the European Communities. 1987. *Council Conclusions Energy: 1171th Council Meeting*, 2 June 1987.

———. 1988. *Council Conclusions Energy: 1246th Council Meeting*, 9 June 1988.

———. 1989a. *Council Conclusions Energy: 1317th Council Meeting*, 11 May 1989.

———. 1989b. *Council Conclusions Energy: 1356th Council Meeting*, 30 October 1989.

———. 1990a. *Council Conclusions Energy: 1404th Council Meeting*, 21 May 1990.
———. 1990b. *Council Conclusions Energy: 1435th Council Meeting, 29 October 1990.*
———. 1991a. *Council Conclusions Energy: 1491th Council Meeting*, 31 May 1991.
———. 1991b. *Council Conclusions Energy: 1526th Council Meeting*, 29 October 1991.
———. 1992a. *Council Conclusions Energy: 1580th Council Meeting*, 21 May 1992.
———. 1992b. *Council Conclusions Energy: 1625th Council Meeting*, 30 November 1992.
———. 1993. *Council Conclusions Energy: 1675th Council Meeting*, 25 June 1993.
Council of the European Union. 1996. *Council Conclusions Energy: 1975th Council Meeting*, 3 December 1996.
———. 1997a. *Council Conclusions Energy: 2009th Council Meeting*, 27 May 1997.
———. 1997b. *Council Conclusions Energy: 2035th Council Meeting*, 27 October 1997.
———. 1997c. *Council Conclusions Energy: 2058th Council Meeting*, 8 December 1997.
Daintith, Terence, and Leigh Hancher. 1986. *Energy Strategy in Europe: The Legal Framework*. Berlin: Gruyter.
Eikeland, Per O. 2004. The Long and Winding Road to the Internal Energy Market: Consistencies and Inconsistencies in EU Policy. *FNI Report* 8.
Eising, Rainer. 2000. *Liberalisierung und Europäisierung: Die regulative Reform der Elektrizitätsversorgung in Grossbritannien, der Europäischen Gemeinschaft und der Bundesrepublik Deutschland*. Opladen: Leske + Budrich.
European Commission. 1968. *First Guidelines for a Community Energy Policy. COM (68)1040.*
———. 1972. *Necessary Progress in community Energy Policy. Communication from the Commission to the Council: COM(72)1200 Final.*
———. 1973. *Guidelines and Priority Actions Under the Community Energy Policy. Communication from the Commission to the Council presented on 27 April 1973: SEC(73)1481.*
———. 1974a. *Community Energy Policy. Objectives for 1985: COM(74)1960 Final.*
———. 1974b. *Towards a New Energy Policy Strategy for the European Community: COM(74)550 final/2.*
———. 1976a. *Community Energy Policy: COM(76)508 Final.*
———. 1976b. *Implementation of the Energy Policy Guidelines Drawn up by the European Council at its Meeting in Rome on 1 and 2 December 1975: COM(76) 20.*
———. 1978. *Energy Objectives for 1990 and Programmes of the Member States: COM(78)613 Final.*
———. 1981. *The Development of an Energy Strategy for the Community: COM(81) 540 Final.*

———. 1985. *Completing the Internal Market. COM(85)310 Final.*
———. 1988a. *Europe 1992. The Overall Challenge: SEC(88)524 Final.*
———. 1988b. *The Internal Energy Market. Commission Working Document: COM (88)238 Final.*
———. 1989. *Towards Completion of the Internal Market for Natural Gas. Communication from the Commission and Proposal for a Council Directive on the Transit of Natural Gas Through the Major Systems: COM(89)334 Final.*
———. 1990a. *Nineteenth Report on Competition Policy*. Luxembourg: Office for Official Publications of the European Communities.
———. 1990b. *The Internal Energy Market. First Progress Report: COM(90)124 Final.*
———. 1991a. *Reports of the Consultative Committees on Third Party Access to Natural Gas Networks*. Brussels: European Communities.
———. 1991b. *XXth Report on Competition Policy*. Luxembourg: European Communities.
———. 1992a. *21st Report on Competition Policy 1991*. Luxembourg: Office for Official Publications of the European Communities.
———. 1992b. *Proposal for a Council Directive Concerning Common Rules for the Internal Market in Electricity. Proposal for a Council Directive Concerning Common Rules for the Internal Market in Natural Gas. COM(91)548 Final.*
———. 1993a. *Amended Proposal for a European Parliament and Council Directive Concerning Common Rules for the Internal Market in Electricity. Amended Proposal for a European Parliament and Council Directive Concerning Common Rules for the Internal Market in Natural Gas: COM(93)643 Final.*
———. 1993b. *List of Proposals Pending Before the Council on 31 October 1993 for Which Entry into Force of the Treaty on European Union Will Require a Change in the Legal Base and/or a Change in Procedure: COM(93)570 Final.*
———. 1993c. *Second Progress Report on the Internal Energy Market: COM(93)261 Final.*
———. 1993d. *XXIInd Report on Competition Policy 1992*. Luxembourg: Office for Official Publications of the European Communities.
———. 1995. *XXIVth Report on Competition Policy*. Luxembourg: Office for Official Publications of the European Communities.
European Council. 1985. *Conclusions of the Presidency: 29–30 March 1985.*
———. 1986a. *Conclusions of the Presidency: 26–27 June 1986.*
———. 1986b. *Conclusions of the Presidency. 06 December 1986.*
———. 1987. *Conclusions of the Presidency: 29–30 June 1978.*
———. 1988a. *Conclusions of the Presidency: 2–3 December 1988.*
———. 1988b. *Conclusions of the Presidency: 27–28 June 1988.*
———. 1989. *Conclusions of the Presidency: 8–9 December 1989.*
———. 1990a. *Conclusions of the Presidency: 14–15 December 1990.*
———. 1990b. *Conclusions of the Presidency: 24–25 June 1990.*

———. 1992. *Conclusions of the Presidency: 26–27 June 1992.*

European Parliament. 1989. *Energy and the Internal Market 1992. Public Hearing. Brussels, 22 and 23 November 1988.* Luxembourg.

Finon, Dominique, and John Surrey. 1996. The Future of EU Energy Policy. In *McGowan 1996a:*165–183.

Fligstein, Neil. 2001. Institutional Entrepreneurs and Cultural Frames: The Case of the European Union's Single Market Program. *European Societies* 3(3): 261–287.

Gao, Anton M.-Z. 2010. *Regulating Gas Liberalization: A Comparative Study on Unbundling and Open Access Regimes in the US, Europe, Japan, South Korea, and Taiwan.* Alphen Aan Den Rijn: Kluwer Law International.

Grunwald, Jürgen. 2003. *Das Energierecht der Europäischen Gemeinschaften: EGKS-EURATOM-EG; Grundlagen—Geschichte—geltende Regelungen.* Berlin: De Gruyter Recht.

Hancher, Leigh. 1990. A Single European Energy Market: Rhetoric or Reality? *Energy Law Journal* 11(2): 217–242.

Helm, Dieter. 2005. The Assessment: The New Energy Paradigm. *Oxford Review of Economic Policy* 21(1): 1–18.

Héritier, Adrienne, Christoph Knill, and Susanne Mingers. 1996. *Ringing the Changes in Europe. Regulatory Competition and the Transformation of the State: Britain, France, Germany.* Berlin: Walter de Gruyter.

Herweg, Nicole. 2015. Against all Odds. The Liberalisation of the European Natural Gas Market: A Multiple Streams Perspective. *In Tosun, Biesenbender, and Schulze* 2015: 87–105.

Herweg, Nicole, Christian Huß, and Reimut Zohlnhöfer. 2015. Straightening the Three Streams: Theorizing Extensions of the Multiple Streams Framework. *European Journal of Political Research* 54(3): 435–449.

Jabko, Nicolas. 2006. *Playing the Market: A Political Strategy for Uniting Europe, 1985–2005.* Ithaca, NY: Cornell University Press.

Jegen, Maya, and Frédéric Mérand. 2013. Constructive Ambiguity: Comparing the EU's Energy and Defence Policies. *West European Politics* 37(1): 182–203.

Jones, Bryan D., and Frank R. Baumgartner. 2004. Representation and Agenda Setting. *Policy Studies Journal* 32(1): 1–24.

Kingdon, John W. 1984. *Agendas, Alternatives, and Public Policies.* Boston: Little, Brown.

———. 2003. *Agendas, Alternatives, and Public Policies.* 2nd ed. New York: Longman.

Lyons, Paul K. 1994. *Energy Policies of the European Union.* London: EC Inform.

Maltby, Tomas. 2013. European Union Energy Policy Integration: A Case of European Commission Policy Entrepreneurship and Increasing Supranationalism. *Energy Policy* 55(100): 435–444.

Matláry, Janne H. 1997. *Energy Policy in the European Union*. London: MacMillan.

McGowan, Francis. 1989. The Single Energy Market and Energy Policy: Conflicting Agendas? *Energy Policy* 17(6): 547–553.

———, eds. 1996a. *European Energy Policies in a Changing Environment*. Heidelberg: Physica-Verlag.

———, eds. 1996b. Ideology and Expediency in British Energy Policy. *In McGowan* 1996a: 130–164.

———, eds. 2011. Putting Energy Insecurity into Historical Context: European Responses to the Energy Crises of the 1970s and 2000s. *Geopolitics* 16(3): 486–511.

Mestmäcker, Ernst J., eds. 1993. *Natural Gas in the Internal Market: A Review of Energy Policy*. London: Graham & Trotman.

Moravcsik, Andrew. 1991. Negotiating the Single European Act: National Interests and Conventional Statecraft in the European Community. *International Organization* 45(4): 19–56.

Nylander, Johan. 2000. *The Power of Framing: A New-Institutional Approach to Interest Group Participation in the European Union*. Uppsala: Uppsala University.

———. 2001. The Construction of a Market. A Frame Analysis of the Liberalization of the Electricity Market in the European Union. *European Societies* 3(3): 289–314.

Padgett, Stephen. 1992. The Single European Energy Market: The Politics of Realization. *Journal of Common Market Studies* XXX(1): 53–75.

———. 2003. Between Synthesis and Emulation: EU Policy Transfer in the Power Sector. *Journal of European Public Policy* 10(2): 227–245.

Palinkas, Peter. 1989. The EC on the Way to an Internal Energy Market. *Intereconomics* 24(5): 246–254.

Pollack, Mark A. 2000. The End of Creeping Competence? EU Policy-Making Since Maastricht. *Journal of Common Market Studies* 38(3): 519–538.

Pollak, Johannes, Samuel Schubert, and Peter Slominski. 2008. *Die Energiepolitik der EU*. Wien: UTB.

Salter, John R. 1994. "Third Party Access to Gas and Electricity Transmission Systems in the Community. Third party Access—Your Flexible Friend?" In *European Community Energy law: Selected Topics*, edited by David S. Mac Dougall and Thomas W. Waelde, 85–98. London: Graham & Trotman.

Scharpf, Fritz W. 1996. Negative and Positive Integration in the Political Economy of European Welfare States. In *Governance in the European Union*, 1st ed., ed. Gary Marks, Fritz W. Scharpf, Philippe C. Schmitter, and Wolfgang Streeck, 15–39. London: Sage.

Schmidt, Susanne K. 1998. *Liberalisierung in Europa: Die Rolle der Europäischen Kommission*. Frankfurt: Campus.

Smeers, Yves. 1993. Aims and Means of European Energy Policy in the Light of the Completion of the Internal Market. *In Mestmäcker* 1993: 19–45.

Stern, Jonathan P. 1992. *Third Party Access in European Gas Industries: Regulation-Driven or Market-Led?* London: Royal institute of international affairs.

———. 1993. The Prospects for Third Party Access in European Gas Markets. *In Mestmäcker* 1993: 183–201.

———. 1998. *Competition and Liberalization in European Gas Markets: A Diversity of Models*. London: Royal institute of international affairs.

Surrey, John. 1990. Beyond 1992—The Single Market and EC Energy Issues. *Energy Policy* 18(1): 42–54.

Talus, Kim. 2013. *EU Energy Law and Policy: A Critical Account*. Oxford: Oxford University Press.

Tosun, Jale, Sophie Biesenbender, and Kai Schulze, eds. 2015. *Energy Policy Making in the EU: Building the Agenda*. London: Springer.

Wälde, Thomas W., eds. 1996. *The Energy Charter Treaty: An East-West Gateway for Investment and Trade. International Energy and Resources Law and Policy Series*. London: Kluwer Law International.

Zahariadis, Nikolaos. 2003. *Political Decision Making in Modern Democracies*. Washington, DC: Georgetown University Press.

———. 2014. Ambiguity and Multiple Streams. In *Theories of the Policy Process*, 3rd ed., ed. Paul A. Sabatier and Christopher M. Weible, 25–58. New York: Westview Press.

CHAPTER 5

The Second Gas Directive Process

In order to unveil when and how common rules for the internal market in natural gas returned on the governmental (and finally decision) agenda, the analysis of the second gas directive process covers the time span between the Council's approval of the first gas directive on May 11, 1998, and the Council's approval of the second gas directive on June 16, 2003. The second gas and electricity directives were negotiated in parallel. The analysis focuses on the gas directive process and only refers to the negotiations of the electricity draft, if required, for analyzing the policy process concerning the gas directive. This chapter is guided by the hypotheses stated in Chap. 2 (for an overview, see Table 2.6) and starts with elaborating how the second gas directive was raised on the governmental agenda and became "up for an active decision" (Kingdon 1984, 4) (Sect. 5.1). This is followed by an analysis of the decision-making process (Sect. 5.2). The chapter concludes with an evaluation of how well the multiple streams framework (MSF) succeeds in explaining these policy processes (Sect. 5.3).

5.1 Agenda Change

This section is structured in the same manner as the section dealing with the first gas directive process in Chap. 4: Sections 5.1.1–5.1.3 test Hypothesis 1 (specified in Definitions 1–3) by summarizing the ripeness of the problem stream, political stream, and policy stream. This is followed by an analysis of how the agenda window opened (Hypothesis 2, alternative causal paths specified in Hypotheses 4–8) and whether a policy-entrepreneur engaged

N. Herweg, *European Union Policy-Making*,
DOI 10.1007/978-3-319-49400-5_5

and succeeded in coupling the streams (Hypothesis 3, specified in Hypothesis 9, Sect. 5.1.4). Finally, I summarize if the hypotheses derived from the MSF in order to explain agenda change can be confirmed or must be rejected for the second gas directive process (Sect. 5.1.5).

5.1.1 Problem Stream

In order for an issue to be detected, it needs to attract attention in the first place. In this regard, the first gas directive's review clauses, contained in Articles 27 and 28, were important (98/30/EC). Both articles tasked the Commission with reporting duties: Article 27 concerning harmonization requirements, which were *not* linked to the directive's provisions, and Article 28 concerning experiences gained on the application of the directive, particularly with regard to public service obligations (PSO) and customer protection. Furthermore, Article 28 explicitly called for the Commission to "consider, in due time, the possibility of provisions for further improving the internal market in natural gas". Thereby, the first gas directive already hinted at the need for evaluation studies and at key points these studies should address.

However, raising attention to a condition does not suffice for the problem stream to become ripe. In order to become ripe, the detected condition must also be perceived as being problematic (Definition 1). By April 1999, the Commission had released two reports regarding the state of energy liberalization, the first in April 1998 (European Commission 1998b) and the second a year later (European Commission 1999b). In terms of interpreting the state of natural gas liberalization as problematic, the Commission's second report was of higher relevance because it was the first report after the gas directive's adoption. The Commission introduced this report with the ascertainment that "[i]t is evident that (...) [the electricity and gas directives are, N.H.] only a start and much remains to be done for the completion of an internal energy market" (European Commission 1999b, 5). In contrast to the gas directive, the date of transposition for the electricity directive had already elapsed (i.e., February 19, 1999). The Commission's report regarding its implementation by member states was very positive: Most member states had implemented the directive fully and properly, which coincided with a fall in electricity prices. Nonetheless, the Commission concluded that this directive did not suffice in order to create a single electricity market because it had just laid down the "groundwork for the liberalization of 15 electricity markets" and "much remains to be done to achieve a single market for electricity" (European Commission 1999b, 20). Put differently, the Commission found it problematic that the directive's provisions created 15 liberalized but unconnected electricity markets instead of one internal electricity market. Given that the gas directive had taken the electricity directive as a blueprint, it was very likely that the Commission's assessment of the internal natural gas market would not be different after the gas directive's date of transposition on August 10, 2000. Thus, the problem stream was ripe as the Commission's evaluation studies had raised attention to energy liberalization in general and interpreted it as problematic.

In addition to this reviewing activity, changes in European Union (EU) primary law had made it more likely for energy issues to be detected and interpreted as problems. The first change was introduced by the Single European Act (SEA), which entered into force on July 1, 1987. The SEA amended the European Economic Community Treaty (inter alia) by inserting a separate title on environment (Article 130r-t, today's Articles 191–193 of the Treaty on the Functioning of the European Union (TFEU)). This provided future policy-entrepreneurs with a means to justify Community action in this policy area. Due to the crosscutting nature of energy issues, this could have easily resulted in internal energy market (IEM) issues being considered problematic. However, this did not happen. It took two more treaty amendments to give environmental protection a higher relevance. The Maastricht Treaty, which came into force on November 1, 1993, changed Article 130r(2) from "Environmental protection requirements shall be a component of other policies" to "Environmental protection requirements *must be integrated* into the *definition and implementation* of other policies" (emphasis added). Since "[t]he notion of 'must be integrated' is much more forceful than the notion of 'shall be a component'" (Jans 2011, 1537, emphasis in original), environmental protection had become more important. The Treaty of Amsterdam, which entered into force on May 1, 1999, followed that line and moved the provision to integrate environmental protection requirements from Article 130r(2) to Article 6 EC Treaty. As a consequence, this integration principle was no longer just an environmental provision but a general principle of EC law (Jans 2011, 1537; Lenschow 2005, 299). In the MSF terminology, this equals to the introduction of a new category, which could be applied in order to interpret a condition as problematic. The Cardiff Process, initiated by the European Council in 1998 (see 5.1.2), aimed at formalizing the application of this integration principle. The centerpiece of this process was the European Council's invitation to "all relevant formations of the Council to establish their own strategies for giving effect to environmental integration and sustainable development within their respective policy areas" (European Council 1998b, 13). Furthermore, it called (inter alia) for the Energy Council to start this process, which it did by including the Cardiff Process and related issues (such as promotion of renewable energy sources and energy efficiency) in its agendas (Council of the European Union 1999a, b). It is noteworthy that the Council did not link the Cardiff Process to the idea of liberalizing the natural gas market. Comparable with the free movement category, which the Commission had introduced during the first gas directive process in its White Paper "Completing the Internal Market" (European Commission 1985), the integration principle provided policy-entrepreneurs with the possibility to define conditions as problematic by documenting that the IEM did not comply with this principle (cf. Nylander 2000, 310). However, there was no indication that policy-entrepreneurs lied in wait for linking the IEM with this principle. In its second implementation report, for instance, the Commission refrained from prominently linking the integration principle with the state of the IEM. Furthermore, the Commission stressed that it expected the IEM to have positive effects on the environment as it would allow for switching over to cleaner energy sources (such as gas) for electricity generation (European Commission 1999b, 3, 20).

Similarly, although some focusing events brought security of supply concerns into focus, they did not call into question the objective to complete the internal market for natural gas. The subsequent events happened in parallel or immediately after the agenda window had opened. They are summarized here since they document that energy security was predominantly dealt with independently from energy liberalization. An example of a prominent focusing event was the Californian supply crisis during 2000 and 2001, which was characterized by accelerating energy prices and blackouts.[1] In September 2001, the Commission explicitly linked this crisis to regulatory disincentives in California, which had not been replicated in EU's energy liberalization policies (*European Voice* September 20, 2001, European Commission 2001a, 46).[2] This is not to say that security of supply was not an issue in Europe. For instance, the Commission released a Green Paper entitled "Towards a European Strategy for the Security of Supply" (European Commission 2000a) in November 2000. Regarding energy liberalization, the Commission concluded that the "integration of energy markets contributes to security of supply, provided that these markets are truly integrated" and that the current provisions (exemplified by the electricity market) need to be revised in order to achieve "greater separation between electricity generators and transport network managers, non-discriminatory network access by new generators and distributors, minimal charges for cross-border trade, clearer public service obligations and widespread establishment of an independent regulator" (European Commission 2000a, 61). Hence, energy liberalization was framed as a way to achieve energy security by the Commission. It presented (in parts) revised provisions of the gas and electricity directives as a solution to this problem. Summing up, the Commission had framed its favorite policy, energy liberalization, not only as a means to increase Europe's competitiveness but also as a means to protect the environment and secure energy supply.

As outlined in Sect. 4.1.1, a key argument for creating the IEM had been the cost of non-Europe, which was documented by the high energy prices in the EU compared with those in liberalized markets (such as the United States). Hence, one rationale behind energy liberalization had been to allow the free play of market forces, which was expected to result in lower energy prices. As a consequence, the development of energy prices was (and still is) an important indicator for this policy field. While the Commission linked the falling electricity prices in 1997 and 1998 compared with those in 1994 to its liberalization policy (European Commission 1999b, 19), this did not work for the gas price, given that the date of transposition for the first gas directive had not elapsed yet and the linkage of the gas price to oil (European Commission 2001a, 25). Nonetheless, the Commission linked the rising gas prices in the United Kingdom to the fact that companies from less liberalized member states increasingly bought natural gas there via the Interconnector since its opening in 1998. Whereas buyers profited from the lower UK prices, their demand triggered price increases in the United Kingdom. Consequently, the price in the United Kingdom started to reflect the higher price level on the continent (European Commission 2001a, 25). This was problematic because the United Kingdom counted as a liberalization pioneer that could not benefit from its liberalization policy.

Thus, the problem stream was ripe due to the Commission's reviewing activities (Definition 1) and energy liberalization was not crowded out from the governmental agenda by environmental or security of supply issues. To the contrary, it was framed as a means to protect the environment and secure energy supply.

5.1.2 *Political Stream*

In order to assess the ripeness of the political stream, the subsequent paragraphs summarize how receptive to energy liberalization the three branches of the EU government—the Commission, the European Council, and the Council—had been.

From June 1998, the passage of the first gas directive, until September 1999, the inauguration of the Prodi Commission, it was unlikely that any further natural gas liberalization attempts would originate from the *Commission*. On the one hand, it would have been difficult to justify why new measures were required before experiences with the existing provisions could have been gained. On the other hand, the Santer Commission resigned in March 1999. The context of its mass resignation, allegations of corruption, and the fact that it did not come along with a personnel turnover but just a rotation between the President (Jacques Santer) and its Vice-President (Manuel Marín) suggested that new large-scale policy projects should stem from a Commission, which had been elected as provided by in Article 214 of the Treaty establishing the European Community. The Prodi Commission, equipped with such a mandate, started its term in office in September 1999. It did not start with elaborated plans for an internal energy agenda. In early January 2000, the Prodi Commission released its policy priorities for the years 2000–2005. Although energy policy was included in these priorities under the label "[a] new economic and social agenda" (European Commission 2000c, 5), the Commission's plans did not become visible because they were formulated too vaguely: "Energy will be an essential factor for Europe's competitiveness and economic development. The Commission will launch a debate on energy and particularly issues of sources of supply which continue to have a strategic importance" (European Commission 2000c, 11). A month later, it published its working program for 2000 and simply stated that "[c]onsideration will be given to whether further action is needed to promote the cross-border supply of energy given the rules which have opened electricity and gas markets to competition" (European Commission 2000d, 15). Put differently, both the Commission's annual and five-year working programs documented its awareness of energy policy in general as well as its interest in achieving competitive energy markets in particular. Referring to the new economic and social agenda (to which it had previously linked energy policy), the Commission expected the forthcoming special European Council meeting in March 2000 to "provide impetus for the reforms needed" (European

Commission 2000c, 11). Thus, the Commission was receptive to agenda change.

At its meetings after the passing of the first gas directive in 1998 and 1999, the *European Council* addressed energy policy in the context of the above-mentioned Cardiff Process (European Council 1998a, 1999a, b, c, d). However, it did not touch the topic of whether further energy liberalization measures were required. In contrast, the *Council* addressed diverse matters related to (or affecting) the IEM between the second half of 1998 and 1999. Basically, these matters can be divided into three broad topics: (1) harmonization requirements for the common rules for the internal market in electricity and natural gas; (2) security of EU gas supply, including the then-ongoing negotiations of the Energy Charter Treaty; and (3) as outlined above, the Cardiff Process and related issues (Council of the European Union 1999a, b). The analysis of the Council Presidencies' working programs for the second half of 1998 to the spring of 2000 replicates this finding. The respective Presidencies, the United Kingdom, Finland, and Portugal,[3] referred to (most of) these issues (United Kingdom 1997; Finland 1999; Portugal 1999). Put differently, the Council was still receptive to IEM matters, but at the same time, environmental and security of supply issues had raised in importance.

To conclude, with regard to stream ripeness, the Commission and the Council were receptive in terms of awareness that further or accompanying measures might become necessary in the future in order to complete the internal market in natural gas. Since the European Council did not explicitly address the issue of energy liberalization, it was neither positively nor negatively connoted.

5.1.3 Policy Stream

In contrast to the first gas directive process, the policy community's participants no longer restricted themselves by concentrating on the generation of energy proposals with a national dimension in mind. Their turn to the EU as a venue relevant to energy legislation can be illustrated by the increase in the number of representative office of the natural gas and electricity sectors at the European level (see Fig. 5.1).

The Commission fostered this development by institutionalizing the dialogue between all actors affected by European energy legislation. It formally set up an *Energy Consultative Committee* in 1996, which was composed of 15 "eminent persons representing energy producers,

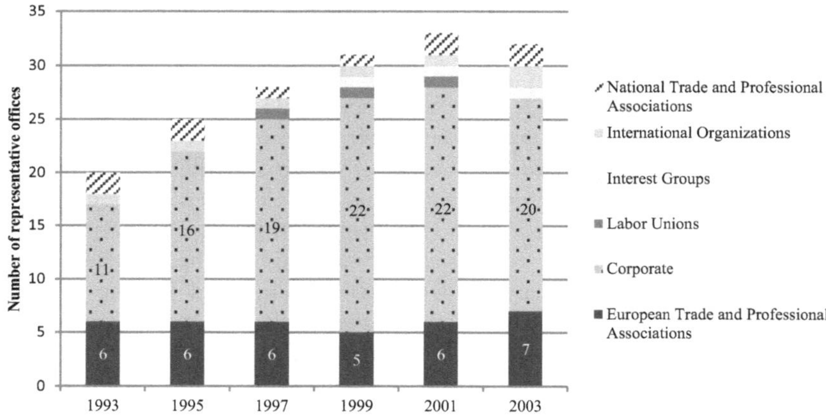

Fig. 5.1 Number of representative offices of natural gas and electricity sectors at European level, 1993–2003. *Source*: Own compilation, based on Landmarks Publications (1992, 1994, 1996, 1998, 2000, 2002)

distributors, consumers and unions, and environmental protection associations" (96/642/EC, Article 1). Its task was to advise the Commission confidentially "on all problems related to Community energy policy" (96/642/EC, Article 2). With regard to natural gas legislation, the Commission met with member states in the framework of the so-called *follow-up group* since October 1998. The goal of this follow-up group was to prevent implementation inconsistencies and to ensure a coherent implementation (European Commission 1998b, 16). It addressed questions such as whether and how the gas directive applied to upstream pipeline networks and ship-or-pay contracts (European Commission 1998a, 1999a). Furthermore, the Commission initiated the European Gas Regulatory Forum in 1999, commonly referred to as the *Madrid Forum*, as a platform to discuss internal gas market issues and develop "consensus amongst all the parties involved in this process; governments, regulators and industry, in order to make rapid progress on these highly technical issues" (European Gas Regulatory Forum 1999, 1).[4] Thus, the Madrid Forum institutionalized the exchange of views immediately after the passing of the first gas directive (and has kept the discussion and development of viable solutions ongoing since then) (cf. Eberlein 2005, 69–75).

Table 5.1 State of implementation of the first gas directive by the end of May 2000

Member state	*Market opening in percentage*			*Access system*	*Unbundling*	*Regulatory system*	*Public service obligations (PSO)*	*Access to storage*
	2000	*2008*	*Later*					
Austria	49	100	100	Regulated	Accounts	Minister of Economic Affairs; by October 2002, national regulatory authority (NRA)	Connect customers, supply	Not covered yet
Belgium	47	66	100	Negotiated	Accounts	Regulatory Commission for Gas and Electricity	Investments	Include in access to transport
Denmark	30	43	43	Distribution: regulated; transmission: negotiated	Accounts	Energy sector–specific regulator	Research and development, storage, network balancing, gas safety, marketing activities of supply obligation companies	Negotiated
France	20	33	33	In general: regulated; in exceptional circumstances: negotiated	Accounts plus Chinese Walls	Regulatory authority for gas and electricity	Prices, supply security, and diversity; developing and operating underground storage; developing transport infrastructure	Subject to competition law and certain priorities (such as storage needs of PSO)
Finland	90	90	90	Regulated	Accounts	Energy market authority	Supply	No storage available

(*continued*)

Table 5.1 (continued)

Member state	*Market opening in percentage*			*Access system*	*Unbundling*	*Regulatory system*	*Public service obligations (PSO)*	*Access to storage*
	2000	*2008*	*Later*					
Germany	100	100	100	Negotiated	Accounts	General competition authority	None	Considered to be part of the gas network
Greece	0	33	33	Not yet decided	legal	Energy regulatory authority	Not yet decided	Not yet decided
Ireland	75	81	81	Regulated	Accounts	Most probably: enlargement of the Commission for Electricity	Not yet decided	No storage available
Italy	96	100	100	Regulated	Legal	Regulatory authority for electricity and gas, and antitrust authority	Connection to the distribution grid, supply modulation and storage	Regulated access
Luxembourg	51,1	75	75	Regulated	Accounts	One regulatory authority for tele-com, gas, and electricity	Security of supply, protection of the environment	Not available
Netherlands	45	100	100	Transmission and upstream pipe-lines: negotiated; distribution: regulated	Accounts and Chinese Walls (Gasunie); legal (distribution)	Energy regulator (subject to competi-tion authority)	Supply of captive and small customers, energy saving, sus-tainability, small fields policy	Included in gas transportation
Portugal	0	33	33	Not yet decided	Not yet decided	Regulatory authority for gas	Not yet decided	Not available

Spain	67	100	100	Regulated	Legal (gas trading); accounts (else)	National Energy Commission and Ministry of Economy	Security of supply, connection and supply, maintenance of quality levels, enhancement of capacity within exclusive supply areas	Allowed for by the law
Sweden	47	100	100	Regulated	Accounts	Network authority	None	Not available
United Kingdom	100	100	100	Regulated	Legal	Office of gas and electricity markets	Social obligations laid down in licenses	Auction, spot market

Source. Own compilation, based on European Commission (2000b)

Given that the member states had to transpose the first gas directive into national law by August 10, 2000, policies addressing the regulation of the natural gas market were worked out at the European level *and* at the member state level. Since the member states had opted for different ways to implement the gas directive into national law, there were many alternatives available with which the policy community was familiar (see Table 5.1). Thus, the policy stream was ripe (Definition 3).

5.1.4 Agenda Window and Coupling

The liberalization of the natural gas market returned on the governmental agenda on February 28, 2000, when the Commission released its contribution to the special European Council meeting in Lisbon in March 2000 (Hypothesis 8). The reason for this special meeting was the intention "to agree a new strategic goal for the Union in order to strengthen employment, economic reform and social cohesion as part of a knowledge-based economy" (European Council 2000b, 1). In its contribution, the Commission defined areas of priority action in order to reach this goal, among others, the reform of underperforming sectors in the internal market. It included the energy market in the list of underperforming sectors and suggested "[t]he date of 2004 to be set for the full liberalisation and integration of European energy markets" (European Commission 2000e, 15).

With this suggestion, the Commission's contribution pushed energy liberalization back on the governmental agenda. However, it is striking that the Commission abstained from presenting concrete energy policy priorities in its policy priorities for the subsequent five years in early January 2000 (as suggested by Hypothesis 5b), just to propose a specific date for fully liberalizing and opening the energy markets less than two months later (see Sect. 5.1.2). That is all the more astonishing, given that, in December 1999, then Energy Commissioner Loyola de Palacio stressed that new propositions regarding further harmonization measures could be expected at the earliest after the completion of the gas directive's implementation phase in August 2000 (*EU Neues Bulletin* November 30, 1999).[5]

Nonetheless, the European Council took into account the Commission's suggestion to increase competition in the IEM at its meeting in Lisbon by addressing the need to speed up legislation in the gas sector in order "to become the most competitive and dynamic knowledge-based economy in the world" (European Council 2000b, Recital 17). In response, the

Commission announced the adoption of proposals for enhancing energy liberalization for June 2001 (*Europe Energy* May 12, 2000).

The likelihood of an agenda change increases if all three streams are ripe, an agenda window is open, and a policy-entrepreneur manages to couple the streams. As outlined above, the streams had been ripe and an agenda window had opened (Hypotheses 1 and 2). As will be shown in the subsequent sections, the policy-entrepreneur did not have to couple the political and problem stream as they converged without further assistance (5.1.4.1). Instead it needed a policy-entrepreneur to link the policy stream to the already converged political and problem stream (5.1.4.2).

5.1.4.1 The Convergence of the Political Stream and the Problem Stream

From the late 1980s until the mid-1990s, the actors affected by energy liberalization had been openly negative toward the idea of liberalizing the natural gas market. In 2000, they supported the idea. More precisely, they shared the same problem perception: The incomplete IEM, which was a result of the present gas directive not going far enough and the fact that France, Germany, and Luxembourg had failed to properly implement it into national legislation (European Commission 2001a, 11, see below). The Commission reacted to the latter by sending letters of reminders to the affected member states (*EU Neues Bulletin* August 9, 2000) immediately after the date of transposition had elapsed, adding weight to seeing the incomplete state of the IEM as problematic.

Referring to the European Council's call to speed up legislation in the gas sector, the *Council* invited the Commission "to present timely proposals for further action" at its meeting on May 30, 2000 (Council of the European Union 2000a, 8). A month later, the *European Council* reaffirmed its push for energy liberalization by inviting the Commission "to present a report by March 2001 on the evolution of energy markets according to the Lisbon strategy" (European Council 2000a, Recital 27). Only a few days later, on June 22, 2000, the Committee on Industry, External Trade, Research and Energy (2000) sang the same song and adopted a motion for a resolution. Mirroring the established problem perception, it included a call for the Commission "to submit specific proposals geared to overcoming all the existing barriers to intra-Community trade, and to take action specifically against those Member States failing to implement the [gas and electricity, N.H.] Directives". One month later, on July 6, 2000, the *European Parliament* (EP) finally passed that resolution (*Official Journal of the European*

Communities April 24, 2001, C121/451-456). While the EP emphasized the need for further liberalization measures, it stressed taking into account the protection of consumers and the environment—the latter particularly with regard to renewable energies. In December 2000, the *European Council* (2000c) announced to address the implementation of the strategy agreed in Lisbon (including energy liberalization) at the European Council meeting in Stockholm in March 2001. The *Commission*, in turn, reported to the Council that it was to table a new gas draft directive on this occasion (Council of the European Union 2000b), which the Commission reaffirmed in its working program for 2001 (European Commission 2001c).

Thus, within ten months after the opening of the agenda window, all branches of the EU's executive and legislature had tasked the Commission to deliver a legislative proposal for a revised gas directive, and the Commission had committed itself to deliver it by March 2001. Thereby, the agenda window remained open (Definition 4). In addition to the EU's executive and legislature, the *industry*, above all energy-intensive users, demanded EU governments to carry gas liberalization further and their suppliers to offer more flexible contracts. They even threatened to take their business elsewhere (*European Voice* November 4, 1999).

5.1.4.2 The Missing Link: Coupling the Policy Stream to the Converged Problem and the Political Stream

As outlined above, the policy stream was ripe, given that the policy community was familiar with a list of options that had been legitimated in one or more member states (Definition 3). Similar to agenda coupling in the first gas directive process, the Commission aimed at coming up with a *European option* instead of pushing for one option that had been implemented in at least one member state. In contrast to agenda coupling in the early 1990s, the Commission succeeded in working out a solution that met the criteria of normative acceptance and receptivity among policy-makers at the European level. The subsequent paragraphs summarize how the Commission succeeded in this endeavor.

The policy community had changed since the 1990s, both in terms of institutionalization and its participants' engagement in working out European alternatives. However, the institutionalization of some key participants was still ongoing: In March 2000, the Commission set up the Council of European Energy Regulators (CEER), which consisted of independent electricity and gas regulators from the member states and was tasked with contributing to the transformation of 15 liberalized markets into one single market (*EU Neues Bulletin* March 9, 2000). Furthermore, following a request of the European Commission, the member states and CEER, the European gas industry founded Gas Transmission Europe (GTE) in July 2000. GTE brought together representatives responsible for the operation of the gas transmission networks in Europe (European Gas Regulatory Forum 2000b). GTE's creation was pivotal to working out alternatives because policy-makers needed GTE's technical input regarding the regulation of gas transmission systems—in particular because the question of whether and how allowing for third-party access (TPA) had been one of the most controversial issues in the first gas directive process (see Chap. 4).

The Commission viewed the Madrid Forum as the "appropriate coordinating forum for discussions" regarding gas liberalization. Furthermore, it expected that discussions taking place in this forum would lead to a "higher convergence of views and regulatory practices" (Commission official quoted in *European Report* May 10, 2000). In fact, the industry confirmed by September 2003 that it viewed the Madrid Forum as a powerful forum, which allowed for consensus-building and generating ideas that could be translated into guidelines and directives (*European Spot Gas Markets* September 24, 2003). Table 5.2 summarizes the agenda items of the Madrid Forum's meetings, before the Commission published its legislative proposal in March 2001 (European Commission 2001c). It shows that along with items such as access to the system, unbundling, and overview of the implementation of the first gas directive, key issues of the gas directive were also addressed. An analysis of the agenda of the first and third meetings of the Madrid Forum[6] reveals the Commission's engagement in working out proposals. Of 32 contributions held at these meetings, the Commission delivered 22 percent ($n = 7$) and the actors whose creation the Commission had initiated, GTE and CEER, delivered 37.5 percent ($n = 12$) (see Annex III). Put differently, almost 60 percent of the contributions were either held or influenced by the Commission, given that it had requested from GTE specific inputs for these meetings and tasked CEER more generally to contribute to the creation of a single energy market.

As outlined above, the member states had used the gas directive's leeway and chosen different ways to implement the directive into national law. If the majority of member states had opted for the same solution regarding specific regulatory aspects, one could argue that this solution also meets the criteria of normative acceptance and receptivity among policy-makers at the

Table 5.2 Overview of the agenda of the Madrid Forum, first to third meeting

No	*Date*	*Agenda items*
1	September 30 to October 1, 1999	Organization of access Access to the system: conditions and pricing principles Storage Harmonization Security of supply
2	May 11 to May 12, 2000	Establishment of a new body or grouping that brings together representatives of all those responsible for the operation of the gas transmission networks in Europe Invitation to the new body to provide the Commission with information Third-party access (TPA)
3	October 26 to October 27, 2000	Overview of the implementation of the gas directive Creation of a new body of European Gas Transmission system operators Unbundling Transparency TPA environment Competition policy issues Transmission tarification Available transmission capacities Congestion management Technical interoperability

Source: Own compilation, based on European Gas Regulatory Forum (1999, 2000a, b)

European level. In this regard, the Commission's presentation of the state of implementation of the gas directive at the third meeting of the Madrid Forum was informative.[7] The Commission found that member states had predominantly opted for regulated TPA, a bigger market opening than envisaged by the first gas directive, independent regulators, and implementation of unbundling, which goes beyond account unbundling.

In addition to exchanging views in the context of the Madrid Forum, the Directorate-General (DG) Energy and DG Transport organized a *public hearing* on the completion of the IEM on September 14, 2000. In sum, 117 organizations and companies participated in this hearing and delivered in total 70 oral and written contributions. This hearing revealed that a majority of the policy community agreed on further solutions regarding specific regulatory aspects (European Commission 2001a, 71–72). Most importantly, it documented:

- Of all respondents, 80 percent favored a full market opening in the short to medium term.
- And 70 percent of respondents suggested strengthening the issue of unbundling; with regard to transmission system operators (TSOs), they preferred legal unbundling.
- In all, 80 percent of respondents supported at least published tariffs, and most supported regulated tariffs for network access.
- And 40 percent of respondents supported trade facilitating mechanisms and wished to work them out in the context of the Madrid Forum.
- All but one respondent found PSO compatible with market liberalization. PSO regarding security of supply, social objectives, and environmental protection were highlighted.
- The interest representation of employees in the energy industry stressed that measures addressing the negative effects of liberalization on employment in the electricity and gas sectors were needed.
- Some respondents suggested paying more attention to the treatment of electricity from renewable energy sources and deleting the provision which allowed member states to introduce thresholds for the eligibility of cogenerators.
- All respondents favored a strongly independent regulatory authority; only a minority favored a European regulatory body.
- Several respondents were concerned about the ongoing consolidation in the energy market.

On this basis, the Commission had sufficient information at hand to come up with a normative acceptable gas draft directive (European Commission 2001a, 3). On March 13, 2001, the Commission tabled its legislative proposal, which consisted of quantitative and qualitative provisions. As a quantitative provision, this draft suggested opening the gas market in two steps: by 2004 for all nondomestic customers, and by 2005, for all customers without exceptions. Qualitative provisions were those regarding the unbundling of vertically integrated gas undertakings (namely, legal and functional unbundling with exemptions for small-scale distribution companies), regulatory oversight (which should be carried out by an independent regulatory authority), PSO (particularly those addressing consumer protection), and a minimum obligation regarding access to the network (which should be regulated TPA based on published tariffs subject of a priori approval by the regulatory authority). A decision window had opened.

5.1.5 *Interim Conclusion*

The MSF does not manage to explain completely why the agenda changed in March 2001 (see Table 5.3). The analysis corroborates Hypothesis 1: The problem stream, political stream, and policy stream had been ripe prior to the agenda change. Although the agenda window had been opened by a change in the political stream (Hypothesis 8), the timing of its opening remains striking. More precisely, it is surprising that the Commission did not include energy legislation in its policy priorities for the years 2000–2005 in early January to suggest its revision in late February 2000. This applies because the European Council had already outlined at its meeting in Helsinki in December 1999 that it would deal with the question of how "to exploit fully the potential of the single market and the single currency" in order to strengthen "employment, economic reform and social cohesion in the framework of a knowledge-based economy" (European Council 1999a, Recitals 32 and 33). As a policy-entrepreneur, the Commission would have seized that opportunity by drawing the executive's attention to energy liberalization, for instance, by including it in the legislative program of the forthcoming year. This did not happen. On the contrary, the Commission had already ruled out the possibility to reflect on revising the current gas directive in November 1999 because it deemed this to be appropriate only after the expiration of its implementation deadline on August 10, 2000 (*EU Neues Bulletin* November 30, 1999). In addition, the Commission stated to be satisfied with the progress and output of implementation at the beginning of 2000 (European Commission 2000b). To conclude, neither the problem nor the political stream had changed in a way significantly enough to explain why the Commission suddenly came up with the idea to push energy liberalization back on the agenda between the publication of its working program and its contribution to the European Council meeting in Lisbon.[8]

After the agenda window had opened, all branches of the EU's executive and legislature stressed the need for a revised gas directive. Due to (1) policy feedback (such as the Commission's report on the state of implementation of the first gas directive and ongoing infringement proceedings) and (2) being included in the Commission's working program and the European Council's, Council's and EP's agenda, the agenda window remained open (Definition 4). Furthermore, it became clear that all relevant actors shared the perception that the incomplete IEM was problematic, and agreed on addressing this problem by means of a revised gas directive.

Table 5.3 How well the multiple streams framework fares in explaining how the second gas directive entered the decision agenda

Directive	*2003/55/EC*
The MSF's necessary conditions for agenda change	
The likelihood for an agenda change increases if	
H1 the problem stream, political stream, and policy stream are ripe;	+
H2 a change in the problem or political stream opens an agenda window; *and*	+
H3 a policy-entrepreneur succeeds in coupling the streams.	–
Specifying H2: Equifinal paths to the opening of an agenda window	
H4 An agenda window opens in the problem stream if	
(a) a relevant indicator deteriorates;	
(b) an evaluation study points to a discrepancy between the program's goal and the program's effects; or	(+)
(c) a focusing event relevant to the policy field in question occurs.	
H5 An agenda window opens in the political stream if	
(a) a new Commission takes office; or	
(b) the Commission publishes a working program.	(+)
H6 An agenda window opens in the political stream if	
(a) a new Council Presidency takes office; or	
(b) one or consecutive Council Presidencies release their working program(s).	
H7 An agenda window opens in the political stream if the European Council publishes acts which provide impetus for the EU's development.	(+)
H8 An agenda window opens in the political stream if (at least) one branch of the EU's executive or legislature tasks one (other) branch of the EU's executive to address an issue.	+ (+)
Specifying H3: Agenda coupling	
H9 The policy-entrepreneur is more likely to successfully couple the streams during an open agenda window,	
(a) the more persistent he or she is; and	n.a.
(b) the more access to key policy-makers he or she has.	n.a.

Source: Own compilation.
Notes: "–" indicates that a hypothesis is falsified, "(+)" indicates that the hypothesis' independent variable had kept the agenda window open, although the policy stream had not been ripe, and "n.a." stands for not applicable.

As a consequence, coupling strategies of a policy-entrepreneur were not required to link the policy stream with the problem and political stream. And since no policy-entrepreneur was required to couple all three streams, Hypothesis 9 is not corroborated by the data. This does not mean that there had not been any policy-entrepreneur engaged during agenda-setting. The

Commission engaged as a policy-entrepreneur in the problem and policy streams. Following Cram (1994, 199), the Commission acted as a "purposeful opportunist". Purposeful opportunists do not just present themselves centrally once an opportunity had arisen but also seek to actively transform the context in a way which makes it more likely that an opportunity emerges in the first place. It was the Commission which inserted a review clause in the legislative proposal of the first gas directive (European Commission 1992, Article 28) and which carried this provision through the decision-making process. Thereby, the Commission had a provision at hand that it could use to draw attention to the problematic state of the IEM. This could result at least in making the problem stream ripe (which had been the case here) and at best in opening an agenda window in the problem stream.

In the policy stream, the Commission pursued the same strategy as during the first gas directive process (see 4.1.4.2): It engaged in institutionalizing and contributing to the policy community. Hence, it did not just create opportunities for the policy community to work out proposals but also influenced the proposals' design by actively participating in the policy community. However, there was no need for investing time, energy, reputation, or money (Kingdon 1984, 188) to couple the three streams since this linkage had already been wished for and anticipated by the involved actors. Thus, in a strict sense, Hypothesis 3 could not be confirmed by the data.

5.2 Policy Change

Decision coupling started with the tabling of the legislative proposal in mid-March 2001 and ended with the Council approving the gas directive in mid-June 2003. With regard to the European policy cycle, this was a time of stability. Agenda and decision coupling took place during the Prodi Commission's term of office and during the same parliamentary term. Consequently, neither the relevant Commissioners in charge during this policy process (Energy Commissioner Loyola de Palacio and Competition Commissioner Mario Monti) nor the rapporteur of the parliamentary committee responsible, the Committee on Industry, External Trade, Research, and Energy (Bernhard Rapkay), changed. The analysis of decision coupling focuses on two aspects: the length of decision coupling (Hypothesis 11, Sect. 5.2.1) and political entrepreneurs' coupling strategies (Hypothesis 10, Sect. 5.2.2).

5.2.1 Length of Decision Coupling

According to Hypothesis 11a, decision coupling is more likely to be lengthy if agenda change has taken place against the will of veto actors. Put differently, decision coupling is more likely to happen quickly if agenda change was supported by the veto actors. The facts provide strong evidence that this hypothesis holds: (1) Decision coupling took around two years, which is rather short when compared with almost six years and three months in the case of the previous gas directive process; and (2) this time, the gas draft directive did not enter the decision agenda against the will of veto actors but even on behalf of them (see 5.1.4.1).

If policy-makers' attention is redirected to other issues, decision coupling is more likely to be lengthy (Hypothesis 11b). Whether policy-makers' attention was distracted can be extrapolated by the analysis of their agendas. The *Commission* referred to the IEM in all working programs it released during decision coupling (European Commission 2001d, 11, 2002c, 11, 21). During that time, the *European Council* met eight times. At four of these meetings, the European Council invited the Commission, the Council, or the EP to progress negotiations on the gas draft directive (European Council 2001, 2002a, b, 2003). The Council meetings during decision coupling were presided over by Sweden (January to June 2001), Belgium (July to December 2001), Spain (January to June 2002), Denmark (July to December 2002), and Greece (January to June 2003). Of these *Council Presidencies*, Sweden (2001, 12), Spain (2002), and Greece (2003, 17) explicitly included the liberalization of the gas market in their working programs. The programs of the Belgian and Danish Presidencies are not available. However, according to secondary sources, the Belgian Presidency worked together with the Swedish and Spanish Presidencies in order to facilitate the decision-making process and get the gas draft directive adopted under the Spanish Presidency (*European Report* May 16, 2001). The Danish Presidency set this draft directive two times on the agenda of the Council, which suggests it was one of its priorities during its term of presidency, too. Between May 2001 and June 2003, the *Council* debated the gas proposal six times (Council of the European Union 2001a, b, 2002a, b, c, 2003b) and adopted it in written procedure (Council of the European Union 2003d) without debate (Council of the European Union 2003c). This leads to the conclusion that the gas draft directive was neither crowded out from the Council's agenda, nor considered to be of low priority. Finally, the *EP* dealt with it intensively: From its referral to the

Committee on Industry, External Trade, Research, and Energy on May 14, 2001, to its first reading in parliament on March 13, 2002, the EP addressed the gas draft directive 11 times. Before the second reading in parliament, the committee dealt with the gas draft eight times between February 13, 2003, and June 4, 2003 (Committee on Industry, External Trade, Research and Energy 2002, 2003). This quantitative overview shows that all policy-makers had their attention focused on the gas draft directive. Consequently, Hypothesis 11b holds: Since the gas proposal remained in the policy-makers' attention, decision coupling was not protracted, but happened quickly, particularly in comparison with decision coupling of the first gas directive.

5.2.2 *Political Entrepreneurs' Coupling Strategies*

The analysis so far has documented that the involved actors agreed on revising the first gas directive in order to boost competition in the market. The gas draft directive in its current version was composed of several ideas the policy community had worked out and (predominantly) considered to be prominent (see 5.1.4.2). In contrast to the first gas directive process, the negotiations dispensed the stage of questioning the legitimacy or feasibility of the entire policy project and entered into technical and political discussions right from the start. This led to a completely different climate for negotiations. As the majority of member states, the Commission, and the EP already supported the gas proposal, there was no fixed (and small) group of political entrepreneurs engaged in pushing it through the decision-making stage. It was more of a joint effort of those policy-makers supporting the gas draft directive to revise it in a way that made it acceptable for all veto actors. Therefore, the subsequent analysis takes another approach to analyzing political entrepreneurs' activities. Instead of searching for political entrepreneurs who promoted the draft directive in its entirety, I concentrate on political entrepreneurs who tried to build support for those provisions of the legislative proposal that were controversial among the veto actors.

However, this does not imply that there had not been any political entrepreneurs who promoted the gas draft directive as such. For instance, Peter Hain, Energy Minister of the United Kingdom in the first half of 2001, actively supported gas market liberalization and pressed the Commission to speed up the revision of the gas directive (*The Guardian* May 9, 2001). Furthermore, he drew attention to the imbalance between continental energy companies taking over British utilities while being shielded from competition in their domestic markets (*Electric Utility Week* May 14, 2001, *The Guardian* May 11, 2001). His successor, Brian Wilson, and Wilson's shadow minister, Crispin Blunt, also pushed for gas market liberalization (*Daily Telegraph* November 26, 2002, *The Guardian* November 26, 2002, *The Sunday Telegraph* November 24, 2002). In a similar vein, Energy Commissioner Loyola de Palacio promoted the entire draft directive on several occasions (cf. *Europe Energy* February 1, 2001, *European Report* May 16, 2001) and visited the capitals of those member states whose agreement on the gas proposal was uncertain before the Energy Council meeting in November 2002 (*European Report* November 20, 2002). Since all Council Presidencies had the negotiation of the gas draft directive as one of their top priorities, they also acted as political entrepreneurs (see previous subsection).

While these political entrepreneurs' actions had been supportive in terms of keeping negotiations ongoing, crucial to policy adoption was achieving the consensus of all veto actors with regard to controversial issues. The veto actors whose approval on specific issues was most questionable were France and Germany, since their resistance against parts of the Commission's legislative proposal was particularly strong (European Commission 2002b: 28, *European Report* May 16, 2001, June 12, 2002) and protracted negotiations in the Council and European Council (*The Guardian* May 11, 2001). This was particularly delicate because the Commission had already sent letters of reminders to France and Germany (as well as to Luxembourg) for not having implemented the first gas directive in due time. Regarding France and Germany, this stipulated in the Commission's initiation of infringement proceedings in the course of 2001 for failure to transpose or transpose completely the gas directive (European Commission 2001a, 11, 2002b, 28). Thus, I concentrate on whether and how political entrepreneurs managed to overcome these member states' resistance and to get the gas draft directive adopted.

In a nutshell, France opposed the provisions regarding market opening and legal unbundling (European Commission 2002b: 28, *Agence France* November 18, 2002, *European Report* November 23, 2002), while Germany particularly disapproved having a regulator imposed upon its own market (European Commission 2002b: 28, *Electric Utility Week* May 14, 2001). The subsequent subsections analyze whether political entrepreneurs accomplished to (1) settle package deals (Hypothesis 10a), (2) offer concessions (Hypothesis 10b), or (3) provide meaning, clarification, and identity to the issue at stake (Hypothesis 10c) with regard to market opening (5.2.2.1), legal unbundling (5.2.2.2), and regulatory oversight (5.2.2.3).

5.2.2.1 Market Opening

The first gas directive had defined the minimum degree of market openness: 20 percent by August 2000, 28 percent by 2003, and 33 percent by 2018 (98/30/EC, Article 18). As a consequence, the market opening varied tremendously between the member states, although most member states had opted to open their markets to a greater extent than envisaged by the first gas directive (cf. European Commission 2001b; see also Table 5.1). However, France had already announced that it would only open its gas market to the required minimum level in order to give its national champion, Gaz de France (GdF), time to adjust to competition (*European Voice* November 4, 1999). On top of that, it failed to implement the first gas directive by the date of transposition in August 2000. By delaying the directive's implementation, France shielded its domestic market from foreign investors and kept the monopoly of GdF intact. As a consequence, member states that had taken the liberalization route purposefully had put their energy companies in a disadvantageous situation: Due to the introduction of competition, their market shares were shrinking (*Energy Economist* December 1, 1996), which qualified them as easy takeover candidates for GdF and Électricité de France (EdF) (given that the French electricity market was equally shielded from competition). GdF and EdF had plenty of resources to do so, thanks to their still prevailing monopoly position (*The Guardian* June 19, 2002). This had led to the isolation of France from the other member states.

The reactions of Spain and the United Kingdom demonstrated the extent of France's isolation. Spain had already passed a law in 1999 which limited foreign investors' voting rights to 3 percent regardless of capital ownership if the companies were publicly owned (*Electric Utility Week* May 14, 2001). In a similar vein, the United Kingdom started thinking about ways to "[hold, N.H.] up European forays into the UK market", conceding that it might "not be possible but, at the very least, we would force Brussels to intervene and impose an investigation on competition grounds, holding up the process" (a senior UK government official, quoted in *The Guardian* May 9, 2001). Moreover, Spain and the United Kingdom explicitly linked blocking French companies from acquiring assets of their domestic energy utilities to France's rejection to open its market as provided for in the first gas directive (*Electric Utility Week* May 14, 2001).

Consequently, it was no surprise that the Commission's suggestion to fully open the gas market for nonhousehold customers by January 1, 2004, and for all customers a year later (European Commission 2001c, Article 2, Recital 12) was met with resistance by France, while it was warmly welcomed by the majority of member states (European Commission 2002b, 28). France even seized the first opportunity to question this schedule, which was only a few days after the Commission had published its legislative proposal (European Commission 2001c) at the European Council meeting in Stockholm in mid-March 2001. On this occasion, France strongly criticized the suggested schedule and made sure that the conclusions did not include a specific date for market opening but a general commitment to consider a timetable for market opening as soon as possible (*Electric Utility Week* May 14, 2001; European Council 2001, Recital 17).

The French government's resistance was based on electoral considerations. In contrast to other member states, France encountered resistance from trade unions and powerful public-sector unions, with the latter fearing that a liberalized gas market could launch the privatization of GdF (*Agence France* May 9, 2001, November 18, 2002, *FT Energy Newsletter* May 14, 2001). Furthermore, local elections in the spring of 2001 revealed waning support for the Socialist-led government. Thus, with parliamentary and presidential elections looming in the spring of 2002, France intended to protract the negotiation of the second gas directive in order to avoid upsetting its electorate (*The Guardian* May 11, 2001, *FT Energy Newsletter* May 11, 2001, May 14, 2001).

How did political entrepreneurs manage to settle an agreement in this situation? The analysis of the negotiation process reveals that political entrepreneurs made use of all strategies contained in Hypothesis 10, as will be shown in the following.

Initiated by Sweden, the current Presidency, the Council addressed a set of yet unsettled questions regarding the Commission's gas draft directive at its meeting in May 2001. However, with regard to market opening, the Council did not manage to agree on how to achieve it. The Swedish Presidency just concluded that "[t]here is broad consensus that the market opening concerning both gas and electricity should be actively pursued and accelerated" and announced to find, together with the incoming Belgian and Spanish Presidencies, "means and ways within the existing Council framework" to accelerate market opening and to "come back with appropriate ideas to be presented to the Council" (Council of the European Union 2001a). The fact that these three successive presidencies agreed on joining forces indicates that they acted as political entrepreneurs and did not just fulfill their duty when their term of presidency had come. In order to push up the negotiations, the Belgian Presidency made use of its power to structure the agenda (Tallberg 2003) and excluded the question of how to open the market from the next Council meeting's agenda in December 2001 in order to concentrate on less controversial issues (Council of the European Union 2001b). Furthermore, it passed the negotiation of market opening on to the European Council, which addressed it at its meeting in mid-March 2002 under the Spanish Presidency. The Spanish Presidency applied salami tactics and set only the negotiation of a date for full market opening for *nonhousehold consumers* on the European Council's agenda and left aside the question of when to open the market for *all consumer groups*. However, this did not suffice to overcome the French blockage on settling on a specific date. Since the French government was concerned that the issue of opening the gas market was highly unpopular among its electorate, it insisted on concessions. The other member states were not willing to grant concessions on this issue—but on an unrelated reform package regarding rail freight arrangements (*Agence France* November 18, 2002). This reform package aimed at liberalizing European railways and was met with harsh resistance equally by French unions and by the French state-owned rail company (*Morning Star* March 15, 2002). Hence, political entrepreneurs proposed and pushed through a package deal, namely, concessions regarding rail freight arrangements, in return for France's agreement on 2004 as the date for market opening for nonhousehold consumers. Although this solution did not shield the French government from electoral pressure regarding energy liberalization, it did decrease electoral pressure regarding railway liberalization. In terms of the likelihood of getting the gas draft directive adopted, the package deal had made it more likely because it had reduced the amount of issues in need of a compromise (Hypothesis 10a).

Simultaneously and independently from the Council Presidencies' entrepreneurial activities, the Commission also acted as a political entrepreneur. As had been the case in the first gas directive process, the Commission threatened to decide on the gas draft directive itself based on its powers under Article 86(3) of the EC Treaty if member states were unable or unwilling to adopt it. The Commission revived this threat on two occasions: in June 2001 and in January 2002 (European Commission 2002b, 29, *World Gas Intelligence* January 28, 2002). The fact that the Commission resorted to this threat showed its dissatisfaction with the entire negotiation process. Its timing can be related to the stalled negotiation regarding the issue of the market opening, which it judged to be the key to completing the IEM. Both times, it happened a month after a meeting of the Energy Council, at which the issue of market openness was either adjourned (in May 2001) or excluded from the agenda (in December 2001). The Commission intended to worsen the member states perceived fallback position by threatening to decide on gas market liberalization itself, since this would have excluded the member states from policy formulation. According to Hypothesis 9c, this should increase the likelihood of policy adoption. However, the Commission's success was mixed. After the Commission had first voiced its Article 86(3) threat in June 2001, neither the Council nor the European Council addressed the issue of market opening at their next meetings. Obviously, this did not increase the likelihood of policy adoption. In contrast, the European Council took the issue up immediately at its next meeting, after the Commission had called to mind its Article 86 (3) option in January 2002. However, this also did not culminate in the European Council settling the issue of market opening conclusively as it just agreed for a date to open the market for nonhousehold consumers.

Since the member states barring France (*European Daily Electricity Markets* November 22, 2002), the EP (*Europe Energy* February 1, 2002), and the Commission agreed that the market should be opened to all customers by January 2005, the Commission retained that date in its amended gas proposal, which was tabled in June 2002 (European Commission 2002a). Nonetheless, at their next Council meetings, the member states could not settle an agreement on market opening for households and listed it as one (out of four) outstanding issues (Council of the European Union 2002b). Before the next Council meeting in December 2002, France said that it would want two to four years longer to open the market for household consumers, which would mean opening the market between 2007 and 2009. Furthermore, it stressed that this provisional time frame would be subject to a number of (yet unreleased) conditions (*European Daily Electricity Markets* November 22, 2002, *Les Echos* November 19, 2002). At this December meeting, France conditioned its agreement on specifying a date for fully opening the market on reviewing the impact of liberalization on the industrial sector (*European Daily Electricity Market* November 22, 2002, *European Report* November 23, 2002) The member states agreed on that condition and tasked the Commission to report by January 1, 2006, on (inter alia) the consequences of the market opening (Council of the European Union 2003a, 4). In return, France agreed to open the market for households by July 1, 2004. The member states had been willing to offer and grant France a concession on the original draft (Hypothesis 10b), which made policy adoption more likely.

Given that France had been unwilling to settle a compromise before, it insisted only on a small departure from the Commission's initial legislative proposal. While it had indicated to insist on delaying market opening for two to four years, it had accepted a six months' delay. Although the political entrepreneurs' coupling strategies might have contributed to increasing France's willingness to compromise, it is not plausible that they alone can explain why France agreed on such a small concession. Indeed, the French agreement on the gas draft directive's provisions on market opening was widely attributed to the election of a center-right government in the summer of 2002 (*The Electricity Daily* December 4, 2002, *The Guardian* November 26, 2002, *The Times* November 26, 2002).

The question of whether the previous government would have settled the same compromise is impossible to answer. However, it seems likely that it would also have agreed to a compromise as a reaction to (1) political entrepreneurs' coupling activities; (2) France's increasing isolation from the other member states, the EP, and the Commission; and (3) the knowledge that France could easily be outvoted in the Council, because in order to pass the gas draft directive, it needed only a qualitative majority, not a unanimous vote in the Council (*Irish Independent* November 26, 2002). At the same time, it is highly probable that a Socialist-led government would have insisted on a less far-reaching compromise than its successor, given that a Socialist-led government would have paid more attention to electoral and ideological concerns.

5.2.2.2 Unbundling Requirements

The first gas directive stipulated that integrated natural gas undertakings were required to separate accounts for their natural gas transmission, distribution, and storage activities, and, where appropriate, for their nongas activities. In its legislative proposal, the Commission suggested remarkable modifications on that issue. These modifications originated from the public hearing preceding the drafting of the legislative proposal and were wished for by an "overwhelming majority of those commenting during the hearing" (European Commission 2001c, 37). More precisely, the Commission suggested functional and legal unbundling of TSO and DSO (distribution system operator) from its integrated parent company. Regarding DSO, the gas draft directive allowed for (1) a delay until 2004 and (2) an exception for integrated natural gas undertakings serving less than 100,000 customers. Furthermore, it tasked the Commission to monitor whether the unbundling requirements were sufficient in order to create a level playing field and, in the case they were not, to submit appropriate proposals for further actions.

As stressed in the explanatory memorandum accompanying the Commission's gas draft directive, these provisions were supported by almost all stakeholders. However, France violently opposed the idea of legal unbundling (*European Report* June 12, 2002). Therefore, this issue turned out to be in need for further discussions at the Energy Council's meeting in May 2001. The Council President concluded that "[t]he principle of unbundling meets general agreement, whereas its concrete modalities still have to be clarified" (Council of the European Union 2001a, 8). The member states agreed that unbundling in the gas sector might be different from unbundling in the electricity sector. The latter was negotiated at the next Energy Council meeting in December 2001, but could not been settled conclusively (Council of the European Union 2001b). While the European Council had settled a compromise regarding market opening for nonhousehold consumers in March 2002, it remained vague on the question of unbundling on this occasion. It just stressed its support for the "separation of transmission and distribution from production and supply" (European Council 2002a, Recital 37) and left the negotiation about how to achieve this in the hands of the Council and the EP.

Between June and November 2002, the Council met three times and addressed the question of legal unbundling (Council of the European Union 2002a, 24, b, 17, c, 5–6). According to Hypothesis 10, I expect to see political entrepreneurs (1) settle a package deal, (2) grant concessions, or (3) manipulate the problem–solution linkage (or a combination of all three strategies). Given the stakeholders' overwhelming support of legal unbundling, manipulating the problem–solution linkage was not a promising strategy. As France had been unimpressed so far from this problem–solution linkage, it was not very probable that reinforcing this linkage would have made it more willing to compromise on that issue. On the other hand, establishing another problem perception would have required any political entrepreneur to invest massive resources without knowing whether the new problem perception would be accepted by veto actors. Consequently, a package deal or concessions were more likely to be within reach. Since France had been by far the strongest opponent of legal unbundling, the question was: How could political entrepreneurs convince France from this provision?

The timing of negotiations could not have been more favorable, because they took place after the French presidential election in April and May 2002. As outlined above, this had led to a change in government. In contrast to the outgoing Socialist-led government, the incoming center-right government had less ideological issues with the idea to introduce competition in the energy market. This can be seen in its decision to privatize partially GdF and EdF, which was announced by the new French Prime Minister Jean-Pierre Raffarin in July 2002 (*Agence France* November 18, 2002). In order to prepare the partial privatization of GdF, it should be divided into three units: (1) infrastructure (transport and distribution networks), (2) upstream activities (exploration, production, research), and (3) commercial operations (*Les Echos* June 12, 2002). France had also elected a new parliament, which reflected the election results of the presidential elections. This newly elected parliament was in favor of legal unbundling in the gas sector and even proposed the French government to anticipate it in its privatization plans for GdF (*European Report* November 23, 2002). From the point of view of political entrepreneurs, these domestic changes in France promised to make it more willing to compromise and to agree on either a package deal or concessions. Since the French government feared that it could test its electorate patience too much with simultaneously pushing for partial privatization in France and accepting an EU obligation to legally unbundle GdF's units, it was more likely that France would accept concessions than agree to a package deal.

At the Council meeting in October 2002, the member states managed to narrow down which concessions might be feasible. The options to introduce legal unbundling while (1) granting some flexibility regarding the implementation deadlines and (2) allowing for slightly different provisions for TSO and DSO were particularly prominent (Council of the European Union 2002b, 17). Before the next Council meeting in November 2002, Energy Commissioner de Palacio visited France in order to promote these options (*European Report* November 10, 2002). At the same November Council meeting, the member states finally managed to settle a compromise (Hypothesis 10b): They agreed to postpone the implementation of unbundling of DSOs until July 1, 2007. Furthermore, they allowed

> some degree of co-ordination between the parent company and its subsidiaries to continue. Unbundling provisions would not imply a requirement to

> separate the ownership of transmission or distribution network assets from vertically integrated companies. (Council of the European Union 2002c, 5)

The compromise included tasking the Commission to produce a report due in 2006, which had to address (inter alia) whether other measures had been developed which had effects equivalent to legal unbundling (Council of the European Union 2002c, 6).

This compromise was criticized by the EP because it favored clearer unbundling provisions (*Europe Energy* February 1, 2002, *European Report* November 26, 2003, *Platts Oilgram News* November 26, 2002). Consequently, the EP's committee in charge came up with amendments. More precisely, it suggested (1) a better definition of functional unbundling, including clarifying that functional unbundling should become compulsory with the directive's entry into force; and (2) greater clarity regarding the possibility for DSOs to derogate legal unbundling up to 2007. In order to get the draft directive adopted, the Commission, Council, and EP entered negotiations in an informal trialogue (*European Report* April 26, 2003). Everybody on the negotiation table granted and accepted concessions concerning the EP's amendments on unbundling (Hypothesis 9b). While the provisions regarding functional unbundling had only slightly been revised, those aiming at clarifying the conditions under which DSO might derogate from legal unbundling more clearly carried the EP's mark (compare, for instance, the EP's suggestion for and the directive's wording of Article 29 [Committee on Industry, External Trade, Research and Energy 2003 versus 2003/55/EC, Article 29]). The EP was willing to compromise on this issue because it had consistently supported greater liberalization (*The Electricity Daily* December 4, 2002) and did not want to risk stopping the entire reform package by insisting on its amendments. Hence, it accepted this compromise and confirmed it in plenary vote on June 4, 2003, which was followed by the Council's approval on June 16, 2003.

5.2.2.3 *Regulatory Oversight*

Regarding the issue of regulatory oversight, the Commission had suggested an encompassing revision of Article 22 of the first gas directive. This article simply stated:

> Member States shall create appropriate and efficient mechanisms for regulation, control and transparency so as to avoid any abuse of a dominant position, in particular to the detriment of consumers, and any predatory behaviour.

> These mechanisms shall take account of the provisions of the Treaty, and in particular Article 86 thereof.

Although not all, the vast majority of member states had opted to assign regulatory responsibilities to general energy or common gas and electricity regulators (European Commission 2001a, 15). By 2001, all contributing stakeholders had pleaded for strongly independent regulatory authorities at the public hearing, which was organized by the Commission in September 2000 (European Commission 2001a, 72). Consequently, the Commission suggested requiring member states to establish national regulatory authorities (NRAs), which should be independent from the interests of the gas industry. The gas draft directive specified a (brief) set of responsibilities that these regulatory authorities should be assigned with, inter alia, approving tariffs and conditions for network access a priori and defining rules for capacity allocation (European Commission 2001c, 38, 60).

This suggestion was heavily criticized by Germany because it was incompatible with its regulatory environment (*European Report* November 20, 2002). Germany's regulatory oversight consisted of a combination of antitrust law, merger control, and voluntary industry agreements (Verbändevereinbarung) (*FT Energy Newsletter* February 6, 2001). This regulatory setup was by far independent from the interests of the gas industry since they were explicitly tasked to negotiate the terms and conditions of network access. However, Germany stressed that these voluntary industry agreements were adequate for the German gas and electricity markets, which, in contrast to other member states' markets, were not characterized by monopolies at the downstream market but by over thousand energy companies. Germany opposed the idea to establish NRAs. In order to make its point, Germany (implicitly) referred to the principle of subsidiarity by asking for respect of the member states' identity and stressing that the Commission's suggestion regarding regulatory oversight clearly failed to respect the German one (*European Report* November 20, 2002). Put differently, Germany intended to change the problem perception by means of framing, which should make the other member states willing to grant Germany concessions (Hypothesis 10c).

In fact, Germany managed to convince the other member states that the provisions regarding regulatory oversight needed more implementation leeway at the Energy Council's meeting in December 2001. At this meeting, the Council concluded that a possible compromise could be to leave the setup of the appropriate institutional frameworks to the member states and to specify "a precise list of regulatory functions to be fulfilled, particularly regarding monitoring, approval of methods and rules, and dispute settlement" (Council of the European Union 2001b, 9) instead. The European Council (2001, Recital 37) confirmed this idea in March 2002 and urged to establish in each member state "a regulatory function, within the appropriate regulatory framework, with a view to ensuring in particular effective control of the tariff-setting conditions". For instance, the Council (2002a, 24) discussed how the effective control of tariff-setting conditions could be ensured in June 2002. At this time, the idea to define regulatory functions had been on the table for a year. Since then, an extensive list of regulatory functions had evolved. Consequently, the Commission's modified legislative proposal (European Commission 2002a), published in June 2002, incorporated the Council's suggestions as well as several amendments the EP had suggested. The text of the final gas directive did not change much until its passage a year later. Hence, the involved actor's willingness to grant concessions on the original proposal made policy adoption more likely (Hypothesis 10b).

The resulting compromise was very detailed and encompassing. This can be illustrated by its mere length. While the corresponding article had a length of 25 lines in the first gas directive (98/30/EC, Articles 21(2)–(3) and 22), it was 106 lines long in the second one (2003/55/EC, Article 25). Since Germany had opposed the provision to set up a regulatory authority because it would not allow for respecting the German identity, it is puzzling that such an encompassing list did not seem to restrict it. This resulted from (1) political entrepreneurs' framing activities and (2) waning support from German policy-makers for their domestic solution.

The German regulatory environment was frequently accused of restricting competition in the gas market. A case in point is the fact that the Commission initiated an infringement proceeding against Germany in June 2001. Furthermore, two evaluation studies, one carried out by Germany's Institute for Applied Ecology and one by the consultancy Accenture, concluded that Germany had failed to deliver the regulatory environment necessary to boost competition (*The Guardian* May 30, 2002). In addition, Germany itself was increasingly embarrassed and isolated from the other member states due to its lack of an energy regulator, which was particularly apparent at the meetings of the Madrid Forum (*European Spot Gas Markets* October 31, 2002). Apart from European pressure, domestic pressure came up when the renegotiations of the voluntary industry agreements stalled in the second half of 2001. This even led federal economics minister Werner Müller to threaten the introduction of a regulatory authority as a substitute to the voluntary industry agreements (*FT Energy Newsletter* June 2001). Similarly, the cartel office criticized the negotiation partners for insufficient progress on introducing competition in the gas market in June 2001 (Klag 2003, 220). By January 2002, the German government distanced itself from its own regulatory environment due to signs of breakdown of gas liberalization talks and considered to give the cartel office additional powers regarding the regulation of gas market (*World Gas Intelligence* January 28, 2002).[9] Thus, the German support of its own solution decreased and made it willing to accept precise provisions regarding regulatory functions.

The EP proposed only a few amendments regarding regulatory oversight (European Parliament 2003), which had overwhelmingly been accepted by the Council and the Commission at trialogue negotiations. The suggestions had been minor ones and predominantly congruent with the Commission's and Council's position. The EP suggested expanding the NRA's (already encompassing) monitoring tasks to also monitor the level of transparency and competition. Furthermore, it suggested assigning NRAs responsible for ensuring competition as well as charging them with the task to publish their opinion on requests for an exemption for major new gas infrastructure from the provisions regarding TPA competition (see European Parliament 2003, Article 22, paragraph 3a, and Article 25, paragraph 1g–h).

5.2.3 *Interim Conclusion*

Only two years and three months after the Commission had published its legislative proposal for a revised gas directive, Directive 2003/55/EC was adopted. This was a (comparatively) short policy process. According to Hypothesis 11, policy adoption is more likely to be lengthy if agenda change has not been supported by veto actors and if policy-makers' attention is redirected to other issues. Since all stakeholders supported the revision of the gas directive and gave it a top priority continuously, the short duration of decision coupling confirms Hypothesis 11.

Since all veto actors had supported setting the revision of the gas directive on the decision agenda, it has proven difficult to identify political entrepreneurs. There are mainly two reasons for this. First, like policy-entrepreneurs, political entrepreneurs "invest their resources (…) in order to promote a position in return for anticipated future gain" (Kingdon 1984, 188). Since the veto actors overwhelmingly agreed on revising the first gas directive in a way that would increase competition in the natural gas market, there was little need for investing resources in order to promote that position. Consequently, discussions remained mostly objective and did not resemble political entrepreneurs pushing for their favorite policy. Second, policy-entrepreneurs and political entrepreneurs are conceptualized as agents of change in the MSF. If the vast majority of involved actors already aim at making a policy change happen, it is rather difficult to delimit policy-makers' engagement in decision-making from policy-makers' engagement in policy entrepreneurship

However, the MSF basically aims at explaining why an issue's time to rise on the agenda and get adopted finally comes. Given the vast support for the gas draft directive, I looked for issues on which at least one veto actor was unwilling to compromise. Since failing to settle a compromise would have led to policy stability, this was where political entrepreneurs mattered most. Therefore, the analysis concentrated on (1) identifying those provisions of the legislative proposal that some veto actors opposed to the point of blockage[10] and (2) explaining how political entrepreneurs tried to build support for them. The provisions regarding market opening and legal unbundling were blocked by France and those provisions regarding regulatory oversight by Germany. Thus, I analyzed whether political entrepreneurs managed to (1) settle package deals, (2) offer and grant concessions, or (3) provide meaning, clarification, and identity. Indeed, political entrepreneurs pursued all three strategies (see Table 5.4).

Interestingly, the Commission's threat to make use of its powers under Article 86(3) did not increase France's willingness to enter negotiations regarding the date for opening the natural gas market (Hypothesis 10c). It seemed as if the affected actors did not believe this threat to be credible. This might relate back to the fact that the Commission participated actively in the policy community, where it (partly) worked together with the same actors it now had to negotiate with. Following its own words and deciding on the issue itself would have constrained its relationship with the stakeholders, on whose (technical) input it depended in order to develop appropriate policy proposals. Since the stakeholders did not even comment on the Commission's threat, this suggests that they did not believe the Commission would follow that road.

I argued in Sect. 2.4.1.2 that national elections do not open an agenda window. The reason is that the Council tends to decide unanimously, which makes it unlikely that, due to a slightly changed composition of this body, a previously unnoticed issue suddenly rises on the Council's agenda. The

Table 5.4 Political entrepreneurs' coupling strategies

Issue	*Package deals (Hypothesis 10a)*	*Concessions (Hypothesis 10b)*	*Provision of meaning, clarification, and identity (Hypothesis 10c)*
Market opening	x	x	x
Unbundling requirements		x	
Regulatory oversight		x	x

Source: Own compilation

Table 5.5 How well the multiple streams framework fares in explaining how the second gas directive was passed

Directive	*2003/55/EC*
Explaining decision-making: decision coupling	
H10 Policy adoption is more likely if a political entrepreneur	
(a) manages to combine viable alternatives embraced by different veto actors into one package;	+
(b) can (and does) offer concessions on the original proposal; and	+
(c) succeeds in providing meaning, clarification, and identity to the issue at stake.	(−)
H11 Decision coupling is more likely to be lengthy if	
(a) agenda change has taken place against the will of veto actors; and	+
(b) policy-makers' attention is redirected to other issues.	+

Source: Own compilation
Note: "+" indicates that a hypothesis holds and "(−)" indicates that a hypothesis does not hold for the entire policy process analyzed

analysis of decision coupling suggested that national elections and feedback on domestic policies might have an impact on the probability of policy adoption. France became willing to settle a compromise regarding market opening under the newly elected center-right government, which had less ideological (and electoral) concerns with this issue. And Germany settled a compromise regarding the provisions for regulatory oversight after it became clear that its regulatory environment did not function properly, which was indicated by stalling (re-)negotiations of the voluntary industry agreements. In conclusion, apart from Hypothesis 10c, the analysis confirmed the hypotheses posed (Table 5.5).

Notes

1. For a summary of this crisis, see US Energy Information Agency (2015), http://www.eia.gov/ electricity/policies/legislation/california/subsequentevents.html, last accessed on April 16, 2015.
2. France and Germany even referred to the Californian supply crisis at the first meeting of the European Council, after the Commission had published its gas draft directive in order to argue against it. The remaining member states, however, did not follow their line of argumentation (*Utility Europe* May 1, 2001).
3. Germany's working program for the first half of 1999 is not available. According to a hearing held on this topic in the German parliament, the German Presidency had three main priorities for its term of office: increased employment for a Europe in a globalized world, introduction of the Euro, and structural reforms (Deutscher Bundestag, Plenarprotokoll 14/10, 549-551).
4. For a detailed analysis of this policy community and its activities, see Herweg (2016).
5. Due to Loyola de Palacio's death in 2006, I could not get firsthand evidence on what had made the Commission set a date for energy liberalization at the European Council meeting in Lisbon. Unfortunately, Loyola de Palacio's fellow Commissioners I managed to get in contact with also had no answer to this question.
6. Unfortunately, the agenda for the second meeting of the Madrid Forum is not available.
7. The Commission's presentation "An overview of implementation of the EU Gas Directive", held by Klaus Geil of DG TREN/A2, is available online at http://ec.europa.eu/energy/ gas_electricity/gas/forum_madrid_en.htm, last accessed on March 25, 2013.
8. For instance, although the follow-up group discussed at its third meeting on February 24, 2000, the state of implementation of the first gas directive, the problem stream did not change tremendously (Andersen 1999). The corresponding summary report was released in May 2000 and documented that the Commission evaluated the implementation process positively so far, particularly since most member states opted for a more far-reaching market opening than stipulated by the directive (European Commission 2000b). Consequently, it does not seem plausible that the Commission's contribution to the European Council meeting in Lisbon resulted from its

information gathering regarding the state of implementation of the gas directive.

9. The industry managed to settle an agreement by May 2002. However, this agreement expired in September 2003 and its renegotiation was suspended since the involved actors were not able to settle a compromise (*Europe Energy* June 3, 2003). Thus, by June 2003, Germany had decided to introduce a regulatory authority. In the summer of 2005, the Federal Network Agency (Bundesnetzagentur) was tasked with regulating the energy sector.
10. This resembles Korpi's (2006, 182) suggestion to differentiate between protagonists (policy initiator), consenters (actors getting involved after policy initiation), and antagonists (actors persisting in opposition).

References

2003/55/EC. *Directive of the European Parliament and of the Council of 26 June 2003 Concerning Common Rules for the Internal Market in Natural Gas and Repealing Directive 98/30/EC.*

96/642/EC. *Decision of 8 November 1996 Setting up an Energy Consultative Committee.*

98/30/EC. *Directive of the European Parliament and of the Council of 22 June 1998 Concerning Common Rules for the Internal Market in Natural Gas.*

Andersen, Svein S. 1999. European Integration and the Changing Paradigm on Energy Policy: The Case of Natural Gas Liberalisation. *ARENA Working Papers* WP 99/12.

Committee on Industry, External Trade, Research and Energy. 2000. *Report on the Commission's Second Report to the Council and the European Parliament on the State of Liberalization of the Energy Markets: A5-0189/2000.*

———. 2002. *Report on the Proposal for a Directive of the EUROPEAN Parliament and of the Council Amending Directive 96/92/EC and 98/30/EC Concerning Common Rules for the Internal Market in Electricity and Natural Gas: A5-0077/2002.*

———. 2003. *Recommendation for Second Reading on the Council Common Position for Adopting a European Parliament and Council Directive on Common Rules for the Internal Market in Natural Gas and Repealing Directive 98/30/EC: A5-00135/2003.*

Council of the European Union. 1999a. *Council Conclusions: 2176th Council Meeting, 11 May 1999.*

———. 1999b. *Council Conclusions: 2230th Council Meeting, 2 December 1999.*

———. 2000a. *Council Conclusions: 2267th Council meeting, 20 May 2000.*

———. 2000b. *Council Conclusions: 2318th Council Meeting, 5 December 2000.*
———. 2001a. *Council Conclusions: 2347th Council Meeting, 14–15 May 2001.*
———. 2001b. *Council Conclusions: 2394th Council Meeting, 4–5 December 2001.*
———. 2002a. *Council Conclusions: 2433rd Council meeting, 6–7 June 2002.*
———. 2002b. *Council Conclusions: 2452nd Council Meeting, 3–4 October 2002.*
———. 2002c. *Council Conclusions: 2456th Council Meeting, 25 November 2002.*
———. 2003a. *Common Position Adopted by the Council with a View to the Adoption of a Directive of the European Parliament and of the Council Concerning Common Rules for the Internal Market in Natural Gas and Repealing Directive 98/30/EC: 29 January 2003.*
———. 2003b. *Council Conclusions: 2507th Council Meeting, 14 May 2003.*
———. 2003c. *Council Conclusions: 2518th Council meeting, 16 June 2003.*
———. 2003d. *Decisions Adopted by Written Procedure: 1–3 February 2003.*
Cram, Laura. 1994. The European Commission as a Multi-Organization: Social Policy and IT Policy in the EU. *Journal of European Public Policy* 1(2): 195–217.
Eberlein, Burkard. 2005. Regulation by Cooperation: The 'Third Way' in Making Rules for the Internal Energy Market. In *Legal Aspects of EU Energy Regulation: Implementing the New Directives on Electricity and Gas Across Europe*, ed. Peter D. Cameron, 59–88. Oxford: Oxford University Press.
European Commission. 1985. *Completing the Internal Market. COM(85)310 Final.*
———. 1992. *Proposal for a Council Directive Concerning Common Rules for the Internal Market in Electricity. Proposal for a Council Directive Concerning Common Rules for the Internal Market in Natural Gas. COM(91)548 Final.*
———. 1998a. *Meeting of Follow-up Group 22 October 1998. Upstream Pipeline Networks.* Brussels.
———. 1998b. *State of Liberalization of the Energy Markets: COM(1998)212 Final.*
———. 1999a. *2nd Meeting of Follow-up Group 29 April 1999. Ship or Pay Contracts.* Brussels.
———. 1999b. *On the State of Liberalization of the Energy Markets. Second Report from the Commission to the Council and the European Parliament: COM(1999) 198 Final.*
———. 2000a. *Green Paper. Towards a European Strategy for the Security of Energy Supply: COM(2000)769 Final.*
———. 2000b. *State of Implementation of the EU Gas Directive (98/30/EC). An Overview: State of Play by the End of May 2000.* Brussels.
———. 2000c. *Strategic Objectives 2000–2005. Shaping the New Europe: COM (2000)154 Final.*
———. 2000d. *The Commission's Work Programme for 2000: COM(2000)155 Final.*
———. 2000e. *The Lisbon European Council—An Agenda of Economic and Social Renewal for Europe. Contribution of the European Commission to the special European Council in Lisbon, 23–24th March.*

———. 2001a. *Completing the Internal Energy Market. Commission Staff Working Paper: SEC(2001)438 Final.*
———. 2001b. *First Benchmarking Report on the Implementation of the Internal Electricity and Gas Market: SEC(2001)1957.*
———. 2001c. *Proposal for a Directive of the European Parliament and of the Council Amending Directives 96/92/EC and 98/30/EC Concerning Common Rules for the Internal Market in Electricity and Natural Gas: COM(2001)125 final.*
———. 2001d. *The Commission's Work Programme for 2002: COM(2001)620 Final.*
———. 2002a. *Amended Proposal for a Directive of the European Parliament and of the Council Amending Directives 96/92/EC and 98/30/EC Concerning Common Rules for the Internal Markets in Electricity and Gas: COM(2002)304 Final.*
———. 2002b. *European Union Competition Policy: XXXIst Report on Competition Policy 2001.* Luxembourg: Office for Official Publications of the European Communities.
———. 2002c. *The Commission's Legislative and Work Programme for 2003: COM (2002)590 Final.*
European Council. 1998a. *Presidency Conclusions: 11–12 December 1998.*
———. 1998b. *Presidency Conclusions: 15–16 June 1998.*
———. 1999a. *Presidency Conclusions: 10–11 December 1999.*
———. 1999b. *Presidency Conclusions: 15–16 October 1999.*
———. 1999c. *Presidency Conclusions: 24–25 March 1999.*
———. 1999d. *Presidency Conclusions: 3–4 June 1999.*
———. 2000a. *Presidency Conclusions: 19–20 June 2000.*
———. 2000b. *Presidency Conclusions: 23–24 March 2000.*
———. 2000c. *Presidency Conclusions: 7–9 December 2000.*
———. 2001. *Presidency Conclusions: 23–24 March 2001.*
———. 2002a. *Presidency Conclusions: 15–16 March 2002.*
———. 2002b. *Presidency Conclusions: 21–22 June 2002.*
———. 2003. *Presidency Conclusions: 20-21 March 2003.*
European Gas Regulatory Forum. 1999. *Minutes: 1st European Gas Regulatory Forum. Madrid, 30 September–1 October 1999:* Available Upon Request from the Author.
———. 2000a. *Agenda of the 3rd Meeting of the European Gas Regulatory Forum: 26–27 October 2000:* Available Upon Request from the Author.
———. 2000b. *Conclusions of the 2nd Meeting of the European Gas Regulatory Forum: 11–12 May 2000:* Available Upon Request from the Author.
European Parliament. 2003. *European Parliament Legislative Resolution on the Council Common Position for Adopting a European Parliament and Council Directive on Common Rules for the Internal Market in Natural Gas and Repealing Directive 98/30/EC: P5_TA(2003)0243.*

Finland. 1999. *Presidency of the Council of Ministers of the European Union: Programme for the Finnish Presidency of the European Union.*

Greece. 2003. *Presidency of the Council of Ministers of the European Union: The Priorities of the Greek Presidency. 1 January to 30 June 2003.*

Herweg, Nicole. 2016. Clarifying the Concept of Policy Communities in the Multiple Streams Framework. In *Decision-Making Under Ambiguity and Time Constraints: Assessing the Multiple Streams Framework*, ed. Reimut Zohlnhöfer and Friedbert Rüb, 125–145. Colchester: ECPR Press.

Jans, Jan H. 2011. Stop the Integration Principle? *Fordham International Law Journal* 33(5): 1533–1547.

Kingdon, John W. 1984. *Agendas, Alternatives, and Public Policies.* Boston: Little, Brown.

Klag, Nadja D. 2003. *Die Liberalisierung des Gasmarktes in Deutschland.* Marburg: Tectum Verlag.

Korpi, Walter. 2006. Power Resources and Employer-Centered Approaches in Explanations of Welfare States and Varieties of Capitalism: Protagonists, Consenters, and Antagonists. *World Politics* 58(2): 167–2006.

Landmarks Publications. 1992. *The European Public Affairs Directory 3 (1993): The Comprehensive Guide to Opinion-Formers in the Capital of Europe.* Brussels: Landmarks Publications.

———. 1994. *The European Public Affairs Directory 5 (1995): The Comprehensive Guide to Opinion-Formers in the Capital of Europe.* Brussels: Landmarks Publications.

———. 1996. *The European Public Affairs Directory 7 (1997): The Comprehensive Guide to Opinion-Formers in the Capital of Europe.* Brussels: Landmarks Publications.

———. 1998. *The European Public Affairs Directory 9 (1999): The Comprehensive Guide to Opinion-Formers in the Capital of Europe.* Brussels: Landmarks Publications.

———. 2000. *The European Public Affairs Directory 11 (2001): The Comprehensive Guide to Opinion-Formers in the Capital of Europe.* Brussels: Landmarks Publications.

———. 2002. *The European Public Affairs Directory 13 (2003): The Comprehensive Guide to Opinion-Formers in the Capital of Europe.* Brussels: Landmarks Publications.

Lenschow, Andrea. 2005. New Regulatory Approaches in "Greening" EU Policies. In *Environmental Policy in the European Union*, 2nd ed., ed. Andrew Jordan, 295–316. London/Sterling, VA: Earthscan.

Nylander, Johan. 2000. *The Power of Framing: A New-Institutional Approach to Interest Group Participation in the European Union.* Uppsala: Uppsala University.

Portugal. 1999. *Presidency of the Council of Ministers of the European Union: Portuguese Presidency of the European Union. 1 January to 30 June 2000. Programme.*

Spain. 2002. *La Presidencia española de la U.E. Las prioridades de la Presidencia española: 1 Enero de 30 Junio 2002.*

Sweden. 2001. *Presidency of the Council of Ministers of the European Union: Programme of the Swedish Presidency of the European Union. 1 January to 30 June 2001.*

Tallberg, Jonas. 2003. The Agenda-Shaping Powers of the EU Council Presidency. *Journal of European Public Policy* 10(1): 1–19.

United Kingdom. 1997. *Presidency of the Council of Ministers of the European Union: Work Programme, January–June 1998.*

CHAPTER 6

The Third Gas Directive Process

The analysis of the third gas directive process spans the time between the Council's approval of the second gas directive on June 16, 2003, and its approval of the third gas directive on June 15, 2009. The third electricity directive (2009/72/EC) was negotiated in parallel and is only referred to if it contributes to explaining the policy process leading to the third gas directive.

The biggest difference between this policy process and those leading to the gas directives in 1998 and 2003 was that this time ten new member states, mostly from Eastern Europe, were represented at the negotiation table due to European Union (EU) enlargement on May 1, 2004. It was not clear from the outset how these member states would position themselves with regard to energy liberalization. On the one hand, it was plausible to expect them to push for the completion of the internal energy market (IEM), which could reduce their dependence on Russian gas (Geden and Fischer 2008). On the other hand, the new member states could also have tried to oppose new liberalization measures, because it would be costly for them to adjust their domestic legislation to EU provisions (Brutschin 2015, 138).

As had been the case in the analysis of the previous two gas directives, the analysis is guided by the hypotheses derived in Chap. 2 (for an overview, see Table 2.6). Sect. 6.1 traces the agenda-setting process, Sect. 6.2 explores the decision-making process, and Sect. 6.3 concludes with a critical evaluation of the multiple streams framework's (MSF) potential to explain the agenda and policy change that had taken place.

N. Herweg, *European Union Policy-Making*,
DOI 10.1007/978-3-319-49400-5_6

6.1 Agenda Change

In order to test empirically whether the MSF manages to explain this agenda-setting process, this section is structured as follows: (1) I address the question of whether the problem stream, political stream, and policy stream were ripe (Hypothesis 1, specified in Definitions 1–3, Sects. 6.1.1–6.1.3). This is followed by the analysis whether an agenda window opened due to a change in the problem or political stream (Hypothesis 2, alternative causal paths specified in Hypotheses 4–8), which a policy-entrepreneur exploited in order to couple the three streams (Hypothesis 3, specified in Hypothesis 9, Sect. 6.1.4). Finally, I conclude with an assessment of the MSF's explanatory potential regarding this agenda change (Sect. 6.1.5).

6.1.1 Problem Stream

Achieving price reductions had been a key driver of the EU's energy policy since its first liberalization attempts. It was natural to measure the first and second gas directives' success on their impact on the natural gas price development. The Commission's second benchmarking report, released in April 2003, documented a fall in gas price for the previous year (European Commission 2003). This price reduction was not interpreted as a success of the Community's energy liberalization policy but as a reflection of the oil price development. By disaggregating the gas price to the member state level and to different consumer groups, the Commission revealed that small consumers had to pay higher gas prices in member states without full market opening (European Commission 2003, 25). In its third benchmarking report, released on March 1, 2004, the Commission confirmed this finding (European Commission 2004, 8–9). Since the benchmarking reports drew attention to the state of the internal gas market and documented that gas prices had been lower in member states with full market opening, incomplete market opening (and liberalization) was interpreted as problematic. As a consequence, the problem stream had become ripe (Definition 1).

Resulting from an increased demand from high-growth economies and growing uncertainties about the supply side due to the international war on terrorism, the oil price began to rise from 2003 onward. Consequently, security of supply concerns became more important (Eikeland 2011, 251). It was clear that the gas price would follow this trend given the oil–gas linkage (which actually happened; see Fig. 6.1). This development had the potential to question the Community's energy liberalization policy as one of its key objectives had been realizing the *gains of Europe*, which refers to Cecchini's calculation of the cost of non-Europe due to the lack of a single European market (see Sects. 4.1.1 and 4.1.4). Furthermore, concerns about growing energy prices could also translate into concerns regarding the supply of natural gas. This did not happen because the Commission succeeded in presenting the completion of the IEM as a prerequisite for securing supply.[1] For instance, in its Communication dealing with coordinated measures on the security of energy supply, the Commission stressed that the IEM, unimpeded by price manipulation and limited third-party access (TPA), was a "necessary basis for measures with regard to security of energy supplies" (European Commission 2002, 5). The IEM was presented as a solution to the problem of supply security (in a similar vein, see European Commission 2006a, 8–9). In addition, by proposing a directive that dealt exclusively with measures to safeguard security of natural gas supply (European Commission 2002, which resulted in directive 2004/67/EC), the Commission managed to delink the discussion of safeguarding measures (other than the completion of the IEM) from the gas directive (for a similar assessment, see Maltby 2013, 439).

6.1.2 Political Stream

According to Definition 2, the political stream is ripe if the EU government is receptive to gas market liberalization. As Sect. 6.1.4 will illustrate, the agenda window opened roughly a year after the second gas directive had been adopted. In terms of stream ripeness, this implies that the EU government was receptive to gas market liberalization, given the facts that (1) there had not been (significant) electoral changes in the meantime and (2) policy-makers had quite recently supported and agreed to further liberalization measures. In this narrow sense, the political stream was ripe. However, in terms of receptiveness to revise the gas directive a third time, there is no indication in primary and secondary data that this had been an issue before the agenda window opened.

6.1.3 Policy Stream

Given the short time span between the closure of the second gas directive's decision window and the opening of the third gas directive's agenda window, the policy stream did not change much. The most far-reaching change was that the institutionalization of the policy community proceeded. In

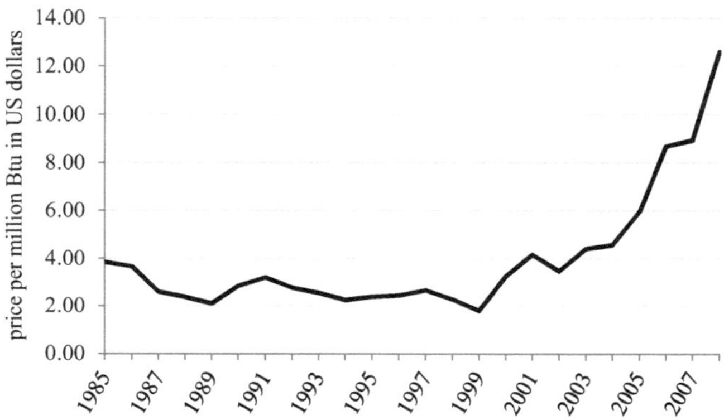

Fig. 6.1 Development of the natural gas price, 1985–2008. *Source*: Own illustration, based on British Petroleum (2009). *Notes*: This figure shows the development of the natural gas price in the European Union, including cost, insurance, and freight in British thermal units (Btu). Data restrictions do not allow for a more disaggregated illustration of the natural gas price development

November 2003, the Commission initiated the creation of the European Regulators Group for Electricity and Gas (ERGEG) (2003/796/EC), which was composed of the heads of the national regulatory authorities (NRAs). Its task was to (1) analyze the given regulatory framework, (2) address shortcomings, (3) develop ideas to overcome them, and (4) make the regulatory framework available to interested parties.[2] However, this process took until March 2004 when ERGEG released its first annual working program, which concentrated on the given regulatory environment and not on providing impetus for additional legislative measures.[3]

Prior to the opening of the agenda window, the Madrid Forum met once. It did not engage in working out new alternatives regarding a future revision of the gas directive but concentrated on the discussion of guidelines for good practice and technical aspects (European Gas Regulatory Forum 2003). Nonetheless, resulting from the exchange of views during the policy processes that had led to the previous gas directives, the policy community was familiar with a list of options that had been legitimated in one or more member states. As a consequence, the policy stream was ripe (Definition 3).

6.1.4 *Agenda Window and Coupling*

The agenda window was opened by the election of Barroso as Commission President in July 2004 (Hypothesis 5b). Due to a lack of political support for Barroso's college from members of the European Parliament (EP), Barroso had to reshuffle it. Among others, the EP opposed the nomination of Lázló Kovács as Energy Commissioner (Eikeland 2012, 48). On November 22, 2004, the EP finally approved Barroso's college, in which Neelie Kroes was in charge for Directorate-General (DG) Competition and Andris Piebalgs for DG Energy. Right from its start, the Commission, acting as a policy-entrepreneur, stressed that the completion of the internal market in electricity and natural gas was high on its agenda (see below). As had been the case in the previous gas directive processes, the Commission attempted to come up with a proposal acceptable to (at best) all stakeholders instead of selecting a policy alternative unilaterally (cf. Sect. 2.3.3). Specifying which policy alternative would be acceptable to the stakeholders required time to enter discussions. However, according to Kingdon (1984), an agenda window closes quickly. Therefore, the analysis starts with a summary of events that held the agenda window open (Definition 4, Sect. 6.1.4.1), before it turns to a policy-entrepreneur's coupling activities (Hypothesis 3, Sect. 6.1.4.2).

6.1.4.1 Events That Held the Agenda Window Open

The agenda window stays open as long as an issue remains on the governmental agenda (Definition 4). In order to rise (or remain) on the governmental agenda, there must be a change in the problem stream or political stream. Until the Commission proposed a third gas directive, there had been changes in both streams, which the subsequent paragraphs summarize.

Regarding the *problem stream*, the Commission directed, on various occasions, attention to the incomplete implementation of the second gas directive. On September 21, 2004, two months after Barroso had been elected Commission President, DG Competition organized a high-level meeting with the national competition and regulatory authorities in order to discuss obstacles to the internal market in electricity and gas and the division of responsibilities between these authorities. On this occasion, the Commission mapped out how it planned to achieve the IEM: by applying competition law and, given that this combined with the proper implementation of the second gas directive on part of the member states would not suffice, by new, more far-reaching legislation (Klotz and Nyssens 2004, 33). Only a few weeks later, the Commission walked the talk and initiated a series of infringement proceedings. In October 2004, three months after the directive's date of transposition, it sent letters of formal notice to 18 out of 25 member states regarding their failure to implement the second electricity and/or gas directive in due time in national law (European Commission 2005e). This was followed by the Commission sending reasoned opinions to ten member states in March 2005 (European Commission 2005g) and bringing five member states before the European Court of Justice while simultaneously sending a reasoned opinion to Portugal in July 2005 (European Commission 2005e). Already in April 2006, the Commission sent 27 letters of formal notice to 17 member states, questioning whether they had transposed the gas and electricity directives in a way which conformed to Community legislation (European Commission 2006g). This culminated in 26 reasoned opinions to 16 member states in December 2006 (European Commission 2006h) and additional two reasoned opinions in June 2007 (European Commission 2007d).[4] Following from the findings of the Commission's energy sector inquiry (see Sect. 6.1.4.2 for details), DG Competition raided 20 offices of major energy companies in Germany, France, Italy, Austria, Belgium, and Hungary in mid-May 2006 (Buchan 2009, 24). It looked for evidence whether these companies had (1) restricted access to pipelines and storage facilities, and (2) signed long-term contracts with gas suppliers (*European Voice* May 24, 2006). To sum up, the intense application of competition law made sure that the incomplete state of the IEM became visible and was interpreted as problematic (Hypothesis 4b).[5] This perception was also reinforced by the release of the Commission's benchmarking report in early 2005 (European Commission 2005h). As required by the gas and electricity directives, the Commission reviewed the state of the internal market in electricity and gas, and published its finding in this report. The main findings of this annual report were: (1) member states needed to intensify the speed and extent with which they implemented the electricity and gas directives, (2) interconnection infrastructure between the member states was underdeveloped, and (3) independence of transmission system operators (TSOs) and separation of distribution system operator (DSO) was insufficiently achieved (European Commission 2005b) (Hypothesis 4b).

Apart from changes in the problem stream, changes in the *political stream* also draw attention to the state of the internal market in gas. In order to summarize them, I concentrate on the analysis of the agendas of the three branches of the EU executive. The inclusion of the internal gas market in their agendas documents best whether they had been paying attention to energy liberalization.

Before the decision window opened, the *Commission* had published three working programs (Hypothesis 5b). In its program for 2005, it announced "a detailed analysis of the current situation with respect to the functioning of the electricity and gas market, identifying improvements and persisting obstacles, [and, N.H.] assessing the need for further measures" (European Commission 2005a, 21). In the following working program, it defined the IEM as a key driver of Europe's growth, which needed to be completed (European Commission 2005i, 5). Furthermore, the Commission announced a Green Paper on a secure, competitive, and sustainable energy policy for Europe based on "the widest possible consultation" (European Commission 2005i, 22). This implies that energy was about to rise on the stakeholders' agenda (in the case it had not already been included in the same) due to their participation at this consultation. In the working program for 2007, the Commission declared that "[e]nergy has climbed on the top of the policy agenda" (European Commission 2006c, 6). The Commission included (inter alia) the revision of the second gas directive in the overview of its planned strategic initiatives, in addition to the first strategic energy review for Europe (European Commission 2006c, 13).

In fact, both the Council and the European Council discussed the IEM consistently at their meetings since the Commission had come forward with its idea of a Green Paper on energy in the autumn of 2005. More precisely, *the Council* gave energy policy and the IEM a high priority since December 2005. At its December meeting, the Council expressed its support for "the Commission's plans for consulting and taking forward the issues (...) [of, N.H.] climate change, energy efficiency, security of supply and furthering of the internal [energy, N.H.] market" (Council of the European Union 2005, 10). Half a year later, the Council discussed at lengths the state of the IEM. It concluded that the impact of existing legislation should be assessed prior to considering further legislation (Council of the European Union 2006, Recital 18). By February 2007, the Council deemed further legislation necessary and invited the Commission to come forward with measures regarding unbundling, regulatory oversight, coordination between TSOs, cross-border trade, incentives for investments, transparency, and consumer protection (Council of the European Union 2007b, 10–12). At the Council meeting in June 2007, the ministers discussed unbundling, effective regulation, and adequate infrastructure investment, and concluded that "[t]he debate will be useful for the Commission in preparation of its legislative package on the internal [energy, N.H.] market which is expected in the autumn" (Council of the European Union 2007c, 9) (Hypothesis 8).

The fact that the Council dealt with the IEM regularly since December 2005 can be only partly explained by the importance the incumbent presidencies had assigned to this issue. Of all member states that presided over the Council, only Finland and Germany, in charge between July 2006 and June 2007, had prioritized the completion of the internal market for electricity and gas highly (Finland 2006, 7; Germany 2006, 5) (Hypothesis 6b). The previous presidencies had remained silent on this issue in their working programs or presidency priorities (Italy 2003; Ireland 2003; Ireland and the Netherlands 2004; Luxembourg 2005; United Kingdom 2005; Austria 2005).[6] Nonetheless, under the British and the Austrian Presidency (in charge between July 2005 and June 2006), gas market liberalization was also debated at the Council meetings.

Since March 2006, the *European Council* also gave energy policy a top priority at its meetings. Between March 2006 and June 2007, the European Council met four times and called for and discussed at each meeting an "Energy Policy for Europe" that aimed at "effective Community policy, coherence between Member States and consistency between actions in different policy areas and fulfilling in a balanced way the three objectives of security of supply, competitiveness and environmental sustainability" (European Council 2006, recital 44). It named ensuring competitiveness as one of its main objectives, which should (inter alia) be achieved by completely opening the electricity and gas markets for all consumers by mid-2007 (European Council 2006, Recital 46b). This culminated in a list of measures required to achieve this, referring to unbundling and regulatory oversight, and an invitation to the Commission "to come forward with relevant proposals, including through the development of existing legislation where possible" (European Council 2007b, Annex I, 17) (Hypothesis 8).

Thus, the impetus for new legislation came from the Commission, but the Council jumped on the bandwagon in February and the European Council in March 2007. In terms of stream ripeness, these dates marked the moment when all three branches of the EU executive were receptive not just to liberalization measures in general (Definition 2) but also to a third gas directive in particular. The EP also passed a resolution on prospects of the internal gas and electricity market on July 10, 2007, in which it supported additional measures aiming at the completion of the IEM (European Parliament 2007).

6.1.4.2 Policy-Entrepreneur's Coupling Strategies

As had been the case in the previous gas directive processes, the Commission aimed at coupling the problem stream and political stream with a policy alternative that was acceptable to (at least) most stakeholders. Therefore, the analysis of agenda coupling is divided into two parts: (1) I turn to the question of how the Commission initiated and contributed to the development of alternatives acceptable to most stakeholders, and (2) I analyze how it managed to make the critical couplings of streams in order for an agenda change to happen. The most important policy-entrepreneurs were Competition Commissioner Neelie Kroes and Energy Commissioner Andris Piebalgs.

Working Out Acceptable Alternatives

The generation and discussion of acceptable alternatives for a revised gas directive took place from July 2004 until September 2007. At the beginning, the involved stakeholders remained mostly vaguely on the design of new alternatives, but they became increasingly specific in the course of time. It was particularly the Commission that initiated and fostered the discussion of details for a revised gas draft directive by (1) setting up the High Level Group (HLG) on Competitiveness, Energy and the Environment (2006/77/EC); (2) launching an energy sector inquiry; (3) preparing a Green Paper on "A European Strategy for Sustainable, Competitive and Secure Energy" (European Commission 2006a); (4) developing a strategy and an action plan for a new European energy policy, which is also referred to as the first strategic energy review (European Commission 2007b); and (5) conducting an impact assessment (European Commission 2007a).

The Commission launched the *HLG* in February 2005. It consisted of members of the Commission for Enterprise and Industry, Competition, Energy, and the Environment, and representatives of the EP and the Council, as well as of relevant stakeholders (European Commission 2006d). Its function was that of an advisory platform for "issues where competitiveness, energy and environmental policies interrelate" (2006/77/EC, art. 2). This documented a shift of focus from competition to supply and environmental issues. Nonetheless, one of the HLG's tasks was to provide advice on how to improve the functioning of the gas market (European Commission 2006d). In this regard, the HLG suggested focusing on the implementation of the second gas directive, effective unbundling, new rules on transparency, and the stricter application of competition law (Eikeland 2012, 66).

Under the impression of continuously rising energy prices, the Commission announced a sectorial screening of the barriers to competition in February 2005 (European Commission 2005c, 8) and decided formally to open a *sector inquiry in the gas and electricity markets* in June 2005 (European Commission 2005d). Further drivers for this inquiry were complaints about entry barriers, limited consumer choice, highly concentrated markets, and insufficient cross-border trade in electricity (Cameron 2007, 295). The Commission particularly investigated the following eight key areas:

> (1) market concentration/market power, (2) vertical foreclosure (most prominently inadequate unbundling of network and supply), (3) lack of market integration (including lack of regulatory oversight for cross-border issues), (4) lack of transparency, (5) price formation, (6) downstream markets, (7) balancing markets, and (8) liquefied natural gas. (European Commission 2007e, Recital 4)

In February 2006, it presented its preliminary findings of this sector inquiry. According to Energy Commissioner Andris Piebalgs, this inquiry's objective was "to reveal further whether [the, N.H.] obstacles [to completing the IEM, N.H.] are due to an insufficient transposition and implementation of the [second electricity and gas, N.H.] directives, or whether we need new legislative measures in order to tackle them" (quoted in European Commission 2006b, 3). Table 6.1 summarizes the inquiries' main findings. While Competition Commissioner Neelie Kroes was convinced of the need for a further liberalization package when the first results of the sector inquiry came in, it took until the presentation of these preliminary findings that Piebalgs came to the same conclusion (Eikeland 2011, 250–51).[7] As a result of the energy sector inquiry, the electricity and gas sectors had the full attention of DG Competition and DG Energy.

Subsequent to the publication of the preliminary findings of the energy sector inquiry, the Commission launched a public consultation with all stakeholders (European Commission 2007e, Recital 11). In its final report, the Commission concluded that there were basically four main fundamental deficiencies in the electricity and gas sector:

Table 6.1 Main findings of the energy sector inquiry

Key areas	*Main findings*
Market concentration	Wholesale gas trade remained national and maintained the high level of market concentration of the preliberalization period.
Vertical foreclosure	Insufficient unbundling of network and supply interests led to a lack of network access for new entrants and a lack of investments in infrastructure.
Lack of market integration	Cross-border sales hardly occurred, among others, because available capacity on import pipelines was limited.
Lack of transparency	Reliable and timely information lacked, for instance, regarding network availability and gas storage.
Price formation	Linkage of the gas price to the oil price was still used in long-term import contracts, which distorted supply-and-demand-based pricing.
Downstream markets	Long duration of retail contracts for industrial consumers and local distribution companies often limited competition at the retail level.
Balancing markets	Balancing markets favored incumbents and the small size of the existing balancing zones led to increased costs (due to complex and divergent rules regarding balancing in each zone and the obligation to reserve capacity at each border point).
Liquefied natural gas (LNG)	Although LNG imports were mainly covered by incumbents, it seemed as if new entrants and producers were beginning to receive more capacity at LNG terminals.

Source: Own compilation, based on European Commission (2007e, Chap. 2)

- Structural conflicts of interest: a systemic conflict of interest caused by insufficient unbundling of networks from the competitive parts of the sector;
- Gaps in the regulatory environment: a persistent regulatory gap particularly for cross border issues (...);
- A chronic lack of liquidity, both in electricity and gas wholesale markets: the lifeblood for our markets is lacking and the market power of the pre-liberalisation monopolies persists;
- A general lack of transparency in market operations in the sector. (European Commission 2007e, Recital 52)

According to the Commission, these problems could be best solved by (1) ownership unbundling or (though complicated by costly regulatory oversight) independent system operator (ISO); (2) more powers for and closer cooperation between independent national energy regulators, more cooperation between TSOs, and an enhanced regulatory consistency between member states; (3) any measure to reduce market concentration, such as competition law enforcement, gas release programs, strict application of use-it-or-lose-it provisions for infrastructure (see Haase 2009 for further information on these issues); and (4) publication of all relevant market information in a timely manner (European Commission 2007e, Recitals 53–64).

In terms of receptivity, most stakeholders agreed with the Commission's findings. However, regarding the interpretation of these findings as problematic, the stakeholders' opinions varied and basically fell into two camps: The vertically integrated undertakings (which did not see the need for further measures and that of consumers, traders, new entrants) and regulatory and competition authorities (which favored further measures) (European Commission 2007e, Recital 12).

As a reaction to the "new energy landscape of the 21st century" (European Commission 2006a, 4), the Commission also published a Green Paper entitled "A European Strategy for Sustainable, Competitive and Secure Energy" in early March 2006. The energy landscape had changed in various aspects: Investment needs had accumulated, import dependency was growing, resources were concentrated in a few countries, global energy demand continued to grow, energy prices were on the rise, climate change was becoming visible, and the IEM was still incomplete (European Commission 2006a, 3). Although this Green Paper also dealt with issues such as energy solidarity, energy efficiency, renewable energy, energy technology, and international cooperation, the IEM received disproportionately high attention (Fischer 2011, 91). With regard to the latter, the Commission planned to base its decision about the need for and the possible design of additional legislative measures on the insights gained from the energy sector inquiry. Nonetheless, it concluded in this Green Paper that five core areas needed to be dealt with, namely: the need for a single European grid, a priority interconnection plan, investment in generation capacity, unbundling, and boosting European industry's competitiveness (European Commission 2006a, 6). With regard to unbundling, the Green Paper stated clearly that the gas directive's provisions needed to be implemented in letter and spirit, and if this did not lead to a level playing field, additional legislative measures would be necessary.

From March 24 until September 24, 2006, the Commission launched a public consultation on the Green Paper on how a European strategy to counter the challenges mentioned above could look like. It received 1680 contributions dealing with six key areas (including competitiveness and the IEM) (European Commission 2006f, 6). Of the member states,

18 submitted contributions to this public consultation. Although they (implicitly) agreed that the current state of competition in the IEM was unsatisfactory, most of them did not support further legislative measures. Instead, they favored the full implementation of the existing legal framework. They opposed the idea to set up a European regulator, while ERGEG's work was appreciated as were the Commission's priority interconnection plan and considerations of how to boost investment in new generation capacities. As had been the case since the mid-1990s, the question of unbundling kept dividing the member states. In particular: Denmark, the United Kingdom, and the Netherlands supported a far-reaching unbundling, while France and Germany opposed ownership unbundling and deemed the existing provisions as sufficient (European Commission 2006f, 16). The EP also contributed to this consultation and stated that, with regard to the IEM, "the responsibilities of governments, regulators and market actors must be better defined in order to achieve a properly functioning market" (European Commission 2006f, 20). Drawing on the analysis of the contributions of all respondents, the Commission concluded it had the support of the majority of stakeholders for new legislative measures (see Fig. 6.2; European Commission 2006f, 48)—though not from the majority of veto actors, since most member states had voiced their opposition against new measures.

Based on the contributions the Commission received for its Green Paper, it developed an *energy policy for Europe* and an action plan on implementation (European Commission 2007b). The Commission put the European energy policy in the context of "combating climate change, limiting the EU's external vulnerability to imported hydrocarbons, and promoting growth and jobs, thereby providing secure and affordable energy to consumers" (European Commission 2007b, 5). Since the IEM contributed to competitiveness, sustainability, and security of supply, the Commission suggested concentrating on actions that would complete it. More precisely, it suggested measures regarding unbundling, effective regulation, transparency, infrastructure, network security, adequacy of electricity generation and gas supply capacity, and energy as a public service (European Commission 2007b, 6–10). For a possible third gas directive, the issues of unbundling and regulatory oversight were particularly important. They were predominantly covered in the current second gas directive.[8] The Commission repeated its assessment that a stricter unbundling regime was required. Notwithstanding that most member states had opposed this idea before, the Commission suggested to revise the current provisions and opt

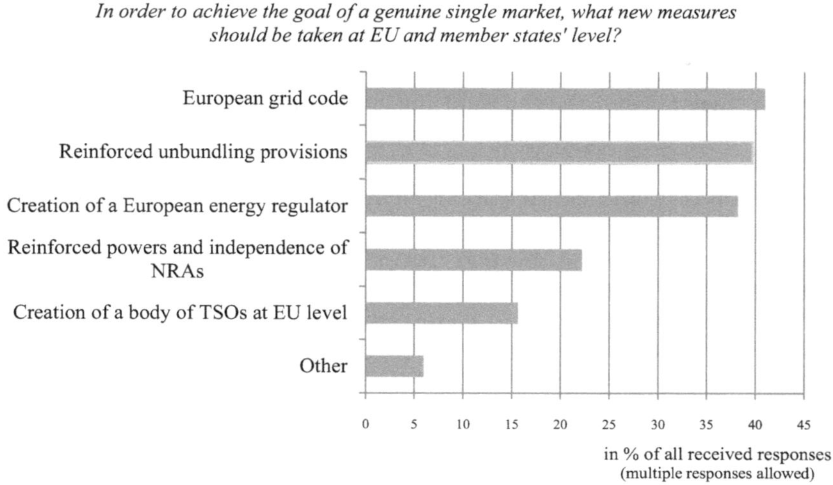

Fig. 6.2 Supported measures for achieving the IEM according to the findings of the Green Paper's public consultation. *Source*: Own compilation, based on European Commission (2006f, 48)

for ownership unbundling and, as a second best option, for ISO. Furthermore, the Commission questioned the exemption of DSO serving less than 100,000 customers from unbundling requirements. The Commission criticized the current regulatory situation because the levels of powers and independence of NRAs differed too much between the member states and needed to be harmonized "on the basis of the highest, not the lowest, common denominator in the EU" (European Commission 2007b, 7). Possible ways to harmonize regulatory oversight were: (1) a gradual evolution of the current approach, in particular reinforcing the coordination between NRAs and granting the Commission a mechanism to review the NRA's decisions that would affect the IEM, (2) formalizing ERGEG and tasking it to structure binding decisions for regulators and market players under the condition of Commission involvement (referred to as "ERGEG+"), and (3) setting up a new, single Community body responsible for making cross-border trade work by deciding on regulatory and technical issues. The Commission judged the first option as insufficient and ERGEG+ as a minimum approach (European Commission 2007b, 8). It concluded this strategy paper with a call to the European Council and the EP to confirm the need for additional legislative measures, particularly (1) introduction of ownership unbundling or a full ISO, (2) harmonization of energy regulators' powers and independence, (3) establishment of a new single regulatory Community body or ERGEG+, (4) establishment of a new Community measure and structure for TSOs, (5) tabling of minimum standards regarding transparency, (6) introduction of a new customers' energy charter, and (7) construction of essential new interconnectors (European Commission 2007b, 20–21).[9]

Since it had become clear to the Commission during the public consultation that new legislative measures were required, it launched an *impact assessment* on possible changes to the existent energy legislation in September 2006.[10] An impact assessment compares ex ante possible policy alternatives with regard to their economic, social, and environmental impacts. It takes place in parallel to policy formulation and preparation, and is meant to enhance policy learning. Contributions to an impact assessment aim at adjusting existing policies, generating new policies, and influencing the stakeholders' value systems in order to achieve a shared problem perception, which should facilitate agreeing on specific policies (Bauler 2006, 278). In early 2007, the Commission consulted with member states, regulators, TSOs, associations of electricity and gas companies, independent producers associations, consumer associations, industrial energy users' associations, traders and new entrants, trade unions, World Wildlife Fund, and additional 56 stakeholders (companies affected by unbundling and possible buyers of such types of assets, financial institutions, and investment funds) regarding the assessment of policy alternatives (European Commission 2007a, 11–12). Table 6.2 provides a brief overview of the discussed alternatives and their assessment.

The *Madrid Forum* met six times during September 2003 and September 2007. In addition to discussing guidelines for good practice (for instance, for storage system operators or balancing) and technical issues (such as interoperability), the participants also exchanged views on the Commission's Green Paper (European Gas Regulatory Forum 2006) and considerations for an energy policy for Europe (European Gas Regulatory Forum 2007a). To conclude, the Commission had initiated and pushed the generation of alternatives tailored to EU gas market specifics. Between mid-2005 and early 2007, it had involved all stakeholders in the discussion of shortcomings of the existing energy legislation and possible ways to tackle them. Since the Commission decided, for instance, which questions stakeholders were confronted with, it influenced the discussion of specific

Table 6.2 Main findings of the impact assessment

Subject	*Assessed policies, best solutions (if available), and/or stakeholder reactions*
Further transmission system operator (TSO) unbundling	Full ownership unbundling: best viable solution independent system operator (ISO): requirement of high regulatory oversight
Role and coordination of regulators	Increasing regulators' powers and independence: extremely beneficial, with a good cost–benefit ratio Set up of a single European regulator: likely to be resisted from a number of member states and stakeholders
Cooperation between TSOs	Introduction of formal coordination between TSOs: balanced solution between regulatory oversight and status quo
Transparency in wholesale markets	Data disclosure: development of a set of pan-European high-level standards of data disclosure for gas and electricity
Regulation of long-term gas contracts	Cost–benefit analysis was not conclusive
Access to storage facilities	Legal unbundling and implementation of European Regulators Group for Electricity and Gas guidelines on gas storage operations
Creation of strategic gas stocks at EU level	Limited support from stakeholders; therefore, no viable solution at the moment
Change of Article 22, 2003/55/EC	Amendment needed in order to create favorable conditions for investment
Distribution system operator unbundling	Further unbundling: benefits only slightly higher than costs; at the moment, no viable solution
Consumer protection	Adoption of an energy charter, aiming in particular at energy poverty
European Union (EU) unbundling requirements and third-country companies	Achieving respect of (EU) unbundling requirements by a combination of regulatory measures

Source: Own compilation, based on European Commission (2007a)

alternatives insofar as it forced stakeholders to start considering them seriously and to position themselves. Since the Commission had "essentially been trying for twenty years to push through the same agenda or to achieve the same goal – open access on energy networks" (Buchan 2010, 364), it was no surprise that the alternatives the Commission brought up for discussion aimed at deepening energy liberalization. In the course of the public consultations, it became clear which alternatives were acceptable (to the policy community and elected decision-makers). Based on this knowledge, DG Energy and DG Competition started authoring a proposal for a revised gas directive (Eikeland 2011, 253).

Making the Critical Couplings

When the agenda window opened, the political stream was receptive to energy liberalization, but, as outlined above, the EU executive meant to achieve it by implementing the existing legislation. It took until late 2005 that Competition Commissioner Kroes was convinced of the need for a third gas directive, followed by Energy Commissioner Piebalgs in early 2006. Therefore, this section starts by analyzing how the Commission and, in particular, these Commissioners managed to couple the problem stream with (the other elements of) the political stream once they were convinced of the need for further legislative measures. This is followed by an analysis of how the Commission managed to add the policy stream to this coupling once an acceptable alternative was available. The analysis focuses in particular on how the Commission managed to include ownership unbundling in the proposed gas directive, since this was the most controversial part of the proposal (Eikeland 2011, 82). This implies that the Commission acted as a policy-entrepreneur. Thus, according to Hypothesis 9, agenda change was very likely since the Commission was persistent and had access to key policy-makers.

An integral part of the Commission's recipe to successfully couple the problem stream and political stream (in the sense of convincing all branches of the EU executive of the need for a third gas directive) was that it related the incomplete internal gas market with an already adopted policy: the Lisbon Strategy. Pushed by Kroes, the Commission put the proposal of the former Competition Commissioner, Mario Monti, into operation and announced an energy sector inquiry as part of the revived competition-oriented Lisbon Strategy in its Communication to the European Council in March 2005 (European Commission 2005c, 8, *European Voice* February 24, 2005). By referring to the energy sector as one key sector in need for (1) improved implementation of the existing EU legislation and (2) an energy sector inquiry (see Sect. 6.1.4.2) "to ascertain the underlying reasons, why [energy, N.H.] markets do not fully function" (European Commission 2005c, 18), the Commission had kept all options open: from stricter monitoring of implementation to additional measures if the energy sector inquiry revealed that the existing shortcomings in the IEM were due to reasons other than the incomplete or inappropriate implementation of EU requirements.

Pushing the IEM on the agenda by giving it a high priority in the revived and widely supported Lisbon Strategy was a clever move because this made it difficult to argue against it. Consequently, the *European Council* (2006, Recital 16) concluded at its March meeting that the integrated guidelines 2005–2008 for jobs and growth[11] remained valid, and that within that framework, defining an energy policy for Europe was a priority. At its meeting in December 2005, the *Council* also discussed the IEM and stressed its importance for Europe's competitiveness (Council of the European Union 2005, 9). As a consequence, the European Council and the Council shared the Commission's view that the IEM was a pivotal part in the revived Lisbon Strategy. From this, the rejection of further integration steps regarding the IEM would have required a plausible explanation. The problem stream and the political stream had converged. By that time, Kroes was already convinced that a third gas directive was needed, and Piebalgs came to the same conclusion in February 2006. A peculiarity of this agenda-setting process was that DG Competition and DG Energy worked closely together and even coauthored the proposal for a third gas directive (Eikeland 2011, 253). How did they manage to add the policy stream to the converged problem and political stream?

By mid-2006, the Commission had opened infringement proceedings against numerous member states and raided 20 offices of major energy companies in six member states (see Sect. 6.1.4.1). Apart from drawing attention to the problematic state of the energy sector, the Commission intended to weaken the member states' resistance against a third directive and against ownership unbundling, in particular, by winning the energy companies over to its side. More precisely, DG Competition offered these energy companies a reduction in fines for infringement of EU competition rules in return for ownership unbundling. Thereby, the Commission hoped that these companies would stop lobbying against ownership unbundling, which would make it easier for member states to accept this unbundling provision (Eikeland 2011, 253).

At the same time, security of supply concerns had grown. These concerns were nourished by (1) the German–Russian agreement of September 2005 to build Nordstream through the Baltic Sea, which was heavily criticized by Poland; (2) the (re-)negotiation of contracts by Gazprom, the Russian state-owned vertically integrated gas company, in order to charge Eastern European states higher gas prices, particularly during 2005; (3) the disputes between Russia and Ukraine over transmission payments in January 2006 (and 2009), which led Russia to hold back gas supplies (Brutschin 2015, 199); and (4) the fact that Gazprom acquired several European wholesale companies, in particular in the period 2006–2008 (Vavilov and Trofimov 2015, 88). While not opposing ownership unbundling in general, the Eastern member states feared that Gazprom would seize the opportunity to acquire even more wholesale companies if they were forced to implement ownership unbundling (*European Report* October 10, 2008, *European Voice* May 21, 2008).

In the first half of 2007, Germany presided over the Council. Since Germany strongly opposed ownership unbundling, it excluded the discussion of a possible revision of the electricity and gas market regulation from its agenda as far as possible (Buchan 2009, 72). It once seriously discussed some regulatory key issues, such as unbundling, effective regulation, infrastructure investment, and cooperation between NRAs at its meeting in June (Council of the European Union 2007c, 9). Ahead of this meeting, the Commission, in cooperation with the German Presidency, sent four questions on energy market regulation to member states, which should guide the discussion at the Council meeting. These questions were:

> (1) Should further unbundling measures, if proposed by the Commission, be applied only to the transmission networks or to distribution networks as well; and should electricity and gas be treated differently? (...)
> (2) Which tasks, competences and responsibilities should be assigned to such a mechanism [independent mechanism for NRAs to cooperate and take decisions on important cross-border issues, N.H.]? (...)
> (3) What measures are necessary in order to expand and develop networks in a manner which is appropriate to requirements, taking account of cost-efficiency at an overall economic level? (...)
> (4) Which tasks, competences and responsibilities should be assigned to such a mechanism [new Community mechanism for TSOs to improve the coordination of network operation and grid security, building on existing cooperation practices, N.H.]? (European Commission 2007f)

The vagueness of the Council's conclusions regarding these questions spoke for itself (Council of the European Union 2007c, 9). The conclusions consisted of a brief note that the four questions were addressed, but did not summarize the member states' answers. Thus, Energy Commissioner Piebalgs concluded that "[t]he majority [of member states, N.H.] is not with me" (quoted in *European Voice* June 14, 2007). In particular, France and Germany were harshly opposing ownership unbundling and were unwilling to except a proposal in which this would be the only option

(*European Voice* June 14, 2007). In the meanwhile, a camp of ownership unbundling supporters had formed, composed of Belgium, Denmark, Finland, the Netherlands, Romania, Spain, Sweden, and the United Kingdom. Two weeks after this Council meeting, these member states sent a letter of support to Piebalgs. They expressed their support for ownership unbundling and stated that a majority in the Council would opt for this alternative, given it would be restricted to the transmission level (Buchan 2009, 73, *Financial Times* June 26, 2007). In July, eight member states in opposition to ownership unbundling (namely Austria, Bulgaria, Cyprus, France, Germany, Greece, Luxembourg, and Slovakia) also wrote a letter to Pielbalgs and stated that "full ownership unbundling would not be able to deliver the necessary positive effects on competitivity, security and sustainability of energy supply" (quoted in *European Voice* August 30, 2007, Buchan 2009, 73). The EP, whose consent was required for a possible third gas directive, also positioned itself in the debate about ownership unbundling. In a nonbinding resolution, it made clear that it considered "transmission ownership unbundling to be the most effective tool to promote investment infrastructures in a non-discriminatory way, fair access to the grid for new entrants and transparency in the market" (European Parliament 2007, Recital 2).

In order to win the support of the member states that were openly opposing ownership unbundling and those that were undecided yet (such as Poland), the Commission came up with several concessions and package deals during the drafting stage of its proposal. The Commission's suggestions can basically be summarized in two points: (1) It allowed for two options regarding further unbundling provisions, namely ownership unbundling and an ISO model. The latter was included due to efforts of DG Energy, which preferred achieving a consensus over pressing for ownership unbundling (Eikeland 2011, 253). However, it was accompanied by increased regulatory requirements, which an official from a pro-ownership unbundling member state commented would produce a "gradual progression to full unbundling" (quoted in *European Voice* September 20, 2007). Furthermore, ownership unbundling was restricted to the transmission level, since some member states had opposed to implement it at the distribution level but supported it at the transmission level (Buchan 2009, 73). (2) The Commission suggested limiting the ability of energy undertakings from third countries to acquire control over transmission system networks from European energy undertakings. More precisely, undertakings based outside the EU should only be allowed to be active in the IEM if they respected EU legislation This implied that undertakings from third countries would also have to comply with EU unbundling provisions. Thereby, the Commission also met the EP's requirement because it had insisted in its resolution that "no third country company should be allowed to purchase energy infrastructure unless there is reciprocity with that country" (European Parliament 2007, Recital 6). Furthermore, the Commission suggested that third-country companies or individuals should only be allowed to acquire control over a Community transmission system or TSO if an agreement was settled between the EU and the third country (European Commission 2007g, 7). The Commission's suggestions regarding third countries made member states from Eastern Europe willing to accept ownership unbundling, since it refuted the danger of Gazprom taking over recently unbundled company segments (Brutschin 2015, 200, Eikeland 2011, 254). As a consequence, the Commission published its legislative proposal for a third gas directive on September 19, 2007, and a decision window opened.

6.1.5 Interim Conclusion

The agenda window opened due to the election of Barroso as Commission President in July 2004 (Hypothesis 5). A few months later, the Commission made clear that it aimed at achieving the IEM, either by implementing the second gas directive properly and applying competition law, or by more far-reaching legislation. As a consequence, the Commission did not start pushing for a revised gas directive immediately after the agenda window had opened. According to Kingdon (1984), a policy-entrepreneur must act quickly once a window has opened; otherwise, the window closes and the opportunity to change the agenda is missed. However, the analysis documented that changes in the problem stream and political stream had not only held the agenda window open (Definition 4), but also reinforced the prevailing problem perception and political receptivity to energy liberalization (Definitions 1 and 2).

By February 2006, the Commission was convinced of the need for a third gas directive. In particular, Energy Commissioner Piebalgs and Competition Commissioner Kroes engaged as policy-entrepreneurs and an agenda change did happen due to their coupling activities (Hypothesis 3). According to Hypothesis 9, coupling success depends on a policy-entrepreneur's persistence and access to key policy-makers. Since both Commissioners had been persistent and were equipped with access to key policy-makers, this hypothesis can be confirmed. Although the Commission did not threaten to make use of its powers under Article 86(3) (cf. Sects. 4.1.4.2 and 5.2.2.1), the member states got the impression that their fallback position had worsened due to the firm engagement of DG Competition. From the member states' point of view, their options seemed to be reduced to negotiating on legislation or to handling with the consequences of the Commission's application of competition law, which was outside their control. This made the member states more receptive to a third gas directive. Furthermore, the fact that Piebalgs was supported by Kroes was an important component of the Commission's coupling success, because by 2007, DG Energy had also the issues of climate change and energy security on its agenda and would have had difficulties to achieve agenda coupling alone, at least within the short time period between recognizing the need for further legislative measures and the tabling of the third gas directive (Buchan 2009, 27).

The policy stream consisted of a multitude of alternatives addressing energy liberalization. As a consequence, it was ripe (Definition 3). Nonetheless, the Commission did not take the chance to pick its favorite policy in order to couple it with the problem stream and political stream. Similar to the previous policy processes, the Commission aimed at fostering the exchange of views in order to figure out which alternatives would be acceptable to (at least) most stakeholders. The Commission nonetheless influenced the discussion of alternatives insofar as it decided which alternatives stakeholders were being debated by stakeholders. In fact, the policy community produced impressively detailed and concrete alternatives. By detailed and concrete, I mean that they were not just discussed as possible alternatives in general but as European solutions specifically. This implied that they were already formulated in a way that enabled the Commission to simply copy and paste them in a legislative proposal. Furthermore, the policy community had also explicitly and systematically assessed the generated alternatives' impact on the European gas market. This did not just help to document which alternatives were viable but also allowed policy-makers to enter negotiations even before the Commission had presented its legislative proposal. Thus, the Commission had already combined viable alternatives embraced by different veto actors into one package (in particular, the inclusion of the ISO model) and offered and granted concessions (most importantly, the restriction of ownership unbundling to the transmission level) while writing the draft directive. This corresponds with Hypotheses 10a and 10b, although they were derived in order to explain decision coupling.

From this, it does not follow that the Commission was insensible to policy-makers' concerns in the previous gas directive processes. For instance, the Commission increased the consumption thresholds for compulsory TPA after having realized how fiercely member states opposed compulsory TPA during agenda coupling of the first gas directive. What was special this time was that the exchange of views on the third gas draft directive did not just take place behind closed doors but also in institutionalized decision-making centers: in the Council, European Council, and EP. This enabled the veto actors to negotiate package deals and concessions even before the formal decision-making process had begun. Since this implies that some compromises had already been found during agenda coupling, this might have made decision coupling easier for political entrepreneurs. Table 6.3 summarizes how well the MSF fares in explaining this agenda-setting process.

6.2 Policy Change

The decision-coupling process of the third gas directive took place between the Commission's publication of its legislative proposal in September 2007 and the Council's approval of the gas directive at second reading in late-September 2009. During this time, the composition of neither the EP nor the Commission changed. Thus, agenda and decision coupling took place under the same Commission President (Barroso), Energy Commissioner (Piebalgs), and Competition Commissioner (Kroes). The responsible EP committee was the Committee for Industry, Research and Energy. It appointed Romano Maria La Russa as rapporteur for the third gas directive in October 2007, who was succeeded by Antonio Mussa in December 2008. The Council meetings were presided over by Portugal (July to December 2007), Slovenia (January to June 2008), France (July to December 2008), and the Czech Republic (January to June 2009). The subsequent analysis focuses on these actors. In the following, I first analyze the length of decision coupling (Hypothesis 11, Sect. 6.2.1) and then turn to policy-entrepreneurs' coupling strategies (Hypothesis 10, Sect. 6.2.2).

6.2.1 *Length of Decision Coupling*

In the third gas directive process, decision coupling took place from mid-September 2007 until late June 2009. Decision coupling was even shorter than in the policy process leading to the second gas directive. This

Table 6.3 How well the multiple streams framework fares in explaining how the third gas directive entered the decision agenda

Directive		*2009/73/EC*
The MSF's necessary conditions for agenda change		
The likelihood for an agenda change increases if		
H1	the problem stream, political stream, and policy stream are ripe;	+
H2	a change in the problem or political stream opens an agenda window; *and*	+
H3	a policy-entrepreneur succeeds in coupling the streams.	+
Specifying H2: Equifinal paths to the opening of an agenda window		
H4	An agenda window opens in the problem stream if	
	(a) a relevant indicator deteriorates;	
	(b) an evaluation study points to a discrepancy between the program's goal and the program's effects; or	(+)
	(c) a focusing event relevant to the policy field in question occurs.	
H5	An agenda window opens in the political stream if	
	(a) a new Commission takes office; or	+
	(b) the Commission publishes a working program.	(+)
H6	An agenda window opens in the political stream if	
	(a) a new Council Presidency takes office; or	
	(b) one or consecutive Council Presidencies release their working program(s).	(+)
H7	An agenda window opens in the political stream if the European Council publishes acts which provide impetus for the EU's development.	(+)
H8	An agenda window opens in the political stream if (at least) one branch of the EU's executive or legislature tasks one (other) branch of the EU's executive to address an issue.	(+)
Specifying H3: Agenda coupling		
H9	The policy-entrepreneur is more likely to successfully couple the streams during an open agenda window,	
	(a) the more persistent he or she is; and	+
	(b) the more access to key policy-makers she or he has.	+

Source: Own compilation.

Note: "–" indicates that a hypothesis is falsified; "+" indicates that a hypothesis holds; "(+)" indicates that the hypothesis' independent variable had kept the agenda window open, although the policy stream had not been ripe; and "n.a." stands for not applicable.

is in line with what should be expected according to Hypothesis 11a. According to this hypothesis, a short decision-coupling process was likely, because all veto actors had supported the agenda change. Furthermore, the veto actors had already entered intense discussions and negotiations about details of the envisaged third gas directive before the formal proposal had been tabled (see Sect. 6.1.4.2). The Commission had seized that opportunity and had already integrated concessions and package deals in the legislative proposal that it tabled in mid-September. These prenegotiation talks surely contributed to reduce the time required for decision coupling.

Furthermore, decision coupling is expected to be lengthy if policy-makers' attention is redirected to other issues (Hypothesis 11b); whether this had happened is tested by analyzing the policy-makers' agendas. During decision coupling, the *Commission* released two working programs. The first one in October 2007, a month after the Commission had published (among others) its proposal for a third gas directive. In this working program, the Commission only referred to the energy package as such and highlighted the second strategic energy review, a revision of oil stocks legislation, and a revision of the directives on energy performance of buildings and of energy taxation (European Commission 2007c, 14–15). In contrast, in its working program for 2009, it stressed that it aimed at completing pending legislation before its mandate would end in 2010 and explicitly underlined "the importance of securing adoption of proposals on the internal market for gas and electricity" (European Commission 2008, 2, quotation on p. 5).

The *Council* discussed the gas draft directive five times (Council of the European Union 2007d, 2008a, d, b, 2009b) after the Commission had released it and before the Council adopted a common position. As outlined above, the Council meetings during decision coupling were presided over by Portugal, Slovenia, France, and the Czech Republic.[12] All of them assigned reaching an agreement on the gas draft directive a high priority (Portugal 2007, 3; Slovenia 2008, 11; France 2008, 7; Czech Republic 2009, 9).

The *European Council* met six times between the release of the gas proposal and the approval of the Council in June 2009. At five of these meetings, it explicitly called for reaching a timely agreement on the third gas directive (European Council 2007a, 2008a, b, c, 2009), and at one meeting, it more generally appreciated the work achieved regarding the entire energy legislative package (European Council 2008d). Finally, the responsible *EP* committee, the Committee on Industry, Research and Energy, discussed the gas draft directive eight times between being appointed as the committee responsible and the EP's first reading, and four times before the EP's second reading. Furthermore, the Committee on Economic and Monetary Affairs as well as the Committee on Internal Market and

Consumer Protection exchanged their views on the draft three and four times, respectively, and delivered their opinions before the EP's first reading (Committee on Industry, Research and Energy 2008, 139, 184–185, 2009, 87). To conclude, all policy-makers dealt with the gas draft directive on numerous occasions, which is why it remained high on their agendas and contributes to explaining why decision coupling was not lengthy. Thus, Hypothesis 11b can be confirmed.

6.2.2 *Political Entrepreneurs' Coupling Strategies*

As had been the case during agenda coupling, the draft directive's provisions regarding ownership unbundling were the most controversial ones. Therefore, the analysis of decision coupling concentrates on the question of whether political entrepreneurs managed to settle package deals, granted concessions, or succeeded in providing meaning, clarification, and identity to the issue of ownership unbundling (Hypothesis 10).

During decision coupling, the camp of ownership unbundling supporters and opponents was composed as follows: In the Council, the United Kingdom and the Netherlands spearheaded the camp of supporters, which also included Belgium, Denmark, Finland, Romania, Spain, and Sweden. The Commission clearly favored ownership unbundling. It was joined by (the vast majority of) the EP (*European Voice* July 28, 2007). Furthermore, Sir John Mogg, chairman of ERGEG and the Council of European Energy Regulators, made clear that he and the institutions he was in charge of also favored ownership unbundling. He also stressed that any other unbundling provision would have to go along with extensive regulatory oversight (*European Voice* August 30, 2007). The most visible actors in opposition to ownership unbundling were Germany and France in the Council. Since these member states hosted some of the world's largest energy companies, it was judged to be a major political challenge to outvote them (*European Voice* June 12, 2008). France and Germany were supported by Austria, Bulgaria, Cyprus, Greece, Latvia, Luxembourg, and Slovakia. However, Cyprus gave up its opposition after the Commission had promised that it could be granted an exception from the unbundling provisions because of its status as a small and isolated market (Buchan 2009, 75). Nonetheless, the opponents' camp had sufficient votes at its disposal to form a blocking majority in the Council. To conclude, the balance in the Council made some kind of package deals or concessions a necessity in order to get the gas draft directive adopted. Furthermore, German and French representatives in the EP as well as a number of energy undertakings opposed ownership unbundling. They criticized that the Commission's impact assessment of ownership unbundling lacked empirical data and was not a suitable basis for a decision on unbundling requirements (Buchan 2009, 75; *European Report* November 26, 2007 and December 7, 2007).[13] Since all Council Presidencies (namely, the Portuguese, Slovenian, French, and Czech one) did not just assign the IEM high priority in their working programs (see Sect. 6.2.1) but also in the Council meetings they presided over, I do not systematically differentiate between them in the following analysis.[14]

At the first meeting of the Council after the legislative proposal had been published, the opponents of ownership unbundling questioned that ownership unbundling was compatible with their national property rights and requested a third alternative of unbundling (*M2 Presswire* December 3, 2007). Thus, the Commission's idea that the inclusion of the ISO option would make the proposal acceptable to those member states that rejected ownership unbundling did not work. The opponents made clear that they were not willing to accept a gas directive, which only allowed choosing between these two options. Although the ISO option would have been "the lesser evil", the opponents of ownership unbundling regarded it "as an even bigger nonsense" (Buchan 2009, 75), because it would have reduced network owners to a financial holding company and increased red tape.

The Portuguese Council President asked the member states in opposition to the current unbundling for suggestions to present a third alternative rapidly so that negotiations could move on (Council of the European Union 2007a, 47, *European Report* December 3, 2007). Energy Commissioner Piebalgs indicated he was willing to discuss other alternatives, provided they involved real structural changes comparable with those that would result from ownership unbundling and the ISO model. In this context, the United Kingdom reminded the opponents of the suggested unbundling provisions that any third alternative had to be consistent with the criteria set by the European Council meeting in the spring of 2007 (*M2 Presswire* December 3, 2007). At this meeting, the European Council had agreed on the need for "effective separation of supply and production activities from network operations (unbundling), based on independently run and adequately regulated network operation systems which guarantee equal and open access to transport infrastructures and independence of decisions on investment in infrastructure" (Council of the European Union 2007b, 17). John Mogg stressed that "[i]f any alternative approach of an ISO surfaces, it must at minimum be a deep ISO model and effectively regulated by independent regulators with appropriate powers" (quoted in *European Voice* August 30, 2007).

Germany announced that it would come forward with a third unbundling alternative, which it finally did together with France, Austria, Bulgaria, Greece, Luxembourg, Latvia, and Slovakia (Bartenstein et al. 2008, *The International Herald Tribune* February 28, 2008). This third alternative was labeled "effective and efficient unbundling" (EEU). *Effective unbundling* referred to the organization and governance of the TSO, more precisely to provisions that should guarantee it was legally independent from its parent company and had the assets, staff, and financial resources to carry out its network responsibilities by itself. Basically, this equaled legal unbundling, although it stipulated more obligations regarding implementation and monitoring. *Efficient unbundling* related to grid investments and market integration. For instance, it required that a 10-year national network development plan would be elaborated, and if a TSO was not willing to realize an infrastructure contained in this plan, the NRA could oblige the TSO to realize it or organize a tender for third investors (Bartenstein et al. 2008, 4).

The Commission rejected this EEU option (*European Report* February 22, 2008), which it described as a watered-down version of the ISO model (*The International Herald Tribune* February 28, 2008). Nonetheless, the Commission specified in a "nonpaper" the conditions EEU as well as any other alternative than ownership unbundling would have to meet in order to be considered as a viable alternative in mid-February 2008 (*European Report* February 22, 2008). According to the Commission, it was essential that (1) unbundling had to apply to gas and electricity, (2) TSO independence with regard to investment decisions and management of the grid was guaranteed, (3) NRAs would have an influence on investment decisions, (4) effective operation of regional cooperation despite vertical integration of some TSOs was guaranteed, and (5) existing requirements set out in the *acquis communitaire* were not reversed (Council of the European Union 2008e, 7). Furthermore, the Commission had summarized a nonexhaustive list of 12 guarantees that it intended to impose on the EEU in order to achieve truly independent TSOs (*European Report* February 22, 2008). The fact that the Commission already considered how EEU would have to be revised in order to be acceptable indicated that it became more willing to negotiate package deals or concessions (Hypotheses 10a and 10b).

Immediately before the Council met in February and June 2008, the Commission settled an agreement with Eon (in February) and with Rheinisch-Westfälisches Elektrizitätswerk (RWE) (in June) regarding the pending infringement proceedings. During agenda coupling, the Commission had offered them to reduce the fines they had to pay for infringement of EU competition rules in return for ownership unbundling. It took until February 2008 that Eon agreed to sell its power grid (*The International Herald Tribune* February 29, 2008) and until June 2008 that RWE agreed to sell its gas grid (Buchan 2009, 77). The German government was annoyed about the fact and the timing of these agreements since they were reached at the same day as it had planned to push for a third option in the Council. The Commission had initially hoped to make governments that opposed ownership unbundling more willing to accept this provision if their domestic energy undertakings had already opted to implement it. This did not work in the case of the German government: it still fought for a third alternative. Nonetheless, it weakened the German position insofar as the involved actors no longer assumed that such a thing as a "unified German position" (senior Commission official quoted in Buchan 2009, 77) existed.

At the first Council meeting after the third unbundling option and the Commission's nonpaper had been revealed, it became clear that EEU was a serious alternative for numerous member states. According to diplomats from the French delegation, unbundling opponents almost managed to settle a compromise that included the suggested EEU option and was only blocked by the United Kingdom, Sweden, and the Netherlands in the last minute (*European Sport Gas Markets* February 29, 2008). However, according to the Presidency conclusions, the member states' opinion varied regarding the options on the negotiating table. Nonetheless, it aimed at achieving a political agreement by June 2008 (Council of the European Union 2008e, 12).

Given the degree of disagreement on the issue of unbundling provisions, the objective to settle a compromise within four months was highly ambitious. The reason for this rush was that, in June 2009, there would be elections to the EP. In order to grant the EP sufficient time to process the draft directive under its current mandate, the Council had to reach an agreement until early 2009(*European Daily Electricity Markets* June 18, 2008). One day before the Council met on June 6, 2008, the Committee on Industry, Research and Energy adopted a report on the proposal for a third gas directive and suggested several amendments. Regarding the unbundling provisions, it rejected the suggestion to include EEU in the proposal as had been made by the German chair of this committee, Angelika Niebler (Europe Energy June 11, 2008). The committee's report suggested deleting the draft directive's provisions regarding the ISO model since it implied bureaucracy and costly regulatory oversight (Committee on Industry, Research and Energy 2008, amendment 71). The members of the EP decided to postpone the final vote on the report's adoption until the next session in July in order to be able to take into account a possible consent member states might reach the next day (*Europe Energy* June 11, 2008). Thus, not only the Commission but also the EP was willing to enter negotiations about package deals and concessions.

Due to the Slovenian Council Presidency's efforts, the Council managed to settle a compromise on June 6, 2008. Based on a Presidency compromise proposal, the Council agreed on two unbundling options: ownership unbundling and the creation of independent transmission system operators (ITSO). The latter option allowed energy undertakings to keep the transmission level vertically integrated as long as the operator, its management, and a supervisory body were effectively independent (Council of the European Union 2008d, 7). It built on the EEU option but differed insofar as this option was combined with more safeguards regarding the TSO's effective decision-making rights. Basically, this was a compromise between the Commission on the one side and France and Germany on the other side (*European Voice* June 12, 2008). They started negotiations with the Commission's offer that member states could derogate from ownership unbundling by opting for the creation of an ISO. However, France and Germany had rejected that their vertically integrated energy undertakings had to detach the transmission level, which was why they opposed ownership unbundling and the ISO option. In this situation, France and Germany mapped out a solution they were willing to accept. They suggested transferring the management of the transmission system to an ITSO, and in return, vertically integrated energy undertakings should be allowed to retain ownership of the transmission system (*European Voice* June 12, 2008). The Commission agreed to accept this ITSO option, provided it was limited to the gas sector and accompanied with extra safeguards which would ensure (1) independence of the TSO from the parent company, (2) avoidance of conflicts of interest, (3) fair and nondiscriminatory network access, (4) undistorted investments in the interconnection infrastructure, and (5) the ITSO would have the means and resources at its disposal in order to work independently (Council of the European Union 2008b, 7). This provision faced opposition from the Council's pro-unbundling camp and contra-unbundling camp. The latter did not want the ITSO option to be limited to the gas sector, while the former insisted on stricter rules on how to ensure the TSO's independence (*European Voice* June 12, 2008). Furthermore, these camps disagreed on the scope of the draft directive's review clause. The Commission had suggested undertaking a detailed review of the implementation of unbundling requirements not later than three years after the directive's entry into force. In particular, the United Kingdom had pushed for an earlier review and that one review criterion should be how unbundling affected competition, with the other criteria being network access, effective regulation, investment, interconnection infrastructure, and security of supply. Although the contra-unbundling camp feared that this review could end up being a sunset clause for the ITSO option, it agreed on (1) limiting the review on the ITSO option, (2) taking ownership unbundling as a benchmark, and (3) accepting two years after the directive's entry into force as a due date for this report (*Europe Energy* June 11, 2008). In return, the pro-unbundling camp and the Commission accepted that the ITSO option applied to the gas and electricity sector (*European Voice* June 12, 2008). Thus, the Council, together with the Commission, had settled a compromise which consisted of various concessions (Hypothesis 10b).

Did the EP adopt this compromise in its legislative resolution regarding the proposal for a revised gas directive? In early July 2008, the EP decided to suggest amending the proposal with regard to the unbundling provisions. It included the ITSO option as agreed upon in the Council and adhered to its decision to delete the ISO option (cf. Committee on Industry, Research and Energy 2008). Since the Council confirmed at its October meeting that it had maintained its decision to allow for the three unbundling options outlined at its June meeting (Council of the European Union 2008c), it became clear that further negotiations between the EP and the Council were necessary in order to settle a compromise. These negotiations took place in six trialogue meetings between January and March 2009 (*European Voice* February 12, 2009). Given how difficult it had been for the Council to settle a compromise between the member states, it was unwilling to renegotiate this compromise with the EP. The EP made clear that if it had to compromise on unbundling, it would insist on concessions in other areas, most importantly regarding regulatory oversight (*European Voice* March 24, 2009). Consequently, the EP and the Council agreed that, in return for the EP's consent to the Council's unbundling provisions, the Council accepted stricter provisions regarding regulatory oversight (such as a reinforcement of the NRAs' competences and the granting of their independence from the governments and industry), some additional rights for consumers (such as switching the supplier within three weeks), and the task to address energy poverty (*EU Neues Bulletin* April 23, 2009, *European Voice* March 24, 2009). This compromise was endorsed in the Council's common position (Council of the European Union 2009a) and at the EP's second reading (European Parliament 2009). Thus, the willingness of all veto actors to offer concessions paved the way for policy adoption (Hypothesis 10b).

The reciprocity clause the Commission had inserted in order to win support for ownership unbundling during agenda coupling was another issue which the involved actors discussed controversially. This clause was designed as a EU investment veto, according to which companies from third countries would not have been allowed to buy assets from EU energy undertakings as long as they did not have the same market access in the third country (*EurActiv* October 13, 2008). Apart from being criticized by Russia (*Nuclear Engineering International* December 12, 2007), doubts regarding the formulation of the reciprocity clause were voiced in the Council and the Commission. According to EU officials, DG Trade questioned whether it was compatible with World Trade Organization rules and the United Kingdom feared that it could keep energy undertakings located in the United States from buying assets in the EU (*European Voice* May 21, 2008). Furthermore, several member states were involved in projects with Gazprom (in particular, Austria, Germany, and Italy), and they all feared that these projects could be jeopardized by the restrictiveness of the reciprocity clause in its current form (*Wall Street Journal* September 21, 2007). The EP in turn barely touched this subject.

At the Council meeting in December 2007, the Council agreed that a reciprocity clause was needed, but "only to guarantee a measure of equal treatment" (Council of the European Union 2007d, 47). How this measure of equal treatment could look like was outlined at the Council meeting in June 2008: "in a non-protectionist way which guarantees that these companies [from third countries, N.H.] respect the same rules that apply to EU undertakings and addresses Member State concerns about third country control" (Council of the European Union 2008b). At the Council meeting in October 2008, the member states agreed that it sufficed if a bilateral agreement between a member state and a third country was settled. Furthermore, they laid down criteria for the assessment of investments by companies from third countries as well as a procedure for certification of investors from third countries that were about taking control of a DSO

(Council of the European Union 2008c). This compromise was included in the third gas directive (2009/73/EC, Article 11). Although the Baltic States and Poland would have preferred a stricter reciprocity clause (*EurActiv* October 13, 2008), they granted these concessions and accepted the compromise (Hypothesis 10b). Their willingness to compromise was, to a certain extent, a result of their weak negotiating position. Given that, in the Council, highly active political entrepreneurs from the pro-unbundling camp (Germany) and the contra-unbundling camp (the United Kingdom) had serious reservations about the reciprocity clause as well as parts of the Commission, it would have been very difficult to force through their position.

6.2.3 Interim Conclusion

Twenty-two months after the Commission had published its legislative proposal, the third gas directive was adopted. This was a rather short decision-making process, given that this directive was a second-order change (Hall 1993) as it not just changed the instruments' calibration (such as a modification of the unbundling provisions) but also introduced new ones (such as the reciprocity clause) (cf. Brutschin 2015, 191). The analysis documented that Hypothesis 11 can be confirmed: Since agenda change did not take place against the will of veto actors and policy-makers' attention was not redirected, it was unlikely that decision coupling would be lengthy.

In addition, a peculiarity of this decision-making process might also contribute to explaining its short duration. This peculiarity was that, swiftly after the Commission had published its legislative proposal, it became clear that (1) the unbundling provisions were the most controversial ones and (2) the Council was split about this issue. Since the supporters' and opponents' camp consisted of sufficient member states to block a decision in the Council, it was apparent that without some kind of package deal or concessions, a policy change would not be within reach. Both camps entered negotiations immediately and concentrated on offering concessions (Hypothesis 10b). Basically, I find two reasons why member states entered negotiations without hesitation:

(1) When the negotiations started, the member states had already exchanged views about the options on the table. As a consequence, they knew which camps existed. This made it easier to organize

negotiations, because (exceptions confirming the rule) they had only to deal with each camp's reservation. In particular, the knowledge about the existence of the two camps facilitated offering concessions, because each camp just had to take into account the others camp's position and not that of several member states. This implies that agenda coupling had a knock-on effect on decision coupling (Chap. 7 returns to this issue in detail). Furthermore, this might also explain why member states did not consider package deals in order to settle an agreement. Since the composition of opponents and proponents varied during decision coupling with the issue at stake, it would have been difficult to find a package deal that was equally attractive to all members of a camp. Consequently, granting concessions was easier to achieve, because the concessions referred to the issue that divided the two different camps from each other.

(2) The European Council had called for the veto actors to reach a compromise in a timely manner at each meeting during decision coupling between December 2007 and December 2008 (European Council 2007a, 2008a, b, c). Since the European Council consists of the heads of state or governments, it has a great deal of authority. This might have increased the Council's commitment to settle an agreement.[15] Table 6.4 summarizes the findings.

Table 6.4 How well the multiple streams framework fares in explaining how the third gas directive was passed

Directive		*2009/73/EC*
Explaining decision-making: decision coupling		
H10	Policy adoption is more likely if a political entrepreneur	
	(a) manages to combine viable alternatives embraced by different veto actors into one package;	
	(b) can (and does) offer concessions on the original proposal; or	+
	(c) succeeds in providing meaning, clarification, and identity to the issue at stake.	
H11	Decision coupling is more likely to be lengthy if	
	(a) agenda change has taken place against the will of veto actors; or	+
	(b) if policy-makers' attention is redirected to other issues.	+

Source: Own compilation
Note: "+" indicates that a hypothesis holds

Notes

1. That the Commission had been successful in framing the IEM as a means to secure energy supply is indicated, for instance, in the fact that the European Council adopted this framing in its conclusion of March 2006, according to which a full, effective, and transparent implementation of the IEM legislation would play "a key role for the security of supply" (European Council 2006, 14). For a similar assessment, see Buchan (2010, 361).
2. Cameron (2007, 108) pointed out that the creation of the European Regulators Group for Electricity and Gas (ERGEG) reduced the Madrid Forum's importance. This might be true in terms of giving national regulatory authorities (NRAs) a stronger voice. Nonetheless, the meetings of the Madrid Forum remained the occasion where all stakeholders came together to exchange views (see Annex III). Due to this function, the Commission explicitly stated that the Madrid Forum would continue to play an important role (*EU Neues Bulletin* November 14, 2003).
3. See *Energie und Management* online (2004): Arbeitsprogramm der europäischen Regulatoren, online available at: http://www.energie-und-management.de/free-archive/Freearchive/feView3/883.html, last accessed on May 1, 2015.
4. The Commission delivered a summary about the state of its infringement proceedings as of April 2006 (European Commission 2006e) and as of December (European Commission 2006h).
5. Note that the Commission profited from the energy sector inquiry (see 6.1.4.2) in order to carry forward the infringement proceedings. In the course of this inquiry, it had obtained in-depth knowledge about the energy sector because it was entitled to obtain information, documents, and statements from companies and trade associations according to Council Regulation (EC) No. 1/2003.
6. The passing of the second gas draft directive fell in the presidency of Italy, which was why Italy (2003) did not include further legislative measures regarding the gas market in its work program. The Irish and Dutch Presidencies referred to the gas market with regard to the need for cross-border regulation (Ireland 2003, 13; Ireland and the Netherlands 2004, 16).

7. For instance, in September 2005, Energy Commissioner Piebalgs did not link the energy sector inquiry to the need for further legislative measures. To the contrary, he stated that the second gas and electricity directives "ought to be sufficient" (quoted in *EU Neues Bulletin* September 23, 2005).
8. With regard to energy as a public service, the Commission planned an Energy Customers' Charter to deal with public service obligations (PSO) and did not link it to the electricity or gas directives (European Commission 2007b, 10).
9. In conjunction with its Communication on an energy policy for Europe, the Commission also released a Communication dealing with the prospects for the internal gas and electricity market (European Commission 2007h). Since the issues discussed in this Communication are also included in the Commission's impact assessment, the former is not included in this overview of the generation of alternatives.
10. For a general introduction to impact assessments, see Adelle et al. (2013).
11. The Commission had worked out these guidelines following a request of the European Council (2005) in the spring of 2005. The guidelines aimed at defining a three-year strategy "that addresses a relatively weak growth performance and insufficient job creation" in the European Union (EU) in the early 2000s (European Commission 2005f, 4). Among others, the Commission had defined the further integration of the IEM as a means to address these problems (European Commission 2005f, 18).
12. Sweden presided over the Council in the second half of 2009. Since the Council had approved the gas directive in late June 2009, Sweden's presidency is not considered in the analysis.
13. This section concentrates on negotiations in the EU's decision-making arena. However, the gas draft directive was also discussed at meetings in the Madrid Forum (European Gas Regulatory Forum 2007b, 2008a, 2008b, 2009).
14. Note that this also applies to France. Although France had threatened that the gas draft directive would be of a low priority during its term of office, it did not act accordingly, but aimed at advancing negotiations (cf. *European Report* June 9, 2008, June 18, 2008).
15. Generally speaking, this applies also to the European Parliament (EP) and the Commission. But since the national ministers are

agents of their head of state or government, it is highly probable that they understand requests stemming from the European Council to be of a highly binding nature.

References

(EC) No 1/2003. *Council Regulation on the Implementation of the Rules on Competition Laid Down in Articles 81 and 82 of the Treaty, 16 December 2002.*

2003/796/EC. *Decision of 11 November 2003 on Establishing the European Regulators Group for Electricity and Gas.*

2004/67/EC. *Council Directive Concerning Measures to Safeguard Security of Natural Gas Supply.*

2006/77/EC. *Decision of 23 December 2005 setting up a High Level Group on Competitiveness, Energy, and the Environment.*

2009/72/EC. *Directive of the European Parliament and of the Council of 13 July 2009 Concerning Common Rules for the Internal Market in Electricityy and Repealing Directive 2003/54/EC.*

2009/73/EC. Directive of the European Parliament and of the Council of 13 July concerning common rules for the internal market in natural gas and repealing directive 2003/55/EC.

Adelle, Camilla, Andrew Jordan, and John Turnpenny. 2013. Policy Making. In *Environmental Policy in the EU: sectActors, Institutions and Processes*, 3rd ed., ed. Andrew Jordan and Camilla Adelle, 209–226. London/New York: Routledge.

Austria. 2005. *The Austrian EU Presidency: January–June 2006.*

Bartenstein, Martin, Petar Dimitrov, Michael Glos, Jean-Louis Folias, Jeannot Krecke, Kaspers Gerhards, and Lubomir Jahnatek. 2008. *Letter to Angelika Niebler, ITRE Chairwoman, European Parliament: 29 January 2008.*

Bauler, Tom. 2006. The Commission's Impact Assessment Process: Handling the External Dimensions of Sustainability. In *The European Union and Sustainable Development: Internal and External Dimensions*, ed. Marc Pallemaerts and Albena Azmanova, 277–290. Brussels: Vubpress.

British Petroleum. 2009. *Statistical Review of World Energy.* London: British Petroleum.

Brutschin, Elina. 2015. Shaping the EU's Energy Policy Agenda: The Role of Eastern European Countries. In *Energy Policy Making in the EU: Building the Agenda*, ed. Jale Tosun, Sophie Biesenbender, and Kai Schulze, 187–204. London: Springer.

Buchan, David. 2009. *Energy and Climate Change: Europe at the Crossroads.* Oxford: Oxford University Press.

———. 2010. Energy Policy: Sharp Challenges and Rising Ambitions. In *Policy-making in the European Union*, ed. Helen Wallace, Mark A. Pollack, and Alasdair R. Young, 357–379. Oxford: Oxford University Press.

Cameron, Peter D. 2007. *Competition in Energy Markets: Law and Regulation in the European Union*. 2nd ed. Oxford: Oxford University Press.

Committee on Industry, Research and Energy. 2008. *Report on the Proposal for a Directive of the European Parliament and of the Council Amending Directive 2003/55/EC Concerning Common Rules for the Internal Market in Natural Gas: A6-0257/2008.*

———. 2009. *Recommendation for Second Reading on the Council Common Position for Adopting a Directive of the European Parliament and of the Council Concerning Common Rules for the Internal Market in Natural Gas and Repealing Directive 2003/55/EC: A6-0238/2009.*

Council of the European Union. 2005. *Council Conclusions: 2695th Council meeting, 1 and 5 December 2005.*

———. 2006. *Council Conclusions: 2735th Council meeting, 8-9 June 2006.*

———. 2007a. *2835th Council meeting. Transport, Telecommunications and Energy. Brussels, 29-30 November/ 3 December 2007: 15891/07 (Presse 274).*

———. 2007b. *Council Conclusions: 2782nd Council meeting, 15 February 2007.*

———. 2007c. *Council Conclusions: 2805th Council meeting, 6–8 June 2007.*

———. 2007d. *Council Conclusions: 2835th Council meeting, 29–30 November and 3 December.*

———. 2008a. *Council Conclusions: 2854th Council meeting, 28 February 2008.*

———. 2008b. *Council Conclusions: 2875th Council meeting, 6 June 2008.*

———. 2008c. *Council Conclusions: 2895th Council meeting, 9–10 October 2008.*

———. 2008d. *Note from Presidency to Delegations: Internal Energy Market, 3 June 2008.*

———. 2008e. *Note from Presidency to Delegations: TTE (Energy) Council on 28 February 2008.*

———. 2009a. *Common Position Adopted by the Council on 9 January 2009 with a View to the Adoption of a Directive of the European Parliament and of the Council Concerning Common Rules for the Internal Market in Natural Gas and Repealing Directive 2003/55/EC.*

———. 2009b. *Council Conclusions: 2953rd Council meeting, 25 June 2009.*

Czech Republic. 2009. *Work Programme of the Czech Presidency of the Council of the EU in 2009: Europe Without Barriers. January–June 2009.*

Eikeland, Per O. 2011. The Third Internal Energy Market Package: New Power Relations Among Member States, EU Institutions and Non-State Actors? *Journal of Common Market Studies* 49(2): 243–263.

———. 2012. *EU Energy Policy Integration–Stakeholders, Institutions and Issue-linkages*. FNI Report 13/2012. Lysaker.

European Commission. 2002. *The Internal Market in Energy: Coordinated Measures on the Security of Energy Supply: COM(2002)488 Final.*

———. 2003. *Second Benchmarking Report on the Implementation of the Internal Electricity and Gas Market: SEC(2003)448.*

———. 2004. *Third Benchmarking Report on the Implementation of the Internal Electricity and Gas Markets.*

———. 2005a. *Commission Work Programme for 2005: COM(2005)15 Final.*

———. 2005b. *Commission's Report Indicates that Governments Should Do More to Implement Energy Market Opening. Press Release: IP/05/11.*

———. 2005c. *Communication to the Spring European Council. Working Together for Growth and Jobs. A New Start for the Lisbon Strategy: COM(2005)24 Final.*

———. 2005d. *Competition: Commission Opens Sector Inquiry into Gas and Electricity. Press Release: IP/05/716.*

———. 2005e. *Energy Markets: Five Member States to be Taken Before the Court of Justice. Press Release: IP/05/853.*

———. 2005f. *Integrated Guidelines for Growth and Jobs (2005-2008). Communication From the President, in Agreement with Vice-President Verheugen and Commissioners Almunia and Spidla: COM(2005)141 Final.*

———. 2005g. *Opening up of Energy Markets: Ten Member States Have Still Not Transposed the New EU Rules. Press Release: IP/05/319.*

———. 2005h. *Report from the Commission. Annual Report on the Implementation of the Gas and Electricity Internal Market: COM(2004)863 Final.*

———. 2005i. *Unlocking Europe's Full Potential. Commission Legislative and Work Programme 2006: COM(2005)531.*

———. 2006a. *A European Strategy for Sustainable, Competitive and Secure Energy: COM(2006)105 Final.*

———. 2006b. *Andris Piebalgs: The Situtation of Internal Markets in Gas and Electricity. Presentation of "Preliminary Findings of the Energy Sector Inquiry": SPEECH/06/94.*

———. 2006c. *Commission Legislative and Work Programme 2007: COM(2006) 629 Final.*

———. 2006d. *Energy, Environment, Competitiveness: Competition Launches High Level Group. Press Release: IP/06/226.*

———. 2006e. *Infringement Procedures Openeed in the Gas and Electricity Market Sector, by Member State: MEMO/06/152.*

———. 2006f. *Summary Report on the Analysis of the Debate on the Green Paper "A European Strategy for Sustainable, Competitive and Secure Energy": SEC(2006) 1500.*

———. 2006g. *The Commission Takes Action Against Member States Which Have Not Opened up Their Energy Markets Properly. Press Release: IP/06/430.*

———. 2006h. *The Commission to Act Over EU Energy Markets: MEMO/06/481.*

———. 2007a. *Accompanying the Legislative Package on the Internal Market for Electricity and Gas. Impact Assessment: SEC(2007)1179.*
———. 2007b. *An Energy Policy for Europe: COM(2007)1 Final.*
———. 2007c. *Commission Legislative and Work Programme 2008: COM(2007) 640 final.*
———. 2007d. *Commission Takes Action Against Luxembourg and Irland Regarding EU Rules on Electricity and Gas. Press Release: IP/07/936.*
———. 2007e. *Inquiry Pursuant to Article 17 of Regulation (EC) No 1/2003 into the European Gas and Electricity Sectors (Final Report): COM(2006)851 Final.*
———. 2007f. *Memo on the Energy Council: MEMO/07/225.*
———. 2007g. *Proposal for a Directive of the European Parliament and of the Council Amending Directive 2003/55/EC Concerning Common Rules for the Internal Market in Natural Gas: COM(2007)529 Final.*
———. 2007h. *Prospects for the Internal Gas and Electricity Market: COM(2006) 841 Final.*
———. 2008. *Commission Legislative and Work Programme 2009. Acting Now for a Better Europe: COM(2008)712 Final.*
European Council. 2005. *Presidency Conclusions: 22–23 March 2005.*
———. 2006. *Presidency Conclusions: 23–24 March 2006.*
———. 2007a. *Presidency Conclusions: 13–14 December 2007.*
———. 2007b. *Presidency Conclusions: 8–9 March 2007.*
———. 2008a. *Presidency Conclusions: 13–14 March 2008.*
———. 2008b. *Presidency Conclusions: 19–20 June 2008.*
———. 2008c. *Presidency Conclusions: 15–16 October 2008.*
———. 2008d. *Presidency Conclusions: 11–12 December 2008.*
———. 2009. *Presidency Conclusions: 19–20 March 2009.*
European Gas Regulatory Forum. 2003. *Programme of the 7th European Gas Regulatory Forum: 24–25 September 2003.* Available Upon Request From the Author.
———. 2006. *Agenda of the 11th Meeting of the European Gas Regulatory Forum: 18–19 May 2006:* Available Upon Request From the Author.
———. 2007a. *Agenda of the 12th Meeting of the European Gas Regulatory Forum: 20–21 February 2007:* Available Upon Request From the Author.
———. 2007b. *Conclusions: 13th Meeting of the European Gas Regulatory Forum. Madrid, 16–17 October 2007:* Available Upon Request From the Author.
———. 2008a. *Agenda of the 14th meeting of the European Gas Regulatory Forum: 22-23 May 2008:* Available upon request from the author.
———. 2008b. *Conclusions: 15th Meeting of the European Gas Regulatory Forum. Madrid, 6–7 November 2008:* Available Upon Request From the Author.
———. 2009. *Conclusions: 16th Meeting of the European Gas Regulatory Forum. Madrid, 28–29 May 2009:* Available Upon Request From the Author.

European Parliament. 2007. *European Parliament Resolution on Prospects for the Internal Gas and Electricity Market (2007/2089(INI)): P6_TA(2007)0326.*

———. 2009. *Internal Market in Natural Gas. European Parliament Resolution of 22 April 2009 on the Council Common Position for Adopting a Directive of the European Parliament and of the Council Concerning Common Rules for the Internal Market in Natural Gas and Repealing Directive 2003/55/EC: P6-TA (2009)0244.*

Finland. 2006. *Preliminary Agenda for Finland's Presidency of the EU: July–December 2006.*

Fischer, Severin. 2011. *Auf dem Weg zur gemeinsamen Energiepolitik: Strategien, Instrumente und Politikgestaltung in der Europäischen Union.* Baden-Baden: Nomos.

France. 2008. *French Presidency of the Council of the European Union. Work programme 1 July–31 December 2008.*

Geden, Oliver, and Severin Fischer. 2008. *Die Energie- und Klimapolitik der Europäischen Union: Bestandsaufnahme und Perspektiven.* Baden-Baden: Nomos.

Germany. 2006. *Europe—Succeeding Together: Presidency Programme 1 January to 30 June 2007.*

Haase, N. 2009. *European Gas Market Liberalisation.* Enschede: Universiteit Twente.

Hall, Peter A. 1993. Policy Paradigms, Social Learning, and the State: The Case of Economic Policymaking in Britain. *Comparative Politics* 25(3): 275–296.

Ireland. 2003. *Programme of the Irish Presidency of the Council of the European Union: 1 January–30 June 2004.*

Ireland, and the Netherlands. 2004. *Operational Programme of the Council for 2004 Submitted by the Incoming Irish and Dutch Presidencies: The Union in 2004: Seizing the Opportunities of the Enlarged Union.*

Italy. 2003. *Programme of the Italian Presidency of the Council of the European Union: 1 July to 31 December 2003.*

Kingdon, John W. 1984. *Agendas, Alternatives, and Public Policies.* Boston: Little, Brown.

Klotz, Robert, and Harold Nyssens. 2004. Energy Day: First Sectoral High-Level Meeting Within the ECN. *Competition Policy Newsletter* 3: 33–35.

Luxembourg. 2005. *The Luxembourg Presidency of the Council of the European Union 2005: The Presidency's priorities, January–June 2005.*

Maltby, Tomas. 2013. European Union Energy Policy Integration: A Case of European Commission Policy Entrepreneurship and Increasing Supranationalism. *Energy Policy* 55(100) 435–444.

Portugal. 2007. *EU Priorities–Portuguese 2007 Presidency of the EU. Summary: 27 June 2007, Portuguese Presidency of the Council: A stronger union for a better world, July–December 2007.*

Slovenia. 2008. *Presidency of the Council of Ministers of the European Union: Slovenian Presidency Programme, January–June 2008.*

United Kingdom. 2005. *UK Presidency of the Council: Presidency Priorities, July–December 2005.*

Vavilov, Andrey, and Georgy Trofimov. 2015. A Phanom Energy Empire: The Failure of Gazprom's Downstream Integration. In *Mirages of Superpower: Gazprom in Pursuit of Expansion and in Need of Rationality*, ed. Andreĭ Vavilov, 72–104. Houndmills: Palgrave Macmillan.

CHAPTER 7

Conclusion

This book contributes to public policy–oriented research on European Union (EU) policy-making in two respects: First, it derived and tested a modified multiple streams framework (MSF) tailored to EU agenda-setting and decision-making. Second, by empirically testing how well the suggested modifications fare in explaining the regulatory shift in the EU natural gas market policy between 1998 and 2009, this book enriches the sparse public policy–related literature on EU natural gas regulation. More precisely, based on the analysis of the policy processes that led to the three directives concerning common rules for the internal market in natural gas (98/30/EC, 2003/55/EC, and 2009/73/EC), it adds to a deeper understanding of the policy dynamics in this field. The subsequent section provides brief answers to the research questions that guided the empirical analysis (Sect. 7.1). This is followed, first, by a summary of the advantages of the MSF over other theories of the policy process, and second, by an assessment of how well the MSF fared in explaining the policy processes analyzed (Sect. 7.2).

7.1 Empirical Findings

Given the resistance of the member states and the energy industry to the liberalization of the natural gas market, this book aimed at answering, first, how the draft directive leading to the first gas directive gained agenda status (RQ 1), and second, why the member states did not use their right to veto in order to avert this policy change once the draft directive had entered the decision-making stage (RQ 2). The analysis revealed that the draft directive

N. Herweg, *European Union Policy-Making*,
DOI 10.1007/978-3-319-49400-5_7

gained agenda status because of the Commission's skillful acting as a policy-entrepreneur. Most importantly, it managed to attach the idea of creating an internal energy market (IEM) to the single market project. This was a clever move because the single market project was wholeheartedly supported by EU policy-makers and industries. Thus, it became difficult to argue that the single market project was wished for but the energy market should be excluded from it. During agenda-setting, the vast majority of stakeholders nonetheless made it clear that they opposed the IEM by not entering a constructive dialogue with the Commission. Thereby, it became complicated for the Commission to work out a legislative proposal since it depended on stakeholders' input.

However, the United Kingdom, a liberalization pioneer and advocate, provided the Commission with information about its energy legislation. As a consequence, the Commission came forward with a proposal that resembled UK legislation. While this explains how the draft directive entered the agenda, it does not explain why the member states did not block it during decision-making. Most importantly, they did not block it because the Commission had threatened to use its powers under Article 86(3) and decide on gas market liberalization by itself. This changed the member states' fallback position as they would have lost any say on this issue. Consequently, it was the lesser evil for the member states to negotiate common rules for the natural gas sector since this granted them the opportunity to influence the design of the gas directive.

Lengthy and complicated negotiations were required in order to get the first gas directive adopted. Therefore, it was surprising that, in 2001 and 2007, the gas draft directive returned on the agenda and was revised extensively. It was particularly surprising because the previous gas directives had only just been implemented. Consequently, the involved actors had only gained little experiences regarding the directives' impact on the creation and completion of the IEM. Thus, the third research question is how can the return of the gas directive on the EU decision agenda be explained (RQ 3). In both cases, it was the Commission that started pushing for the revision of the gas directive. The reason was that the Commission had been aiming at achieving open access on energy networks since the late 1980s. Since the gas directives were compromise solutions, the member states had only opened the networks to a certain extent but less than what the Commission had envisaged (cf. Buchan 2010, 364).

Furthermore, the Commission was convinced that an IEM was not just a goal in itself but would also tackle the problems of energy security and climate change (cf. Buchan 2010, 362). As had been the case in the first gas directive process, the Commission linked the gas directives to a broader and widely supported policy project, namely the Lisbon Strategy. In contrast to the first gas directive, it managed to include the IEM in the Lisbon Strategy from the very beginning. At the heart of the Lisbon Strategy was the idea to increase the EU's competitiveness; thus, the Commission just had to reveal that the state of the internal natural gas market was problematic in this respect. Resulting from a Commission's initiative, the first and second gas directives contained a review clause. The clause tasked the Commission to review the directives' application, to submit reports on the experiences gained, and to consider whether provisions for further improving the internal market in natural gas were required (98/30/EC, Article 28; 2003/55/EC, Article 31). These provisions gave the Commission room to closely monitor the gas directives' implementation and impact. The Commission documented observed deviations from a fully liberalized internal natural gas market in its annual benchmarking reports. The knowledge gained from this close monitoring made it easier for the Commission to apply competition law, which it did in the form of infringement proceedings and (in case of the third gas directive) an energy sector inquiry. As a consequence, the incomplete state of the natural gas market had become apparent, which was why there was no ground for excluding this market from the Lisbon Strategy.

The fourth research question deals with the length of the decision-making processes that led to the three gas directives. Although from directive to directive, the political and regulatory complexity increased, the decision-making processes required less time. Thus, the last research question aims at explaining why these processes had shortened substantially (RQ 4). Put differently, it focuses on reasons that made policy-makers more willing (and capable) to compromise. At least the following three observations contribute to explaining policy-makers' increased willingness: (1) While they had equaled the liberalization of the natural gas market with "the end of civilization" (Stern 1998, 91) during the first gas directive process, they accepted this idea in the second and third gas directive processes. Although there was no consensus regarding how to achieve an IEM, the project was no longer questioned. Thereby, the IEM had shifted from high to low politics (although some overlap persisted). (2) The first gas directive had induced changes, which undermined "mechanisms capable of producing path-dependent continuity" (Beyer 2010, 9). This fostered the member states' interest to agree on common rules, as documented by the following example: The extent and the speed with which the member states implemented the gas directives differed. As a consequence, companies from those member states that had taken the liberalization route purposefully were in a disadvantageous situation. Due to the introduction of nondiscriminatory third-party access despite existent take-or-pay commitments, the market shares of vertically integrated gas giants shrunk. This qualified them as easy takeover candidates from barely liberalized member states, which had plenty of resources to do so, thanks to their still prevailing monopoly. Hence, once they opted for the liberalization route, it became vital for those member states that a level playing field was created to eliminate the disadvantages for their domestic companies. (3) The extent and manner as to how the stakeholders exchanged their views on the natural gas market regulation in general and with regard to the draft directives on the negotiating table had changed tremendously since the late 1980s. The most prominent and visible example of this change was the institutionalization of the Madrid Forum. At its meetings, all stakeholders exchanged their views and experiences, and aimed at developing consensus in order to achieve rapid progress on the highly technical issue of natural gas market regulation (European Gas Regulatory Forum 1999, 1). This went along with the institutionalization of European industry associations, such as Eurogas. Since the stakeholders' input was (and still is) pivotal in order to prepare a proposal for a revised gas directive, their turn to the European level made it easier for the Commission to come up with proposals that were (more) congruent with their demands. This reduced member states' incentives to block or prolong negotiations.

7.2 Theoretical Findings

In this book, I applied the MSF in order to explain agenda change and policy change in energy policy-making in the EU between mid-1980 and 2009. Thereby, I applied the MSF to another issue, jurisdiction, policy stage, and time frame than covered by the original formulation of the framework (Kingdon 1984). Although applying the MSF outside its original scope is common practice, only a few contributions explicitly address the question of whether this renders necessary theoretical adjustments. Since EU policy-making differs markedly from policy-making in the United States, I defined functional equivalents for the framework's elements and translated its necessary conditions for agenda change to EU policy-making. Given the mixed findings regarding interest groups' influence on the EU policy process and indications in the secondary literature that interest groups' influence had been limited in the three gas directive processes (see Sect. 2.3.2), I dealt with them only marginally. Thus, the question of how interest groups affect the EU policy process and how this knowledge can be incorporated in a MSF requires further research. The same applies to the question of how EU policy-makers' partisan affiliation affects which ideas are considered during agenda-setting and decision-making (see Sect. 2.3.2). Regarding the analysis of the gas directive processes, this question did not need to be answered since the national affiliation was more important than the partisan one, given that energy was perceived to be a high-politics issue.

Due to my research interest, I also suggested a way to analyze the decision-making stage of the gas directive processes using a multiple streams lens: by introducing a second coupling process. Since there are different legislative procedures to adopt a policy, the MSF might call for different revisions depending on the legislative procedure under which an issue falls. The refinements suggested in this book were derived with the ordinary legislative procedure in mind. In order to systematically test whether my theoretical refinements hold in the empirical analysis and to make my results coherent and comparable, I derived and tested a set of hypotheses, which has been "a little trodden path" (Cairney and Jones 2016, 53). Before summarizing how well these theoretical adjustments fared in the empirical analysis (for an overview, see Tables 7.1 and 7.2) and which new questions arise from my findings, I outline the advantages of the applied multiple streams perspective when compared with other theories.

7.2.1 *Advantages of the Multiple Streams Framework*

Following Zahariadis (2013, 809, 814), the most promising frameworks of the EU's policy process to date are: advocacy coalition framework, constructivism, multilevel governance approach, MSF, normative power Europe, policy learning, principal–agent theory, and punctuated equilibrium theory (PET). Instead of applying multiple frameworks simultaneously or a synthesis of some of them, Zahariadis suggests using the lens that best captures the institutional and issue complexity by which the object of research is characterized. Institutional complexity is defined as the "multitude of rules governing close interactions among a high number of structurally differentiated units across different organizational levels", and issue complexity can best be understood as the degree of information overload concerning a specific issue (Zahariadis 2013, 811). By comparing the framework's assumptions with regard to these two dimensions, researchers

Table 7.1 Explaining agenda change in EU policy-making by applying the multiple streams framework

Directive	*98/30/EC*	*2003/55/EC*	*2009/73/EC*
The MSF's necessary conditions for agenda change			
The likelihood for an agenda change increases if			
H1 the problem stream, political stream, and policy stream are ripe;	–	+	+
H2 a change in the problem or political stream opens an agenda window; *and*	+	+	+
H3 a policy-entrepreneur succeeds in coupling the streams.	+	–	+
Specifying H2: Equifinal paths to the opening of an agenda window			
H4 An agenda window opens in the problem stream if			
(a) a relevant indicator deteriorates;	(+)		
(b) an evaluation study points to a discrepancy between a program's goal and the program's effects; or	(+)	(+)	(+)
(c) a focusing event relevant to the policy field in question occurs.			
H5 An agenda window opens in the political stream if			
(a) a new Commission takes office; or			+
(b) the Commission publishes a working program.	+ (+)	(+)	(+)
H6 An agenda window opens in the political stream if			
(a) a new Council Presidency takes office; or			
(b) one or consecutive Council Presidencies release their working program(s).			(+)
H7 An agenda window opens in the political stream if the European Council publishes acts which provide impetus for the EU's development.	(+)	(+)	(+)
H8 An agenda window opens in the political stream if (at least) one branch of the EU's executive or legislature tasks one (other) branch of the EU's executive to address an issue.	(+)	+ (+)	(+)
Specifying H3: Agenda coupling			
H9 The policy-entrepreneur is more likely to successfully couple the streams during an open agenda window,			
(a) the more persistent he or she is; and	+	n.a.	+
(b) the more access to key policy-makers he or she has.	+	n.a.	+

Source: Own compilation

Note: "–" indicates that a hypothesis is falsified, "+" indicates that a hypothesis holds, "(+)" indicates that the hypothesis' independent variable had kept the agenda window open, and "n.a." stands for not applicable

Table 7.2 Explaining policy change in EU policy-making by applying the multiple streams framework

Directive	*98/30/EC*	*2003/55/EC*	*2009/73/EC*
Explaining decision-making: decision coupling			
H10 Policy adoption is more likely if a political entrepreneur			
(a) manages to combine viable alternatives embraced by different veto actors into one package;	+	+	
(b) can (and does) offer concessions on the original proposal; and	+	+	+
(c) succeeds in providing meaning, clarification, and identity to the issue at stake.	(−)	(−)	
H11 Decision coupling is more likely to be lengthy			
(a) if agenda change has taken place against the will of veto actors; or	+	+	+
(b) if policy-makers' attention is redirected to other issues.	+	+	+

Source: Own compilation
Note: "+" indicates that a hypothesis holds and "(−)" indicates that a hypothesis does not hold for the entire policy process analyzed

can identify that framework which best suits their research interest, including the possibility to identify competing and complementary frameworks.

Energy issues are multidimensional (cf. Prontera 2009, 3–9) and intersect multiple policy areas, such as environment, competition, and security policy (cf. Hoogeveen and Perlot 2005). Thus, European natural gas regulation is characterized by high issue complexity. Resulting from being a cross-cutting issue, energy regulation is dealt with in different units (for instance, ministries or Directorate-Generals responsible) across different organizational levels (for instance, at the member states' and EU level). Thus, European natural gas regulation is also characterized by a high institutional complexity. The frameworks that capture best high institutional and issue complexity are PET and MSF.

Basically, for two reasons, the MSF is better equipped to explain the regulatory shift in EU's natural gas market policy than the PET: First, the MSF is better suited to explain the *timing* of a change. According to the PET, change results from positive feedback, which occurs if an issue's dominant policy image is challenged and other venues become active on that issue. Thereby, it reinforces the redefinition of the up-to-now-dominant policy image (cf. Baumgartner et al. 2014, 64–68; Princen 2013, 857). Positive feedback is triggered either by a change in preferences or a change in attentiveness (True et al. 2007, 163). However, as Tosun (2013, 26) rightly notices, the PET "(...) only makes general reference to possible exogenous factors [initiating positive feedback, N.H.] without specifying which of these are more relevant or under which conditions they become particularly effective" (for a related critique, see Princen 2013, 867). In contrast, the MSF specifies when opportunities for an agenda change arise (namely, when changes in the problem stream or political stream open an agenda window) and which conditions must be met to make an agenda change more likely (namely, stream ripeness and successful coupling activities of a policy-entrepreneur).

Second, the PET's distinction between incremental and radical change is difficult to apply with regard to regulatory policies because they are, by nature, multidimensional. Depending on the dimension the regulatory policy touches, change can be incremental and radical at the same time (Princen 2013, 866). This does not mean that the PET is not equipped to analyze a change regarding regulatory policies in general, but this multidimensionality needs to be incorporated in the theory, which very probably makes measuring change a methodologically demanding endeavor. In comparison, the MSF does not differentiate change according to its degree.

Furthermore, the empirical analysis revealed another advantage of the modified MSF: By differentiating between two coupling processes, it enables researchers to analyze whether there is a knock-on effect between agenda-setting and decision-making. Put differently, it allows for analyzing whether there is a causal connection between the way agenda-setting takes place and the lengths of decision coupling (see Sect. 7.2.3).

7.2.2 *Agenda Change*

Regarding agenda-setting, I derived three sets of hypotheses. The *first set* has the likelihood of an agenda change as its dependent variable (Hypotheses 1–3), the *second set* specifies which equifinal paths to the opening of an agenda window exist (Hypotheses 4–8), and the *third set* deals with policy-entrepreneurs' success metrics (Hypothesis 9).

According to Hypothesis 1, the likelihood of an agenda change increases if the problem stream, political stream, and policy stream are ripe. Put differently, if one or more streams are not ripe, the agenda window closes quickly. While this hypothesis holds for the second and third gas directive processes, it does not for the first one because the problem stream had not been ripe when the agenda window opened (Definition 1). However, the immature problem stream did not lead to the closure of the agenda window because the IEM remained in the Commission's center of attention (Definition 4). Only three-and-a-half months after the agenda window had opened, the Commission published its IEM document. In addition to keeping the agenda window open, this document also made the problem stream ripe (Definition 1).

I raised the question as to when the political stream is ripe (Definition 2). In contrast to national executives, the EU executive consists of three branches: the Commission, the European Council, and the Council. In the first gas directive process, only the Commission was receptive to natural gas liberalization before the agenda window opened. In the second gas directive process, the Commission and the Council were receptive to this issue, and in the case of the third gas directive process, they were joined by the European Council. Consequently, these cases suggest that it suffices for the political stream to be counted as ripe if the Commission is receptive to an issue.

Regarding policy stream ripeness, I defined this stream to be ripe if the policy community is familiar with at least one alternative to the policy problem in question (Definition 3). This had been the case in all three agenda-setting processes. Furthermore, the analysis documented that, with the ongoing institutionalization of the policy community, policy-entrepreneurs had more worked-out *European* solutions at their disposal. In the late 1980s, the policy community was not prepared to work out European solutions, given that the regulation of the natural gas market had fallen under the member states' responsibilities until then. The institutionalization of the policy community at the EU level started a year after the passage of the first gas directive with the Madrid Forum. Since then, the discussion and generation of European alternatives has become very vivid. This indicates, for instance, the evolution of representative offices of the gas and electricity industry in the EU (see Fig. 7.1) or the composition of participants at the meetings of the Madrid Forum (see Annex III). The empirical analysis revealed that, with each gas directive process, the intensity with which the policy community discussed worked-out alternatives had increased.

Building on the above and on the observation that decision-making took less time from directive to directive, this prompts the question of whether

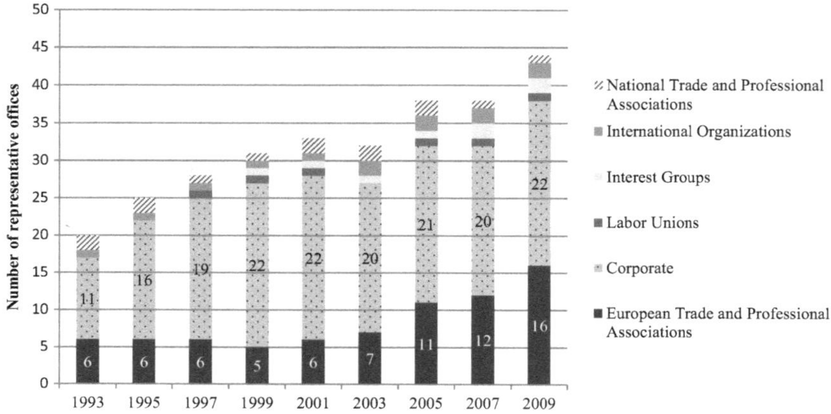

Fig. 7.1 Number of representative offices of natural gas and electricity sector at European level, 1993–2009. *Source*: Herweg (2016, 136); reproduced by permission of ECPR Press

there exists a causal connection between the lengths of decision-making and, first, the extent to which all branches of the EU executive have been receptive to an issue right from the start and, second, the dynamics in the policy stream.

According to Hypothesis 2, the likelihood of an agenda change increases if a change in the problem stream or political stream opens an agenda window. In fact, the analysis documented that in all three agenda-setting processes, the agenda window opened due to a change in the political stream (Hypotheses 5 and 8). More precisely, the political stream changed due to the publication of the Commission's working program (first gas directive), the Commission's contribution to the European Council's meeting at Lisbon (second gas directive) and the Commission's inauguration (third gas directive). Regarding the second gas directive process, it is striking that the Commission did not mention the IEM in its working program in early January 2000, only to suggest liberalizing this market fully by 2004 in its contribution to the European Council's meeting at Lisbon in late February.

According to Kingdon (1984), an agenda window closes quickly. Nonetheless, after the agenda window had opened, it took between 13 months (second gas directive) and 49 months (first gas directive) for the gas draft directives to rise on the decision agenda. The analysis documented that, in all three agenda-setting processes, some of the mechanisms that open agenda windows (more precisely, those captured in Hypotheses 4a and 4b, 5b, 7, and 8) managed to hold the agenda window open during agenda coupling (Definition 4). As a consequence, policy-entrepreneurs had more time at their disposal for coupling the streams. This observation raises the question whether it is a general feature of the EU agenda-setting processes that agenda windows do not close quickly—and in the case it is so, whether prolonged coupling opportunities influence the coupling strategies employed by policy-entrepreneurs.

Hypothesis 3 expects that the likelihood of an agenda change increases if a policy-entrepreneur succeeds in coupling the streams. In the first and third gas directive processes, the analysis revealed that, in particular, the Commission counted as a policy-entrepreneur that succeeded in coupling the streams. In the case of the second gas directive process, I could not identify such a policy-entrepreneur.[1] Since all policy-makers had supported setting the revision of the first gas directive on the decision agenda, it needed no policy-entrepreneur to make critical couplings for this agenda change to happen. The second gas directive only calibrated existing instruments (first-order change) (Brutschin 2015, 191). Compared to the introduction of new instruments (second-order change) or the establishment of new goals (third-order change) (Hall 1993), this was a minor change only - which might have made it easier for policy-makers to address the revision of the first gas directive. Furthermore, since the vast majority of involved actors aimed at changing the agenda and the policy, it is rather difficult to delimit policy-makers' engagement in policy-making from their engagement in policy entrepreneurship.

Hypothesis 9 specifies a policy-entrepreneur's success metrics. Since I did not identify a policy-entrepreneur who coupled the streams when the agenda window opened in the second gas directive process, this hypothesis could only be assessed for the first and third gas directive processes. The chance that a policy-entrepreneur couples the streams is higher if he or she (1) is persistent and (2) has access to key policy-makers. In both policy processes, the Commission was the most visible and most important policy-entrepreneur. Thus, due to its role and function in the EU policy process, it had access to key policy-makers. Furthermore, agenda coupling took place during the Commission's term of office, which was why there had not been a change in personnel. As a consequence, the Commission was also a persistent policy-entrepreneur. Therefore, Hypothesis 9 is confirmed by empirical analysis.

According to Kingdon (1984), any actor can be active in all three streams, although he assumed that he or she tends to limit his or her activities to one stream. A peculiarity of the three gas directive processes was that the Commission had been active in all three streams. It engaged in problem definition and recognition in the problem stream, set the IEM high on its agenda in the political stream, and engaged in institutionalizing the policy community and in contributing to the generation of alternatives in the policy stream. I follow Kingdon (1984) insofar as the streams' dynamics were different enough to maintain the assumption of stream independence. Since the Commission is known to be the driving force of integration and entrusted with monitoring tasks due to its exclusive role as guardian of the treaties, it is highly probable that the Commission's engagement in more than one stream is rather the norm than the exception. This makes agenda change even more likely if the Commission acts as a policy-entrepreneur. A comparison of agenda coupling processes in which the Commission acted as a policy-entrepreneur with processes in which it did not would be a valuable contribution to the further theoretical refinement of the MSF for the EU policy process.

7.2.3 *Policy Change*

In order to analyze the gas directive processes using a multiple streams lens, I derived two hypotheses: one deals with the likelihood of policy adoption (Hypothesis 10) and the other with the length of decision coupling (Hypothesis 11). Regarding the former, I differentiated three strategies political entrepreneurs could apply in order to make policy adoption more likely: offering (and granting) package deals (Hypothesis 10a) and concessions (Hypothesis 10b), and providing meaning, clarification, and identity to the issue at stake (Hypothesis 10c). In the first and second gas directive processes, political entrepreneurs applied all three strategies, whereas they only offered and granted package deals in the case of the third gas directive. Did these strategies make the adoption of the three gas directives more likely?

Package deals and concessions indeed contributed to making veto actors more willing to compromise and policy adoption more likely. In all gas directive processes, political entrepreneurs granted concessions, and in the first and second gas directive processes, they also negotiated package deals. Given that the draft directives combined different measures into one package, the veto actors' willingness to enter negotiations varied with the issue at stake. Since the MSF is particularly interested in explaining change, I suggested concentrating on conditions and processes that make *agenda change* more likely and on conditions and processes that make *policy change* less likely. The idea behind this differentiation is that, during agenda coupling, policy-entrepreneurs are willing to take any chance to get their favorite policy on the governmental agenda and eventually on the decision agenda. But once it is on the decision agenda, political entrepreneurs are interested in getting their favorite policy through the decision-making process. Thus, they concentrate on overcoming possible blockages. As a consequence, it is sufficient to identify those aspects of a legislative proposal that at least one veto actor is unwilling to compromise on and to analyze how political entrepreneurs try to make this veto actor (or those veto actors, provided there is more than one) enter negotiations.

Although this suggestion worked well in principle, it did not suffice to explain policy adoption in the second gas directive process. In this policy process, France and Germany were veto actors that blocked specific aspects of the draft directive. Although the analysis documented that political entrepreneurs' coupling strategies made them more willing to compromise, it needed considering domestic developments to explain why they accepted a compromise on market opening and regulatory oversight, respectively. The analysis revealed that France's and Germany's willingness to negotiate increased after a change in government in France and after receiving negative feedback on a contemporary domestic policy regarding natural gas regulation in Germany. Thus, it might be worth considering in future research whether it is possible to specify events in the member states' problem stream and political stream that might increase veto actors' willingness to settle compromises in EU negotiations. However, it would pose considerable difficulties to researchers to learn about the peculiarities of the (today's) 28 member states' problem streams and policy streams as well as being familiar with the EU's problem, political, and policy streams. Therefore, I suggest restricting this additional analysis to those member states that block negotiations.

In the first and second gas directive processes, the Commission threatened to decide on gas market liberalization by itself by applying its powers under Article 86(3). This was an attempt to worsen the veto actors' (in particular, the member states') fallback position. Thus, this was an example of providing meaning (Hypothesis 10c). This strategy was only partly successful. In the first gas directive process, the involved actors commentated on this threat and voiced their discontent. Since the European Court of Justice had previously sanctioned the Commission's use of its powers under Article 86(3) in the telecommunication sector, the political entrepreneurs had no reason to believe this threat to be incredible on legal grounds. Although it made member states willing to enter negotiations, it did not make them willing to compromise, given that the threat did not spur negotiations. In contrast, the veto actors did not even comment on this threat at the two occasions the Commission raised it during the second gas directive process, while the European Council reacted to it only at one occasion by settling a compromise on one aspect regarding the question of market opening. One explanation for this finding is that the Commission's threat had lost its credibility in the second gas directive process. A reason for this could be the Commission's engagement in the policy stream and, in particular, its efforts to institutionalize a policy community. Policy-makers could have come to the conclusion that a confrontation policy would do too much damage in the long run as it would most probably reduce the policy community's willingness to engage in generating EU alternatives. This might also explain why the Commission had not revived the threat to make use of its powers under Article 86(3) in the third gas directive process. Since the Commission promoted and contributed to the generation of alternatives during agenda coupling and invited a huge variety of stakeholders to participate in the discussions, it would have been disconcerting if the Commission nonetheless had opted to not consider their concerns and to decide on the issue by itself. This implies that there is a knock-on effect of agenda coupling on decision coupling: First, the more vivid the discussions in the policy stream are; second, the more stakeholders (in particular from member states) contribute to these discussions; and third, the greater the Commission's involvement in the policy stream is, the less likely it becomes that the Commission threatens to decide on an issue by itself during decision-making (provided the legal grounds for this threat are given regarding the issue at stake).

Hypothesis 11 aims at explaining the length of negotiations (see Fig. 7.2 for an overview of the actual length of each decision coupling process). I hypothesized that decision coupling is more likely to be lengthy (a) if agenda change has taken place against the will of veto actors and (b) if policy-makers' attention is redirected to other issues. Both subhypotheses

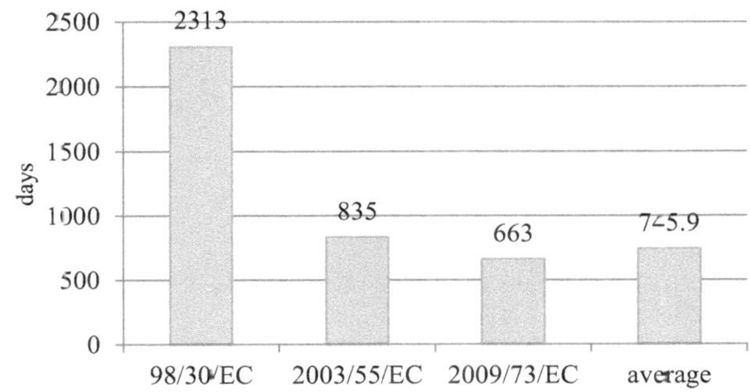

Fig. 7.2 Overview of the length of the EU decision-making process. *Source*: Own compilation. *Notes*: The graph informs how many days it took from adoption by the Commission to the end of procedure for each gas directive. This is compared to the average duration to pass a directive (irrespective of the policy area) between January 1992 and April 2008. The on-average value was calculated from the dataset provided by Kovats (2009)

were confirmed in the empirical analysis. While in the first gas directive process, almost all member states had harshly opposed the idea of liberalizing the natural gas market during agenda coupling, they supported the revision of the gas directive in the case of the second and third gas directive processes. This is reflected in the duration of decision coupling. It took 2313 days for the first gas directive from adoption by the Commission to the end of procedure, while it took only 835 and 663 days, respectively, for the second and third gas directive processes.[2] If one compares these durations with the average duration to adopt a directive, one finds that it took 310 percent more time for the first gas directive to be adopted than it took on average to adopt a directive between January 1992 and April 2008. The second directive needed only 10 percent more time to get adopted and the third directive 11 percent less time than the average directive. It is highly plausible that the long duration of the first directive's decision-making process reflects not only that agenda coupling had taken place against the will of veto actors but also that breaking down the "legitimacy barrier" (Wilson 1979, 41) requires prolonged negotiation.[3]

The analysis of the second and third gas directive processes suggests that three aspects contributed to the fact that decision coupling was shorter for the third gas directive: (1) the EU policy cycle, (2) the attention the European Council devoted to the internal market in energy or natural gas,

Table 7.3 Frequency with which the European Council referred to the policy process (or the internal energy market)

Coupling process	*98/30/EC*	*2003/55/EC*	*2009/73/EC*
Agenda coupling	1	1	5
Decision coupling	1	4	5
Sum	2	5	10

Source: Own compilation, based on the Conclusions of the European Council for its meetings between December 1984 and June 2009

and (3) the introduction of impact assessments. Regarding the EU policy cycle, the negotiations of the second gas directive fell in the European Parliament's (EP) session from 1999 to 2004. Since this directive was adopted in mid-2003, there was no pressure on the policy-makers to rush through negotiations in order to avoid postponing a decision due to EP elections. The negotiations of the third gas directive took place in the 2004–2009 parliamentary term. Given that the legislative proposal had been published in September 2007, policy-makers had less than two years to negotiate it before the end of the EP's mandate. Thus, policy-makers started feeling the pressure to settle an agreement in the course of 2008 so that the outgoing legislature could still decide on the issue. This is in line with Kovats' (2009, 251) finding, according to which there is a peak in adoptions in the codecision procedure before the EP election date. He explains this finding with political actors pushing even harder to complete ongoing procedures, given the uncertainty about the future composition of the EP. Put differently, the policy-makers anticipated that their attention would be redirected by EP elections and feared that a differently composed EP could render necessary renegotiating the compromises settled with the outgoing EP.

With regard to the attention the European Council paid to the gas directive processes, it is notable that this increased with each gas directive process (see Table 7.3). Although the first gas directive had been the most controversial one, the European Council referred to it only on two occasions. It referred to the second gas directive five times and to the third gas directive ten times. Furthermore, its contributions were far more precise in the third gas directive process than in the previous ones, even during agenda coupling.

Finally, the Commission has been doing impact assessments for major policy proposals since 2002.[4] Thus, the third gas directive process was the first one accompanied by an impact assessment. Impact assessments include (inter alia) the identification of different policy options and the comparison of their positive and negative impacts before the Commission starts working out a proposal. As a consequence, there is an intense exchange of views before the publication of a legislative proposal. This had been the case in the third gas directive process, even to the point that the institutionalized decision-making venues started negotiating compromises. As a consequence, it took less time to settle an agreement once the legislative proposal was published.

With regard to the question of how suitable the MSF is for explaining the EU policy process, this book documented that, by applying this lens, a deeper understanding of the policy processes could be gained. At the same time, a range of new research questions evolved, for instance, regarding the Commission's participation in all three streams. However, these new questions do not imply that the MSF is not suitable for explaining the EU policy process. To the contrary, considering that the MSF's concepts were transferred one to one from the United States to the EU, there are relatively few assumptions that call for theoretical refinements. By documenting where theoretical refinements are required in order to tailor the MSF to the EU policy process, this book contributed insights to the MSF literature that allow for a more systematic theory development.

Notes

1. This refers to the identification of policy-entrepreneurs that engaged in coupling the streams once the agenda window had opened. Before the agenda window opened, the Commission acted as a policy-entrepreneur in the problem stream and in the policy stream. However, *Hypothesis* 3 is interested only in policy-entrepreneurs' activities during times of open agenda windows.
2. Consequently, Hall's (1993) differentiation between first-, second-, and third-order policy change does not contribute to explaining why the policy process of the second gas directive (first-order change) was longer than that of the third gas directive (second-order change).
3. This might also apply to policy changes that were wished for by veto actors during agenda coupling, since they know that departing from a path once taken is difficult.
4. Usually, major policy projects are those included in the Commission's working program, proposals with identifiable economic, social, and

environmental impacts, nonlegislative measures such as White Papers, and implementing measures (Adelle et al. 2013, 218).

References

2003/55/EC. *Directive of the European Parliament and of the Council of 26 June 2003 Concerning Common Rules for the Internal Market in Natural Gas and Repealing Directive 98/30/EC.*

2009/73/EC. *Directive of the European Parliament and of the Council of 13 July Concerning Common Rules for the Internal Market in Natural Gas and Repealing Directive 2003/55/EC.*

98/30/EC. Directive of the European Parliament and of the Council of 22 June 1998 Concerning Common Rules for the Internal Market in Natural Gas.

Adelle, Camilla, Andrew Jordan, and John Turnpenny. 2013. Policy Making. In *Environmental Policy in the EU: Actors, Institutions and Processes*, 3rd ed., ed. Andrew Jordan and Camilla Adelle, 209–226. London, New York: Routledge.

Baumgartner, Jones R., Bryan D. Jones, and Peter B. Mortensen. 2014. Punctuated Equilibrium Theory: Explaining Stability and Change in Public Policymaking. In *Theories of the Policy Process*, 3rd ed., ed. Paul A. Sabatier and Christopher M. Weible, 59–103. New York: Westview Press.

Beyer, Jürgen. 2010. The Same or Not the Same. On the Variety of Mechanisms of Path Dependence. *International Journal of Social Sciences* 5(1): 1–11.

Brutschin, Elina. 2015. Shaping the EU's Energy Policy Agenda: The Role of Eastern European Countries. In *Energy Policy Making in the EU: Building the Agenda*, ed. Jale Tosun, Sophie Biesenbender, and Kai Schulze, 187–204. London: Springer.

Buchan, David. 2010. Energy Policy: Sharp Challenges and Rising Ambitions. In *Policy-making in the European Union*, ed. Helen Wallace, Mark A. Pollack, and Alasdair R. Young, 357–379. Oxford: Oxford University Press.

Cairney, Paul, and Michael D. Jones. 2016. Kingdon's Multiple Streams Approach: What is the Empirical Impact of this Universal Theory? *Policy Studies Journal* 44 (1): 37–58.

European Gas Regulatory Forum. 1999. *Minutes: 1st European Gas Regulatory Forum. Madrid, 30 September–1 October 1999:* Available upon request from the author.

Hall, Peter A. 1993. Policy Paradigms, Social Learning, and the State: The Case of Economic Policymaking in Britain. *Comparative Politics* 25(3): 275–296.

Herweg, Nicole. 2016. Clarifying the Concept of Policy Communities in the Multiple Streams Framework. In *Decision-Making Under Ambiguity and Time Constraints: Assessing the Multiple Streams Framework*, ed. Reimut Zohlnhöfer and Friedbert Rüb, 125–145. Colchester: ECPR Press.

Hoogeveen, Femke, and Wilbur Perlot. 2005. *Tomorrow's More: The International System, Geopolitical Changes and Energy CIEP 02/2005.* The Hague: Clingendael International Energy Programme.

Kingdon, John W. 1984. *Agendas, Alternatives, and Public Policies.* Boston: Little, Brown.

Kovats, Laszlo. 2009. Do Elections Set the Pace? A Quantitative Assessment of the Timing of European Legislation. *Journal of European Public Policy* 16(2): 239–255.

Princen, Sebastiaan. 2013. Punctuated Equilibrium Theory and the European Union. *Journal of European Public Policy* 20(6): 854–870.

Prontera, Andrea. 2009. Energy Policy: Concepts, Actors, Instruments and Recent Developments. *World Political Science Review* 5(1, Art. 7): 1–30.

Stern, Jonathan P. 1998. *Competition and Liberalization in European Gas Markets: A Diversity of Models.* London: Royal institute of international affairs.

Tosun, Jale. 2013. *Environmental Policy Change in Emerging Market Democracies—Central and Eastern Europe and Latin America Compared.* Toronto: University of Toronto Press.

True, James L., Bryan D. Jones, and Frank R. Baumgartner. 2007. Punctuated-Equilibrium Theory: Explaining Stability and Change in Public Policymaking. In *Theories of Policy Process*, 2nd ed., ed. Paul A. Sabatier, 155–187. Boulder, Colorado: Westview Press.

Wilson, James Q. 1979. American Politics, Then and Now. *Commentary* 67: 39–46.

Zahariadis, Nikolaos. 2013. Building Better Theoretical Frameworks of the European Union's Policy Process. *Journal of European Public Policy* 20(6): 807–816.

Annex I: Structure of the Gas Directives

Chapter heading	*98/30/EC*	*2003/55/EC*	*2009/73/EC*
Subject matter* Scope and Definitions	Chapter 1	Chapter 1	Chapter 1
General Rules for the Organisation of the Sector	Chapter 2	Chapter 2	Chapter 2
Transmission, Storage and LNG	Chapter 3	Chapter 3	Chapter 3
Distribution and Supply	Chapter 4	Chapter 4	Chapter 5
Independent Transmission Operator	–	–	Chapter 4
Unbundling and Transparency of Accounts	Chapter 5	Chapter 5	Chapter 6
Organisation of** Access to the System	Chapter 6	Chapter 6	Chapter 7
National Regulatory Authorities	–	–	Chapter 8
Retail Markets	–	–	Chapter 9
Final Provisions	Chapter 7	Chapter 7	Chapter 10

Source: Own compilation
Note: One asterisk (*) indicates that the title differs in Directive 2009/73/EC, while the content remains comparable; two asterisks (**) indicate that the title differs in Directives 2003/55/EC and 2009/73/EC, while the content remains comparable

N. Herweg, *European Union Policy-Making*,
DOI 10.1007/978-3-319-49400-5

Annex II: Articles of the Gas Directives

Title of articles	*98/30/EC*	*2003/55/EC*	*2009/73/EC*
Subject matter and scope	Article 1	Article 1	Article 1
Definitions	Article 2	Article 2	Article 2
Public service obligations and customer protection	Article 3	Article 3	Article 3
Authorisation procedure	Article 4	Article 4	Article 4
Monitoring of security of supply	–	Article 5	Article 5
Regional solidarity	–	–	Article 6
Promotion of regional cooperation	–	–	Article 7
Technical rules	Article 5	Article 6	Article 8
Designation and certification of transmission system operators	Article 6	Article 7	Article 10
Tasks of transmission, storage and/or LNG system operators	Article 7	Article 8	Article 13
Unbundling of transmission systems and transmission system operators	–	Article 9	Article 9
Designation and certification of transmission system operators	–	–	Article 10
Certification in relation to third countries	–	–	Article 11

(*continued*)

N. Herweg, *European Union Policy-Making*,
DOI 10.1007/978-3-319-49400-5

Title of articles	*98/30/EC*	*2003/55/EC*	*2009/73/EC*
Designation of storage and LNG system operators	–	–	Article 12
Independent system operators	–	–	Article 14
Unbundling of transmission system owners and storage system operators	–	–	Article 15
Confidentiality for transmission system operators and transmission system owners	Article 8	Article 10	Article 16
Assets, equipment, staff and identity	–	–	Article 17
Independence of the transmission system operator	–	–	Article 18
Independence of the staff and the management of the transmission system operator	–	–	Article 19
Supervisory body	–	–	Article 20
Compliance programme and compliance officer	–	–	Article 21
Network development and powers to make investment decisions	–	–	Article 22
Decision-making powers regarding the connection of storage facilities, LNG regasification facilities and industrial customers to the transmission system	–	–	Article 23
Designation of distribution system operators	Article 9(1)	Article 11	Article 24
Tasks of distribution system operators	Article 10	Article 12	Article 25
Unbundling of distribution system operators	–	Article 13	Article 26
Confidentiality obligations of distribution system operators	Article 11	Article 14	Article 27

(*continued*)

Title of articles	*98/30/EC*	*2003/55/EC*	*2009/73/EC*
Closed distribution systems	–	–	Article 28
Combined operator	–	Article 15	Article 29
Right of access to accounts	Article 12	Article 16	Article 30
Unbundling of accounts	Article 13	Article 17	Article 31
Third-party access	Articles 14–16	Article 18	Article 32
Access to storage	–	Article 19	Article 33
Access to upstream pipeline networks	Article 23	Article 20	Article 34
Refusal of access	Article 17	Article 21	Article 35
New infrastructure	–	Article 22	Article 36
Market opening and reciprocity	Articles 18 and 19	Article 23	Article 37
Direct lines	Article 20	Article 24	Article 38
Regulatory authorities	Articles 21(2) and (3), and 22	Article 25	Articles 39 and 41
Designation and independence of regulatory authorities	–	Article 25(1), 1st and 2nd sentence	Article 39
Duties and powers of the regulatory authority	–	Article 25 (rest)	Article 41
General objectives of the regulatory authority	–	–	Article 40
Regulatory regime for cross-border issues	–	–	Article 42
Compliance with the guidelines	–	–	Article 43
Record keeping	–	–	Article 44
Retail markets	–	–	Article 45
Safeguard measures	Article 24	Article 26	Article 46
Level playing field	–	–	Article 47
Derogations in relation to take-or-pay commitments	Article 25	Article 27	Article 48
Emergent and isolated markets	Article 26	Article 28	Article 49
Review procedure	–	Article 29	Article 50
Committee	–	Article 30	Article 51
Reporting	Articles 27 and 28	Article 31	Article 52

(*continued*)

Title of articles	*98/30/EC*	*2003/55/EC*	*2009/73/EC*
Repeal	–	Article 32	Article 53
Transposition	Article 29	Article 33	Article 54
Entry into force	Article 30	Article 34	Article 55
Addressees	Article 31	Article 35	Article 56
Measures on consumer protection	–	Annex A	Annex I
Correlation table	–	Annex B	Annex II

Source: Own compilation, based on Annex B of Directive 2003/55/EC and Annex II of Directive 2009/73/EC

Annex III: Contributors to Meetings of the European Gas Regulatory Forum

N. Herweg, *European Union Policy-Making*,
DOI 10.1007/978-3-319-49400-5

Contributors to Meetings of the European Gas Regulatory Forum (Madrid Forum)

Number of meetings	1	3	4	5	6	7	8	9	10	11	12	13	14	15	16	Sum
Date	September 30 to October 1, 1999	October 26 to October 27, 2000	July 2 to July 3, 2001	February 7 to February 8, 2002	October 30 to October 31, 2002	September 24 to September 25, 2003	July 8 to July 9, 2004	December 3, 2004	September 15 to September 16, 2005	May 18 to May 19, 2006	February 20 to February 21, 2007	October 16 to October 17, 2007	May 22 to May 23, 2008	November 6 to November 7, 2008	May 28 to May 29, 2009	
European Commission	1	6	4	6	4	3	2	1	1	6	4	3	3	4	7	55
Council of European Energy Regulators		6	8	7	6	5	5	1	1							39
Gas Transmission Europe		6	5	5	6	6	2	1							1	32
European Regulators' Group for Electricity and Gas								1		3	4	2	4	4	8	26
European Federation of Energy Traders		1		2	5	4							1	3	1	17
European Council Presidency		1	1	1	1	1	1	1	1	1	1	1	1	1	1	14
International Federation of Industrial Energy Consumers		1	1	3	4	4										13
Eurogas		1	1	6	4											12
Comisión Nacional de la Energía						1			1	1	1	1	1	1	1	8
EASEE-Gas					1	1	1		1	1		2	1			8
Eurelectric				2	3	2										7
Fundación de Estudios de Regulación	1	1	1	1	1											5
Gas Infrastructure Europe									1			2	1			4
Gas Transmission Europe (GTE+) (precursor of ENTSOG)													1	1	2	4
GEODE					1	2										3
				1	1	1										3

International Association of Oil & Gas Producers																
Brattle Group		1		1	1											3
Gas Storage Europe														1	1	2
Representative of Germany						1	1									2
European Chemical Industry Council						2										2
BG Storage	1															1
BP Gas & Power Europe			1													1
Centrica Energy Management Group			1													1
Edison Gas	1															1
Gas Industry Standards Board			1													1
Gas LNG Europe															1	1
Gas Natural	1															1
Gasunie	1															1
Gazprom					1											1
German gas industry association			1													1
Marcogaz															1	1
Ofgem	1															1
OXERA	1															1
Representative of the United Kingdom									1							1
Sum	8	24	25	35	39	33	12	5	7	12	10	11	13	15	24	273

Index

Note: Page numbers followed by "n" denote endnotes.

N. Herweg, *European Union Policy-Making*,
DOI 10.1007/978-3-319-49400-5

M

N

O

P

Kolibri 360 GmbH
Ferdinand-Jühlke-Straße 7
99095 Erfurt, Deutschland
produktsicherheit@kolibri360.de